FATHERS' LIBERATION ETHICS

A HOLISTIC ETHICAL ADVOCACY FOR ACTIVE NURTURANT FATHERING

Gary Ritner, Ph.D.

UNIVERSITY
PRESS OF
AMERICA

Lanham • New York • London

Copyright © 1992 by
University Press of America®, Inc.
4720 Boston Way
Lanham, Maryland 20706

3 Henrietta Street
London WC2E 8LU England

Paraphrase of the tale of *Iron John* translated by Robert Bly,
used with permission of Addison-Wesley Publishing, Co., Inc.

Library of Congress Cataloging-in-Publication Data
Ritner, Gary.
Fathers' Liberation Ethics : a Holistic Ethical Advocacy
for Active Nurturant Fathering / by Gary Ritner.
p.   cm.
Includes bibliographical references and index.
1. Fatherhood—United States.
2. Fathers—United States—Psychology.
3. Father and child—United States.
4. Sex role—United States.
5. Househusbands—United States   I. Title.
HQ756.R57   1991
306.874' 2—dc20   91-28593 CIP

ISBN 0-8191-8465-9 (cloth : alk. paper)
ISBN 0-8191-8466-7 (pbk. : alk. paper)

ACKNOWLEDGEMENTS

An earlier version of this book was first presented in 1981 as a doctoral dissertation at Union Theological Seminary in New York City for a Ph.D. in Christian Social Ethics. Thanks to Union Professors Beverly Harrison, Roger Shinn, Robert Neale, and Donald Shriver for their advice, direction and support in the early stages of this project which led to the oral defense and the degree.

Thanks to Professor Joseph Mow of West Virginia Wesleyan College who encouraged me to present a series of lectures on this subject as part of a statewide ethics lecture series at West Virginia Wesleyan in 1984. I had the opportunity to return to classes there and share my learning with the next generation of fathers.

Thanks to James Levine of the Families and Work Institute, whose writing in 1976, launched me from living the issues of fatherhood to reading and reflecting on the field of fathering research. In 1989, a lecture he gave to working parents on their lunch break in Downtown St. Paul moved me to renew my quest for answers to the problem of low father involvement in childcare.

Thanks to Professor James Nelson of United Theological Seminary of the Twin Cities who encouraged me, more than anyone else, to bring this work to publication. He also encouraged me to share my research with his classes in "Men's Liberation" in 1982 and 1985.

Thanks to United Theological Seminary of the Twin Cities for giving me the opportunity in 1990 to explore the issues further while teaching there as an adjunct professor in a class on "Ethics and Social Justice Issues."

Thanks to Carter Heyward of Episcopal Divinity School who helped me to find University Press of America at a time when other publishers insisted upon my meeting their standards of profitability (especially providing a more popularized style and deleting most of what I consider to be an invaluable bibliography on the subject). Carter and I met at Union Seminary in New York while working on our doctoral studies there in the late '70's. Her inspiring writing and courageous social witness helped me to lead others toward the commitments outlined in this book.

Thanks to Beverly Harrison for her support and encouragement in the summer of 1990. She and James Nelson convened an ethics course together at Union Seminary in New York City during which I refined some approaches and arrived at the conclusion that fathers, mothers and children could benefit by this book now more than ever.

I am grateful to Jon, my fifteen-year-old son by a first marriage, and to Jessica, my seven-year-old daughter by a second marriage, for heightening the satisfactions of fathering and teaching me what I have come to understand about nurturing myself and others.

Thanks to Jessica's mother, Martha, and Jon's mother, Janet, who have both shown extraordinary love for their children by facilitating the opportunity for them to relate regularly and frequently with me as their father through joint custody. Such cooperation has made it possible for me to complete this project with satisfaction rather than turn away from it out of pain about the loss and separation of divorce. For fathers to remain close to their children after divorce, such cooperative and healing love is essential.

Thanks to my local church, Central Park United Methodist Church, for sabbatical leave in 1990 that allowed me to complete this book. Thanks to Sean Gordon, who typed on two chapters. Thanks to Sean, Marcial, Tony, Mark and Nancy, who instructed me when I was stumped in doing this camera-ready manuscript with Microsoft Word software.

Thanks to my parents, Bill and Virginia Ritner, who gave to me invaluable emotional gifts, but especially the gift of unconditional love. They helped me to know the unconditional love of God through their caring. That is what I treasure most in life and what I want to pass on to my children.

Thanks to Pam Armstrong with whom I share marriage and and a blended family. Her capacity for empathy and her healthy self-esteem have reduced the possibility for discord in a blended family to the bare minimum. Her loving support while I have been completing the final stages of this project has been wonderful. Without her encouragement, I could not have completed this journey.

CONTENTS

INTRODUCTION

To become an "active nurturant father" takes a commitment to share equally with the mother in the care of one's child. It takes a desire to be compassionate toward children who may not always be at their best. It takes an appreciation of forgiveness of oneself and others and the capacity to accept grace and love in spite of the failures. Most of the time, just being "pretty good" as a "Daddy" has to be good enough. A father who can live with that, can grow close enough and remain close enough for his child to experience him as "Daddy." For all that it takes to be a "Daddy" and for all that it requires from a man, the rewards are precious moments to treasure. A "Daddy" is a man who can fully appreciate the value of these fulfilling moments and maintain composure in the not-so-fulfilling moments.

A "Daddy" is one who is clear about just how much is at stake for him and for his children in his providing consistency in nurturing rather than neglecting his children. "Daddy" is the affectionate badge of honor that a well-nurtured child pins on his/her active nurturant father from time to time. One of the priceless awards for fathering comes when his child says "I love you, Daddy."

The subtitle, "A Holistic Ethical Advocacy for Active Nurturant Fathering" sets this work apart from previous works on fathering. Some social researchers have organized their data to point in the direction of encouragement of greater involvement by fathers, but they have not developed more than a vaguely suggestive ethical approach based on the good benefits of fathers getting more involved. I will develop a holistic and multi-faceted ethical approach for advocating active nurturant fathering, which I believe is essential to provide motivation for fathers to become and remain equally involved in parenting.

The part of the whole that has been emphasized by social researchers is "observation." That part is vital and researchers should not be faulted for that. But other parts need to be incorporated into the total body of a work that encourages fathers to be more involved. Those parts include the openly stated commitment of the writer to the goal of active fathering, overt rather than covert ethical argumentation, educational methods, political strategies, legislative force, religious motivations, and other incentives. This forms a whole that is far more comprehensive than the parts that have previously been utilized in the area of writing on fathers. This is *not* an argument for researchers to use these methods. This book is *different* from social research. It is an ethical argument. It is a plea for social change. It is a *FATHERS' LIBERATION ETHICS* that attempts to convince fathers as well as mothers, employers, social planners, legislators and relevant others that active nurturant fathering is of vital importance to the society. It is also a critique designed to assist in developing more successful efforts at bringing this ideal into more widespread reality.

The most frequent ethical conclusion built into studies on fathers is that active fathering should be done because all members of the family are more satisfied and better off when fathers take an equal part with mothers in parenting responsibilities and joys. This ethical point in itself is too vague and brief to provide much motivation for fathers to do more parenting; to give adequate encouragement to educators, legislators and employers who could help; or to accomplish significant movement toward greater equality for those mothers who are doing most of the parenting.

While researchers have backed away from providing an ethical argument, one of the primary motivations for many works has been to further the cause of equality. Part of the reason for this reluctance is that social researchers have been trained to seek "scientific objectivity." It is not an acceptable part of their work to approach the study from an ethical perspective or to take a strong advocacy position in their work. Unlike social researchers, I am free (as a Christian social ethicist) to utilize social research, religious motivations, and ethical approaches in a holistic way. While I am still bound to standards of accuracy in research, I am not restrained from working toward and from an ethical goal of encouraging fathers to become equally involved with mothers in caring for their children.

Some researchers have focused their studies of fathers on those who are getting *more* involved than their own fathers and more involved than they used to be, but these fathers are still not doing anywhere near half of the work of parenting. The goal I seek is *EQUALITY* between men and women in parenting as well as in the workplace and society in general. The words, "active nurturant" indicate a level of involvement that approximates equality with the way women care for infants and children rather than "helping" the mother in her role as if she ought to be the primary parent. Achieving of the goal of "active nurturant fathering" would mean that fathers as well as mothers would be the primary parents.

In 1971, I was among two men and thirty women who studied child care and development in a college classroom at West Virginia Wesleyan College. It was a course in the home economics department which dealt with childbirth, infants' clothing, medical issues, feeding, diapering, disciplining, and nurturing children. I was also taking another course in the psychology department to study developmental stages of children's lives.

There were many women in the home economics course who understood it as a class in motherhood. I was disturbed and somewhat embarrassed because only one other man in a school of one thousand males was taking the course which I understood to be preparation for fatherhood. During that semester, I wondered why males generally did not raise children in Twentieth Century American society and why so few men enrolled in a course that would be so vital for their future as fathers.

Four years later, I participated in Lamaze classes and prepared to be in the delivery room for the birth of my first child. The birth took place at a large New York City hospital. There were complications. The delivery was done by forceps and I was asked to leave the room. I was told that it was standard procedure not to allow fathers into the room during a forceps delivery. I was anxious and disappointed. Finally, a nurse and doctor appeared with my newborn son. He was beautiful. It was a religious experience. I felt at one with the miracle of life itself and God's creative power. I held my son as much as hospital routine would allow. It was not enough! I spent many hours staring at him through the glass of the nursery in the hospital before we could finally take him home. There I could finally be close and enjoy him.

"I am a father!" Those words were ringing delightfully in my mind the day my son Jonathan was born, November 10, 1975. In the years before his birth, I realized that I wanted to be a father, but not like the father known in traditional families. I wanted to provide frequent emotional and physical care for my child, not just financial support. I wanted to participate first-hand in my child's growth and development, not just hear about it at the end of my working day. I wanted to share equally in the joys and responsibilities of parenting, not just help the mother of my child to do what many referred to as "her job" (i.e., primary parent). These were my hopes as I held my son for the first time.

During the early months after Jonathan's birth, a bond developed between us which helped me to care for him. He smiled at me as I cuddled him in my arms. He imitated the sounds I made and I imitated the sounds he made. He stopped crying when I changed his diaper or fed him. We influenced each other's behavior and were drawn together. We became attached to each other and those early months of closeness helped me to remain involved, to be patient in caring for him, to understand his needs, and to meet them adequately.

However, in the five years after Jonathan's birth, I faced some formidable resistance to my being actively involved, as a man, in caring for his physical and emotional needs on a frequent basis. Several people strongly suggested that I was obligated to provide financially for him, but that meeting his emotional and physical needs (e.g. bathing, diapering, feeding) were the proper tasks of his mother and not his father.

The people who resisted my efforts to be actively involved acted not simply from their own personal preferences but in defense of a more widely held view of the proper roles of mothers and fathers, which restricts both men and women and deprives children of quality interaction with both parents.

Such resistance is not purely individual. It has become highly institutionalized and yet we hardly recognize it in daily political and economic life. When we do recognize how women are pressured to care for children and men are restricted from child care, most of us are inclined to accept it as an unchangeable character of the society or nature without questioning whether it is a just or unjust state of affairs and whether it can be changed.

Believing that this state of affairs is both unjust and changeable, I have, since 1977, worked to analyze how and why society separates fathers from their children and explored ways of bringing them together again with greater justice and love between men, women, and children. This book is the result of research and reflection which began, at least intentionally, in 1975, when I sought to combine paid employment with taking care of a newborn during part of the day while his mother worked. Soon after that, James Levine published *Who Will Raise the Children?* This helped me to realize that my concerns were not private problems but part of a larger human malaise for which millions of people were seeking a solution. Then I began researching in earnest.

My father, who served as a model with whom I identified strongly, broke through some traditional barriers of sex-role specialization of his generation. He frequently cooked for the whole family. He provided warm hugs, kisses, massages and tucked us in at night. He has taken care of infants and did not shy away from cleaning up after us, bathing us and changing diapers. As a grandfather, he has taken three or more grandchildren temporarily into his sole care with pleasure, ease and confidence.

His fathering has helped me to father and to feel good about myself in that capacity. I have learned parenting from him and felt deeply satisfied and confident as a father because of the caring attitudes he has expressed toward me.

But, there was another side of my experience of growing up in the 1950's and 1960's. In some ways, our relationship was much like other fathers and sons who are generally emotionally distant with each other. When I had an emotional crisis, I seldom took it to him. Whether he was prepared to help, I cannot be sure. Today, he is the one that I take my emotional crises to. We have both become better at talking through emotions together. When I was growing up, we did not talk enough about my feelings, or his, for me to learn how to deal with my feelings or with my children's feelings. I have learned a lot by trial and error, but I have also regretted that I did not have more skills and lifelong habits of talking through feelings.

I was born into a blue-collar family in 1949. My mother stopped working for a while to care for three children. My father worked in a job category that contained mostly men---a local post office mail clerk. My mother worked in a category that contained mostly women then---department store sales clerk. I became closely acquainted with inequality between men and women in the work world through their reports to me about the institutions for which they labored.

I have come to see how inequality between my parents tended to bring me closer in daily life to my mother and to separate me from my father. For several years, he was out of town working mail on the train every other week, and she was at home with the children. He could earn a lot more by working than she could, and she was home more than he was to care for the children. This arrangement was not simply a personal preference. They did what they had to do, given the limitations and expectations placed upon them by structures of the society.

These are the roots of my moral indignation toward inequality between men and women which separates fathers and children such that women are compelled to care for children and men are restricted from doing so.

Since 1980, I have been divorced from Jonathan's mother. I felt strongly that Jonathan should not be cut off from the continuing love and care of either his mother or his father. He could benefit from relatively equal time with each parent and cope with the adjustments necessary to make this equal time possible.

I felt the need and responsibility to continue in an active role in his growth and development, play and discipline, laughter and tears. I believed it would be unfair to his mother to deprive her of similar opportunities by seeking custody. A legal separation agreement was filed and later a divorce decree was obtained, granting custody to both Jon's mother and me. We both would have legal custody and Jon would live half of the time with me and half of the time with his mother.

During this time, I spoke with several divorcing fathers, none of whom were sharing custody of their children. Most of them either did not want to share custody or could not get their former spouse to agree to it. But I read many accounts of fathers who did share custody, and I followed their lead without knowing how it would work out.

After three satisfying years of joint custody, life became more complicated in 1981. Employment opportunities for clergy were rare in New York City. Housing costs were skyrocketing. Jon's mother had remarried and moved an hour away. It was possible for me to be with my son only on the weekends as he entered first grade. The travel was traumatic for all of us. I had remarried and my wife (at the time) wanted us to return to her home in Minnesota to live and work. For ten years, my son has lived with me during ten weeks of the summer and during another two-week vacation from school. Opportunities for employment were in Minnesota, and New York opportunities were very limited in ministry. It was a painful decision to move, but I felt that it was also the only way that I could provide for my son financially. I frequently wished that we could have lived close enough to continue sharing the care of Jon in that joint custody arrangement.

In 1984, my second child, Jessica, was born in a small town hospital. It was such a contrast to my first experience. Delivery took place in our hospital room. I stayed in the room overnight for three days until the three of us went home together. I could hold Jessica as much as I wanted. She was apart from us for only a few minutes during the hospital stay. It was the experience I had dreamed about. In the months after, as I cared for this newborn, I felt a deep sense of bonding.

Her mother and I served three churches each as ministers. Our schedules were exhausting at times. Sharing child care equally was vital to our career satisfaction and our well being. After a few months, it became clear that there was just too much stress in the situation. We relocated to one church in St. Paul. I worked full time. She worked half time and studied for another graduate degree. Changing the schedule helped some things, but the relationship was disintegrating over issues unrelated to child care. In 1988, we legally separated and worked out joint custody arrangements amicably. Jessica has lived with me three nights and parts of four days and with her mother four nights and parts of five days a week. The arrangement has worked to everyone's satisfaction and given us opportunities for a rhythm of child care and work, rest and parenting, family time and time alone.

In 1991, I married Pam Armstrong. She and I talk about having children together. She is 31. At 42, I am better prepared to be a good father than I was at 25. I am more realistic now about just how much energy it takes to be a good father. I realize that trials are a part of parenting in ways I never imagined at 25. I am even more prepared now to see nurturing children as immensely rewarding and vital to the family, the children, the parents, and the society.

Between 1975 and now, my mind has changed toward greater realism about the difficulties of getting fathers to share equally in child-care-giving with mothers. In 1975, I saw so many positive signs of change on the streets of Manhattan. Fathers were in the park with their infants. Fathers were involved where I went to seminary. *Kramer Vs. Kramer* was a popular movie. However, my optimism was cut short by some hard evidence that I found in research.

I began with the hypothesis that innovative work opportunities, in themselves, could be adequate encouragement for men to take a greater role in child-care-giving. In 1975, I did not fully understand the economic realities that would continue to be formidable barriers to fathers changing in the direction of more involvement in parenting on an equal basis. I did not have a holistic view of the strategies needed to initiate and sustain active nurturant fathering.

By the time I produced an earlier version of this work for a doctoral dissertation in 1980, I had realized the need for a holistic ethical advocacy that utilizes several approaches, including, work innovations, early socialization, ethical argumentation, motivating images, adult education in parenting skills, negotiation techniques, legislative support and encouragement from spouses and others.

Facing barriers honestly is essential to bringing about real change rather than living with the illusion that "it" is happening easily. I believe that the society must bring fathers into sharing equally in child-care-giving with mothers in order to bring about greater satisfaction for children, mothers and fathers. Active nurturant fathering is vital for a healthy society. No "kinder, gentler society" is possible as long as there continues to be private and public resistance (as well as a lack of support for) equality within families and between men and women. The nation must override the veto of those who find this equality to be a threat to their exploitative way of life. The work that follows explores the subtleties of why our society must do that and what it will take to accomplish such radical liberation of fathers.

Chapter One critiques traditional roles and argues that these roles are unjust. Chapter Two critiques the syndrome of the absent father while searching for clues to bring him back. Chapter Three argues from relevant ethical perspectives that active nurturant fathering is the right relationship between fathers and children and husbands and wives.

Chapter Four weaves together motivating mythical images for a father's equal involvement. Chapter Five analyzes and commends various educational, psychological, and political strategies. Chapter Six critiques the various employment options that have been assumed to create more involvement and prescribes a more comprehensive strategy for transforming the society. Chapter Seven analyzes the reasons for the growing reduction in father involvement due to divorce and argues for joint custody cooperation as a remedy to reduce the loss of fathers. The conclusion spins out a vision of the kind of society that is possible if the "prodigal father" can be brought back into an equal and caring involvement in the lives of his children. Lastly, the most extensive bibliography published to date in the field of fathering research directs the reader to a vast array of resources for more detailed exploration of the issues addressed in *Fathers' Liberation Ethics*.

CHAPTER ONE

A CRITIQUE OF TRADITIONAL ROLES

In modern industrial society, both Christian ethics and the social sciences have been heavily influenced by a "traditional" view of the right relatedness or properly functional relationship between men and women, especially between fathers and mothers. Proponents of this view have espoused that fathers make better breadwinners and that they should work outside the home to provide for the family's financial needs, while mothers make better parents and that they should work inside the home and care for the children.

A pivotal figure for illustrating this influence in Christian ethics is Lyman Abbott, a Social Gospel preacher regarded as "the virtual chaplain of Theodore Roosevelt's Progressivism."[1] Abbott addressed social questions with the normative ethics he understood to come from the Gospel. He was both influenced by the "traditional" view on families prevalent in

---

[1] Sydney E. Ahlstrom, *A Religious History of the American People, Vol. 2* (Garden City, N.Y.: Image Books, 1975), p. 253.

his society and influential toward establishing this viewpoint as "the Christian perspective."

With the publication of *The Home Builder* in 1908, Abbott set forward a Christian endorsement of the sex-role differentiated family. "Love drove [the husband] from [his wife] that [he] might prove [himself] more worthy of her."[2] The father is the breadwinner because he loves his wife, and he remains away working to show his love for her and the family.

The child's language "thrills the mother's heart," but to the father it is an "unknown tongue."[3] He does not know how to care for the children, nor is he supposed to, for the care of the children is the "sacred task" which he entrusts to her. For the mother who fulfills this sacred task, "one child is not enough. She wishes a brood."[4]

The wife remains at home, keeping it and preparing it as "a rest and refuge from the strenuous and stormy life outside, and a tonic to virtue and an inspiration to vigor in that life" for her husband.[5] As homemaker, her role is to help her husband "fulfill the purpose of his life, and to make [his purpose] a nobler and yet nobler purpose."[6]

It is significant that Abbott was, in part, responding to the woman suffrage movement as a threat to the role allocation which he considered to be constitutive of the Christian family. Abbott's idealized role of the wife and mother "laughs at the virgin reformers who have never known the mystery of love and are protesting against the subjection of women."[7] "She

---

[2]Lyman Abbott, *The Home Builder* (New York: Houghton Mifflin Co., 1908), p. 121.

[3]Abbott, p. 47.

[4]Abbott, p. 46.

[5]Abbott, p. 13.

[6]Abbott, p. 32.

[7]Abbott, p. 25.

cannot understand how any woman should not want children."[8] "She has no ambition to be a public woman."[9] "She has as little use for masculine women [i.e., suffragists] as for feminine men."[10]

A pivotal figure for illustrating the influence of the traditional view in social sciences is Talcott Parsons. For over thirty years his sociological analysis of middle class nuclear families in contemporary urban industrial society has served as a social scientific justification of a sex-linked division of labor in families and society. He has reflected the dominant view, the traditional view, of families in the social sciences. Furthermore, his work was influential toward establishing sex-role differentiation as a paradigm and norm for understanding families.

In the late 1940's and early 1950's, Parsons claimed that the sex-role differentiated nuclear family (i.e., the "traditional family") is a modern adaptation well suited to the new environment of urban industrial society and that it is functional for both society and the individual family members. He observed that an industrial economy requires labor mobility, income stability and (for fathers and growing infants) personal relationship reliability.[11] The traditional allocation of roles provides these, according to his evaluation.[12]

---

[8]Abbott, p. 45.

[9]Abbott, p. 77.

[10]Abbott, p. 78.

[11]Rhona Rapoport, Robert N. Rapoport and Ziona Strelitz with Stephen Kew, *Fathers, Mothers and Society* (New York: Basic Books, 1977), p. 62.

[12]Talcott Parsons, "The Social Structure of the Family," in *The Family: Its Function and Destiny,* ed. R.N. Anshen (New York: Harper and Row, 1949), p. 171.

The father's responsibility to his family is primarily discharged by doing well in his occupational role. The wife/mother holds primary responsibility for the activities and care of family members in the home, e.g. child rearing, housekeeping and shopping.[13] These separate roles were identified as two kinds of leadership and task orientation (i.e., "instrumental" and "expressive"[14]). The husband/father, as the instrumental leader, earns the family living and assures the social status of the family which is necessary for its members to succeed in life. In return, his home is made a place of refuge, privacy, personal satisfaction and emotional security by his wife.

The wife/mother, as the expressive leader, is expected to be at home as her first priority, though she may engage in hobbies, volunteerism or even some minimal paid labor. But these are to be subordinated to her primary role of "good mother" for her children and a "good companion" and housekeeper for her husband. In return for this, she receives from her husband not only economic security but social status as well.

Parsons illustrates the ways in which their roles complement each other and suggests that their leadership in the family is equal overall. He describes the tasks which they perform and claims that there is an equal balance between the mother's tasks and the father's tasks, since they complement each other.

This division of labor, according to Parsons, is rooted in nature:

---

[13]Talcott Parsons, "The Father Symbol: An Appraisal in Light of Psychoanalytic and Sociological Theory," in *Social Structure and Personality* (Glencoe, N.Y.: Free Press, 1964), p. 49.

[14]Talcott Parsons and R.F. Bales, *Family, Socialization and Interaction Process* (New York: Free Press, 1955), pp. 35-131.

> In our opinion the fundamental explanation of the allocation of the roles between the biological sexes lies in the fact that the bearing and early nursing of children establish a strong *presumptive primary* relation of mother to the small child and this in turn establishes a presumption that the man, who is exempted from these biological functions, *should* specialize in the alternative instrumental direction.[15]

This particular discrimination of roles is "necessary" in order to make the nuclear family a "stable social system."[16] The father is the instrumental leader because he has more mobility than the mother. "The concentration of the mother on the child precludes a primacy of her attention in this direction although she always performs some instrumental tasks."[17]

Relying upon Freudian theory, Parsons minimizes the father's role in nurturing and emphasizes the mother's:

> In addition to the managerial aspects of the (father's) role there are certain discipline and control functions.... consider, again, why *two* parents are *necessary at all.* The initial mother-child subsystem *can do without the father* (except that he provides food, shelter, etc., for this subsystem so that it need not split up to perform many of its own instrumental tasks). But some significant member of the nuclear family must "pry the child loose" from the mother-dependency so that it may "grow up" and accept its responsibilities as an "adult."

---

[15]Parsons and Bales, p. 23.

[16]Parsons and Bales, p. 315.

[17]Parsons and Bales, p. 314. Italics added.

There is necessarily a coalition of father and mother in this, or no stable socialization pattern develops.[18]

Parsons is a biological determinist in so far as he assumes that women are the nurturers of children and men are breadwinners *because* women can bear children and nurse them while men cannot. He takes a biological function as the determinant of differentiated sex-roles.

Abbott is a biological determinist in assuming that men and women are very different in temperament and capacities by virtue of their being created by God to be physiologically and emotionally different. In this assumption, Abbott correlates the religious/moral imperative with the biological differences and claims that they should act according to the nature of their creation as male and female. Their biological makeup and Divine calling as male or female determines what they should do vis-a-vis each other with regard to employment and child care.

The positions of Abbott and Parsons represent a "soft biological determinism," meaning that human beings can, in their view, defy these roles. For Parsons, societies are comprised of symbol networks which people create and people can, at least on a hypothetical level, change them (though it may be "antisocial" or "disruptive" to defy the sex-role conventions). For Abbott, free will means people can and do act against such role prescriptions (though it may be "sinful").

Parsons and Abbott also presented a case for cultural determinism. By identifying the needs of the society and evaluating how well the sex-role differentiated family meets these needs, Parsons suggests that the existence and character of differentiated sex-roles are also determined by the needs of the culture.

---

[18]Parsons and Bales, p. 314. Italics added.

Abbott believed that the cultural context (i.e., "the strenuous and stormy life"[19] for men in employment) also *determined* the differentiated roles between men and women. Thus, women would *have to* stay home. The need for the husband/father of the turn of the century to have support for his work and and help in strengthening his moral fiber required a wife/mother to provide inspiration and conscience as well as child care, food preparation and housework.[20]

But this cultural determinism was also a "soft determinism." In the view of Abbott and Parsons, deviation was possible, however inappropriate. Efforts to reverse roles or to eliminate sex-roles would not only fail in the long run but lead to social disaster, according to the traditional view.

Of course it is easier in today's context (i.e., after a revitalization of feminist critique in the 1960's) to find fault and take issue with the traditional views of Abbott and Parsons. And perhaps the condemnation of their work must be mitigated with appreciation of the fact that they lived and wrote in a more rigid theoretical context than recent sociology, theology and ethics provide.

On the other hand, it should also be noted that both Abbott and Parsons were confronted with the issues by their peers and both defended their own conservative views. Abbott criticized the turn-of-the-century women suffragists,[21] career women[22] and the "First Wave" of feminists with those who supported their causes in quest of equality.[23] Indicating that he was well aware of the issues at stake, Abbott defended the

---

[19]Abbott, p. 13.

[20]Abbott, p. 32.

[21]Abbott, p. 25.

[22]Abbott, p. 45.

[23]Abbott, p. 78.

status quo of sex-role differentiated labor in families and stood firmly against any change in the patriarchal tradition.

Not all Social Gospel preachers and scholars took this traditional line. At least one of Abbott's contemporaries, Shailer Matthews, found the scriptures to be supportive of equality between men and women. For example, he believed that Jesus, in his relating to Martha and to his Disciples, "carried his teaching into the heart of housewifery care and ... lifted women's life above cooking (and beyond parenting) as he lifted men's above money-getting."[24] Matthews published his views in support of a more liberated perspective one year after Abbott's *Home Builder* was published.

Parsons added in a footnote that he was well aware of Margaret Mead's cross-cultural studies and that he refused to accept her evaluation that sex-role reversal had in fact taken place (i.e., "in view of the feminine functions in child care"[25]). He regarded sex-roles as generic to all human societies, while assuming that bearing and nursing children would, of course, require women in every culture to be the more involved parent and fathers the breadwinner.

A critique of Abbott and Parsons is important as much for what others have made of their position and the traditional view in general, as it is for what these two figures wrote in their own lifetimes. While Parsons closely observed the inequality between men and women in the society, the conclusions he drew about this situation gave to the facts a static quality. By objectifying the dynamics as he saw them into a principle of all social systems, Parsons gave the weight of science to legitimate the fact of sex-role differentiated families into an *ought* for future generations.

---

[24]Shailer Matthews, *The Social Teaching of Jesus* (New York: Macmillan, 1909), p. 99.

[25]Parsons, "The Father Symbol," p. 44.

Abbott and Parsons carried the traditional view of family relationships in a parallel direction, within Christian ethics and social sciences, respectively, to the culminating point of establishing this view as normative in their disciplines and in the cultural mores generally.

It is clear that Abbott intended to endorse the traditional family as an ethical norm, but it is not clear whether Parsons intended to establish an ethical norm. Parsons, as a sociologist, initially set out to describe a social norm, but his description took on the character of an ethical norm when he began to claim that the traditional role allocation was the *best* way to meet the needs of urban industrial society as well as the needs of the individual family members.[26] The "Parsonian Model" had clearly become an ethical norm in the way Parsons utilized it to endorse and defend the sex-role division of labor in families.

While Abbott primarily espoused the traditional family structure to be *the* Christian family which fulfills God's will, Parsons claimed this family structure to be the one which *best* meets the needs of society. Both assumed men and women are *very* different and should perform different roles, but that their respective tasks are of equal value. Both assumed that the traditional role allocation is fair, because the husband/father and wife/mother offer each other a fair exchange.

However, as a result, neither Abbott nor Parsons adequately raised the issue of *fairness*, especially the issue of inequality between fathers and mothers. Nor did they seriously question their assumption, whether, in fact, men and women are different enough by nature, or nurture, or both, to warrant a division of labor along sex-role lines in families and in society at large.

---

[26]Parsons and Bales, pp. 35-131.

IS THE TRADITIONAL FATHER REALLY FAIR?

Over against the traditional view, the issue of fairness must be raised about the traditional division of labor in families. Is it *fair* to place the primary responsibility for child care and homemaking upon women alone? What happens to their opportunities for satisfying paid employment when they must take primary responsibility to care for the children and the home? Is it *fair* to place the primary responsibility for breadwinning upon men alone? What hazards to their health result when work and the pressure to succeed at work consume the greatest part of their time and energy?

How is each parent's relationship with their children affected when the father is away most of the time and the mother spends nearly all of her time with the children? What are the costs of the traditional arrangement to the father, mother and children in terms of dissatisfaction, boredom, fatigue and emotional pain?

Is it fair to the father, mother and children to divide labor in the particular family along sex-role lines if such division imposes heavy emotional and physical burdens upon each of them which might be reduced by more equal sharing of family responsibilities?

The traditional division of labor in families is *unfair* to women because it places them in an inferior position relative to men in terms of opportunities for success in paid employment and for the multiple benefits of esteem and power to actualize the self associated with the most humanizing forms of employment.

It is *unfair* to men because it generally places them under inordinate pressure to succeed in paid employment and frequently deprives them and their children of opportunities for a satisfying and caring relationship with each other.

Some further consideration of these basic points clarifies how the different roles played out by mothers and fathers in the traditional arrangement are not simply equal and complementary but unequal and unfair. By perpetuating inequality of opportunity and results in the distribution of satisfactions, power and self-esteem, the traditional division of labor in families is an injustice.

Because the traditional father works outside the home, the benefits of his work generally include pay, insurance coverage, pension, promotion opportunities, power and influence, reliable human contact, solidarity and shared interests with co-workers, job satisfaction (including variety, change of pace, self-development, etc.). These are absent from the traditional mother's work at home, where she is not paid and is not promoted. She is isolated from other adults while carrying out her duties. Her economic and social power relative to society is dependent upon her husband's work status.

In families where both parents work outside the home, where the mother works similar hours and earns less, and where she carries major responsibility for child care and housework (the "dual-role wife"), there is a greater burden carried by her vis-a-vis her husband. Generally, she receives less power, prestige and financial reward from her work and gives more energy, time and labor at home than does her husband.

Because the traditional mother works at home, her work is characterized by the absence of extreme pressures, by freedom from job competitiveness and from domination by supervisors. She has more and better opportunities than the father to receive satisfaction through personal relationships with their children. In the father's work setting outside the home, on the other hand, much of his work is characterized by functional relationships, high pressure, domination by employers and competitiveness to succeed on the job.

For the dual-role wife, the double demand of work at home and outside the home together provide a stressful "overload." Her husband, rather than relieve her stress by sharing the child care and housework, gives his time elsewhere, e.g. to longer hours of work or to recreation away from home.

The husband may work longer hours or compete more fiercely for success in order to provide financially for the family because discrimination against women in the job market prevents his wife from obtaining a job equal to his in pay. Because she earns less, he feels compelled to earn more to meet the needs of the family.

For the woman who drops out of the job market while she raises her young children and then returns years later, there is a substantial loss of opportunity for employment success. If a woman does not return to work after five years of parenting, she is likely to feel underemployed and superfluous in the home after the children no longer live there (the "empty nest syndrome").

While economic and political power are more or less available to people who work outside the home, they are only indirectly available to women who work in the home without wages. The power to actualize oneself, to affirm one's goals, to impress upon society (and against the resistance of other people) one's own direction and values is generally enhanced by paid labor with the status, income and influence it provides. Men at work, while they have differing degrees of power and influence between them, have far greater power of this sort than women who work in the home as housewives/mothers.

Self-esteem follows from the exercise of power to actualize one's values. But not all self-esteem is derived from working outside the home, and domination of workers in the workplace is a major destroyer of self-esteem.

Fathers who work outside the home have greater opportunities to develop the economic, political and vocational power to acquire a sense of self-esteem and prestige. Mothers working inside the home may receive fewer threats than paid workers to their daily sense of self-esteem, but feel less self-esteem in general. The male-dominated definitions of prestige include the traditional mother in a high place (i.e., on a "pedestal"); however, this position affords her no opportunities for exercising political and economic power, determining public policy or resisting domination.

Emotional pressure on the job, especially that related to getting promotions, obtaining higher salaries or maintaining one's employment status, "may result in greater vulnerability [to health hazards] for men" than women in families where men are the breadwinners and women are not.[27] Men have a higher mortality rate, in part, because of illnesses related to stress in their employment and to the pressure men are under as breadwinners for their families.

Approximately three-fourths of the difference in life expectancy between men and women in the United States can be attributed to the behaviors of men in fulfilling a traditional male role.[28] One third of the differences involve smoking and one-sixth involve coronary prone behavior (e.g., hostility, aggression, impatience, difficulty relaxing, preoccupation with advancement approval).[29] Most of these behaviors are associated with being the breadwinner. Being the only breadwinner in the traditional family, the husband/father is under greater stress than his spouse.

---

[27]K. Slobin, "Stress," *New York Times Magazine,* November 20, 1977, pp. 48-50, 96, 98, 100, 102, 104, 106.

[28]I. Waldron, "Why Do Women Live Longer Than Men?", *Journal of Human Stress,* No. 2 (1976), pp. 1-13.

[29]Waldron, pp. 1-13.

In examining evidence on the comparative patterns of health and illness in men and women, a "psychosocial" perspective helps to explain the differences with more accurate attention to operative factors than a "biogenetic" perspective. The "psychosocial" perspective provides "a conception of causality involving interacting systems in which biological, psychological and social factors are related in a complex matrix."[30] In contrast, the "biogenetic" perspective is a linear view of causality linking the differences to biological/genetic factors alone.[31] Even at a hypothetical level, the "biogenetic" perspective does not allow for the possibility that health patterns could change as more women share the breadwinning responsibilities and more men share responsibilities for work in the home.

In a series of studies conducted by Harvard University and the National Institute of Mental Health, it was concluded that young married mothers working in low-level jobs and poor women who head single-parent families show the greatest rise in the national rate of depressive symptoms-- both treated and untreated.[32]

"Sociopsychological" explanations were found to account best for the "differential rates of depression in men and women, the rise in such rates, and the particular group of women that appears to be the most at risk for [depressive] symptoms."[33] For these women whose work satisfaction is low

---

[30]James Harrison, "Warning: The Male Sex Role May Be Dangerous to Your Health," *Journal of Social Issues,* Vol. 34, No. 1 (1978), p. 70.

[31]Harrison, p. 70.

[32]Marcia Guttentag and Susan Salasin, "Women, Men, and Mental Health," in Libby Cater et. al., eds., *Women and Men: Changing Roles, Relationships, and Perceptions* (New York: Aspen Institute for Humanistic Studies, 1976), p. 153.

[33]Guttentag and Salasin, p. 175.

and whose parenting responsibilities are heavy, stress is very high. Stress alone does not lead to depression. However, when combined with powerlessness to change the sources of stress both at work and at home, depression frequently results for these women.[34] The traditional, unequal distribution of family labor and paid employment between these women and their husbands or ex-husbands maintains conditions which lead to greater frequency of depressive symptoms for women.

Betty Friedan reported on "the problem that has no name" (or the "trapped housewife") and pointed to the painful experiences of exploitation felt by many housewives/mothers who held sole responsibility for child care and housekeeping.[35]

These women felt depression and then intense anger and desperation, particularly in response to losing their own personality to the demands of the family. They felt trapped as people who service other's ambitions and keep others going: moving them upward, outward and forward. They perceived themselves as moving in circles, doing the same routines day in and day out as housewife/mother and receiving *n o gratitude* for doing what was only expected of them in their role.

At different points in their lives and with varying levels of intensity, great numbers of housewives/mothers rebelled against the prescribed roles that would keep them at home. They have responded to a voice from within: "I want something more than my husband and my children and my home."[36] These women have given a resounding critique of the injustices of traditional role allocations by their refusal to fill the role and their efforts to find something "more."

---

[34]Guttentag and Salasin, p. 153.

[35]Betty Friedan, *The Feminine Mystique* (New York: Dell Books, 1963), p. 15.

[36]Friedan, p. 27.

In 1973, the Berkeley Men's Center Manifesto, which recorded the proclamation of a few, reflected the protest of an increasing number of men:

> We no longer want to strain and compete to live up to an impossible oppressive masculine image .... We want to be equal with women and end destructive competitive relationships between men .... We are oppressed by conditioning which makes us only half-human .... We are oppressed by working in alienating jobs, as "breadwinners" .... We want men to share their lives and experiences with each other in order to understand who we are, how we got this way, and what we must do to be free.[37]

Men, as well as women, realized that to some extent they have helped to perpetuate the traditional roles that they have found themselves living out. While easy alternatives to these roles were not readily available, many men were experiencing dissatisfaction and wanting some relief.

As many women were "finding it hard to fight an enemy who has outposts in your head,"[38] so also were many men having difficulty getting perspective on the problem which included themselves:

> However heavy the burden of supporting a family or being boss, men weighed their worth by those masculine roles. When did self-fulfilling achievement

---

[37]Berkeley Men's Center, Berkeley, California, 1973, reprinted in Joseph Pleck and Jack Sawyer, eds., *Men and Masculinity* (Englewood Cliffs, N.J.: Prentice-Hall, Inc., 1974), pp. 173-174.

[38]Quoted in Peter Gabriel Filene, *Him/Her/Self: Sex Roles in Modern America* (New York: New American Library, Inc., 1974), p. 216.

become   self-impoverishing   ambition?   Few
"breadwinners"   would   have   a   ready   answer,   but,
precisely   because   they   played   a   conventional   role,   they
usually   did   not   have   to   ask.   When   a   man   stepped
outside   of   the   role's   ready-made   definitions,   however,
he   could   not   help   asking   and   could   not   easily   answer.[39]

IS BIOLOGY REALLY DESTINY?

The   traditional   assumption   that   biology   is   destiny   must   be
more   seriously   evaluated   in   light   of   the   evidence   to   the
contrary.   Social   science   research   has   been   helpful   in
ascertaining   whether   there   are   biological   determinants
significant   enough   to   account   for   the   low   level   of   male
involvement   in   child   care   today   as   well   as   the   related   unequal
participation   of   women   in   paid   employment.

The   first   of   two   basic   questions   (are   men   and   women   very
different   in   their   capacities   to   nurture   children?)   is   raised   over
against   the   traditional   argument   of   biological   determinists   who
claim   that   women,   rather   than   men,   raise   children   because
women   are   endowed   with   a   child-bearing   physiology,
including   the   capability   of   lactation   as   well   as   a   temperament
more   suited   to   caretaking   activities.

The   second   question   (are   men   and   women   very   different
in   their   capacities   for   success   in   paid   employment?)   is   raised
over   against   the   traditional   argument   of   biological
determinists   who   claim   that   male   success   in   the   work   world
vis-a-vis   women's   lower   work   status   and   women's   less
frequent   participation   in   paid   employment   is   due   largely,   if
not   entirely,   to   some   generic   endowments   more   prevalent   in

---

[39]Filene, p. 216.

men (e.g. physical strength, rationality, bravado and aggression, etc.).

The two divergent schools of thought on why particular human societies have been characterized by sex-role division of labor are the "naturist" position and the "nurturist" position. This debate between the two positions, popularly referred to as the "nature vs. nurture" controversy, is in fact, only occasionally a clear debate between a particular "naturist" who believes *strictly* that biology is the only determining factor and a particular "nurturist" who believes *strictly* that social conventions/environment are the only determining reasons for the sex-role division found in some societies. More frequently, the debate is over *which* are more significant, biological or social factors, and *how strongly* they determine human behavior toward the living out of sex roles.

Isolating the physiological factors from the environmental factors would be quite arbitrary, since these two interact so closely in the development of human personality. As James Harrison explains:

> Both the biochemical environment and the social environment seem to have an effect on the structure of the organism. The resulting human being is the product of multiple forces which play a role in his/her development and differentiation. It seems safe to conclude from [the research Harrison reviews] that the effort to determine the absolute primacy of either biological or social factors is essentially a misguided quest.[40]

---

[40] James Harrison, "A Critical Evaluation of Research on 'Masculinity/Femininity' and a Proposal for an Alternative Paradigm for Research on Psychological Differences and Similarities Between the Sexes," Dissertation, New York University, 1974, p. 229.

Therefore, it is necessary to understand the notion of "capacity" being utilized in these two questions as a construct indicating the present abilities of a person based upon *both* physiological *and* social antecedents.

ARE MEN AND WOMEN VERY DIFFERENT IN THEIR CAPACITIES TO NURTURE CHILDREN?

They are not, according to those social researchers who have concluded that men *can* nurture children unless restricted from doing so or unless unmotivated to do so. In general, "nurturing" refers to the behaviors associated with providing affectionate care and attention, e.g. feeding, dressing, bathing, diapering and cuddling.

Ross Parke and Douglas Sawin investigated whether the traditional views about fathering are observed to be true in a laboratory setting or whether these traditional hypotheses are contradicted and qualified by research observations. They restated the traditional views of fathering as follows:

(1) Fathers are uninterested in and uninvolved with newborn infants.

(2) Fathers are less nurturant toward infants than mothers.

(3) Fathers prefer non-caretaking roles and leave caretaking up to mother.

(4) Fathers are less competent than mothers to care for newborn infants.[41]

---

[41]"The Father's Role in Infancy: A Re-Evaluation," *The Family Coordinator*, Vol. 25, October 1976, p. 365.

Contrary to proposition number two, fathers in two studies by Parke were observed to be "just as nurturant as mothers."[42] In the first study, they touched, looked, vocalized and kissed their newborn as often as the mothers did.[43] In the second study, the fathers exhibited "an equal amount of nurturing when alone with the baby."[44]

In a study of the feeding of infants, Parke and Sawin found that fathers tend to spend less time overall in feeding activities, but that the fathers were "as sensitive as the mothers to infant cues in the feeding context."[45] Infants provide some indication (e.g. crying in certain ways) when they need to be fed, or to have feeding discontinued, or to be patted for a burp. Sensitivity to these cues was interpreted as competency in nurturing. Results of the study established that fathers can display equal competency in feeding infants, contrary to proposition four.

Overall, it was concluded that the traditional hypotheses are contradicted and qualified in the following ways:

(1) Fathers are interested in newborns and, if provided with the opportunity, do become involved.

(2) Fathers are just as nurturant as mothers in their interactions with newborns.

---

[42]Parke and Sawin, "The Father's Role in Infancy," p. 369.

[43]Parke, S. O'Leary, and S. West, "Mother-Father-Newborn Interaction: Effects of Maternal Medication, Labor and Sex of Infant," *Proceedings of the American Psychological Association* (1972), pp. 85-86.

[44]Parke and Sawin, "Infant Characteristics and Behavior as Elicitors of Maternal and Paternal Responsibility in the Newborn Period" (Paper presented at the Annual Convention of the American Psychological Association, Chicago, September 1975).

[45]Parke and Sawin, "The Father's Role in Infancy," p. 369.

(3) Fathers do apparently engage in less caretaking, but;

(4) Fathers can be capable and competent in caretaking activities.[46]

In at least seven American studies, using a variety of measures and methodologies, infants were observed to exhibit attachment behavior toward both their mothers *and* their fathers. These fathers did not prove to be unacceptable to the infants as providers of affection and comfort.[47] In several other studies, infants in stress-free situations showed no preference for either parent over the other.[48]

While some researchers observed infants who preferred their mothers under stressful circumstances,[49] these findings may say more about the effects of unequal distribution of the day-to-day responsibility for child care in the families participating in the study than any differences between men and women in capacities to nurture children. The infant's preference for the mother under stressful circumstances is, in these studies, due more, perhaps, to the greater quantity (and possibly higher quality of time) spent by the mothers in caretaking activities in that family. Their fathers, generally, spent less time interacting with their infants outside the laboratory setting, and the infants' mothers were more frequently the comforters, affection givers and care providers than the infants' fathers. It is, perhaps, due to the low level of previous involvement with their fathers that the infants

---

[46]Parke and Sawin, "The Father's Role in Infancy," pp. 369-370.

[47]Michael Lamb and Jamie Lamb, "The Nature of the Father-Infant Relationship," *The Family Coordinator,* Vol. 25, October 1976, p. 380.

[48]Lamb and Lamb, p. 380.

[49]Lamb and Lamb, p. 380.

prefer their mothers under stressful conditions and not because their fathers have less capacity for nurturing them.

Prior to the work of Parke and Sawin, researchers did not distinguish between whether fathers have a capacity for nurturance and whether many fathers actually do nurture young children on a frequent basis. While men are capable of nurturing activity, they do not generally spend very much time and effort in caretaking activities with young children. Ross Parke explains the mistaken traditional assumption:

> Too often the fact of low father involvement throughout history in the caretaking of children has been extended to the conclusion that the low level of involvement was equivalent to a low level of competence. However, the fact that historical, social and economic arrangements meant that fathers were allocated to other roles need not necessarily imply that they are incapable of assuming a caretaking function.[50]

Men have been observed to be competent and involved in caring for children in some non-Western cultures. These include the Trobianders of Melanesia, the Taira of Okinawa, the Nyansongo of Kenya, and the Ilocos of the Philippines.[51] This cross-cultural evidence suggests that men either have or may acquire the capacity to care for children if the culture encourages such behavior.

Studies on the parenting behavior of animals not only show that some males, particularly some non-human primates, engage in nurturant activity toward infants in the wild,[52] but

---

[50]"The Father's Role in Infancy," p. 366.

[51]Parke and Sawin, "The Father's Role in Infancy," p. 366.

[52]G.D. Mitchell, "Paternalistic Behavior in Primates," *Psychological Bulletin,* Vol. 71 (1969), pp. 399-417.

that others who do not care for infants in the wild may be motivated to do so in a laboratory setting.[53] Male rhesus monkeys, who rarely exhibit nurturing behavior in their natural habitat, were found to be capable of caring for infants when they were motivated to do so by changing their environment and the conditions influencing their non-parenting behavior. When the female was not present and not caring for the young in the laboratory, male rhesus monkeys performed the nurturing activities.[54]

Neither male hormones nor previous socialization, according to this study, could absolutely restrict the capacity of rhesus monkeys in caring for infants. Changed environmental and motivational factors, on the other hand, enabled these male primates to become more actively involved in caring for the young.

While hormones that are more concentrated in females (those associated with pregnancy, childbirth and lactation) help to arouse parental behavior, these hormones are not necessary for the appearance of parental behavior.[55] Some males in sub-human mammals and the human species, can and do display nurturing behavior without pregnancy, childbirth or lactation. While "female" hormones can help arouse parenting behavior, neither the lack of these hormones nor the prevalence of "male" hormones restricts males from caretaking activity.

According to available evidence, it is reasonable to conclude that males *can* raise babies. But if males *can* "raise

---

[53]Mitchell, W.K. Redican and J. Gomber, "Males Can Raise Babies," *Psychology Today*, 7 (1974), pp. 63-67.

[54]Mitchell et. al., "Males Can Raise Babies," pp. 63-67.

[55]E. Maccoby and C. Jacklin, *The Psychology of Sex Differences* (Stanford: Stanford University Press, 1974), p. 219.

babies," then why don't they do so more often? This question is the subject of the analysis in the next chapter.

ARE MEN AND WOMEN VERY DIFFERENT IN THEIR CAPACITIES FOR SUCCESS IN PAID EMPLOYMENT?

In the traditional view, women are endowed with softness, subjectivism, emotionality, sensitivity and intuitiveness which make them ill-suited for the "strenuous and stormy life"[56] of paid employment outside the home and naturally constituted to fulfill the expressive functions inside the home. In this view, fulfilling the role of nurturer is considered *necessary* to the "personality-equilibrium of the woman."[57] Being the active parent helps her to be a more complete person. The needs of the occupational system, on the other hand, require the father's attention to be elsewhere.

While Parsons pointed out that there was a trend toward more women working, he was unwilling to admit that sex-role differentiation is not generic to human societies. According to Parsons, because this difference of roles is rooted so deeply in the social system (i.e., being biologically and socially determined) it cannot be significantly altered. As he went so far to claim:

> Even if, as seems possible, it should come about that the average married woman had some kind of job, it seems most unlikely that this relative balance (between the male role as primary breadwinner and the female role

---

[56]Abbott, p. 13.

[57]Parsons and Bales, *Family, Socialization, and Interaction Process*, p. 154.

as primary active parent/homemaker) would be upset; that either the roles would be reversed, or their qualitative differentiation in these respects completely erased.[58]

Over against the traditional interpretation of the lower position of women in the labor force, a basic preliminary question must be addressed: are men and women very different in their capacities for success in paid employment? In a monumental study published in 1974, *The Psychology of Sex Differences,* Eleanor Maccoby and Carol Jacklin compiled and evaluated research which seriously addressed this question.[59]

In measures of dominance, competitiveness and overall activity level, which might become significant in evaluating potentials for career success, men and women do not exhibit salient differences.[60] But many other measures of ability and personality must be considered.

It has been "fairly well established" that girls "as a group" have greater verbal ability than boys. This difference begins to appear in test scores about age eleven, increasing through high school and perhaps beyond.[61] However, the significance of this difference can be misconstrued. The *difference* is in mean scores of males and females on various tests of verbal ability, but there is a large overlap in the individual scores of males and females. As Harrison has warned in his critique of measures of masculinity and femininity:

---

[58] Parsons and Bales, *Family, Socialization, and Interaction Process,* p. 15.   Parenthetical explanation added.

[59] Stanford: Stanford University Press, 1974.

[60] Maccoby and Jacklin, p. 353.

[61] Maccoby and Jacklin, p. 351.

The convention of reporting only the difference between means has perpetuated an impression that differences between the sexes is far more important than similarities on psychological variables.[62]

In verbal ability, males and females are more alike than they are different. While males excel as a group in visual-spatial tests in adolescence and adulthood, this finding does *not* indicate that all males are better at visual-spatial tasks than all females. It does indicate that the mean scores of the males are higher than the mean scores of the females. However, the large overlap is much more significant than the differences.[63] The number of men and women who are similar in these abilities is much larger than the number of men and women who are different. It is also possible that this difference has as much to do with socialization and learning as it does with biochemical variations between males and females.

In light of this logical consideration, Maccoby and Jacklin conclude:

Intellectual aptitudes are similarly distributed by sex, at least enough so as to rule out reserving certain occupations for one sex or the other on the basis of ability patterns.[64]

It has been determined that the "greater aggressiveness of males" is "one of the best established and most pervasive of all

---

[62] "A Critical Evaluation of Research on 'Masculinity/Femininity'...," p. 236.

[63] Maccoby and Jacklin, p. 367.

[64] Maccoby and Jacklin, p. 370.

psychological sex differences."[65] And there appears to be a biological/hormonal component underlying this difference. However, Maccoby and Jacklin doubt that dominance, leadership and employment success are linked to aggressiveness in such a way as to account for the advantaged position of men in the economy.

They reason that since aggression is not a modern method most usually employed in leadership and in achieving a high level of success in employment, aggression is not a significant determinant of male advantage in jobs. Leadership is now exercised by being supportive of others with whom one works and guiding a group toward consensus through negotiation. When aggression is necessary to accomplish the job, males may have an advantage. But when the job requires skill in setting goals, planning, organizing, persuading, conciliating and conveying enthusiasm (as most jobs presently require), there is little reason to believe that men are holding their advantaged position in the work world because of their greater aggressiveness as a group.[66]

While there are some jobs that require great physical strength and men can be expected to predominate in them, the increasing use of tools and machinery has reduced the legitimacy for employing only males in heavy work. Men are assisted in multiplying their strength by the use of machinery, and so also can women multiply their strength by using tools to perform the same tasks as men. No one looks down on a man who uses a forklift to carry a ton of metal, nor should anyone be critical of a woman who uses tools and machinery to do jobs that might be done by some men with fewer tools.

Biology is not destiny, according to Maccoby and Jacklin. Societies can minimize sex differences rather than maximize

---

[65]Maccoby and Jacklin, p. 368.

[66]Maccoby and Jacklin, p. 368.

them through the socialization process.[67] Differences in test scores can be better understood and interpreted without reifying them into a liability for which individual men and women are categorically discriminated against.

The existence of different capacities in men and women significant enough to justify a sex-linked division of labor in society is *not* confirmed by social science research. Quite to the contrary, findings from this research suggest that social structures and *social restrictions* against women working and fathers nurturing, *not* differences in capacities, are largely responsible for the profound differences in the roles men and women presently play in paid employment and in child care.[68]

By virtue of these findings, it is now possible to refocus the issue. The central question is no longer whether men *can* nurture children and whether women *can* succeed in paid employment, but rather, how and why are the opportunities of men to nurture children and of women to succeed in paid employment limited by social, personal and institutional constraints?

---

[67]Maccoby and Jacklin, p. 374.

[68]Joseph Pleck, "The Psychology of Sex Roles: Traditional and New Views," *Women and Men: Changing Roles, Relationships, and Perceptions,* ed. Libby Cater, et. al. (New York: Aspen Institute for Humanistic Studies, 1976), pp. 181-199.

CHAPTER TWO

A CRITIQUE OF THE ABSENT FATHER

In the majority of two-parent families in the United
States, the father is not significantly involved in the physical
care and emotional nurture of children. Most fathers are
absent from all but the financial responsibilities of parenting
while mothers fulfill the role of primary parent.[1] Very few
divorced fathers have an opportunity to maintain more than a
"visiting" relationship with their children.[2]

As David Blankenhorn observed and concluded:

To understand today's major trend, picture a father who
is absent from the home altogether, divorced or never
married, having little or no steady contact with his
children. The dramatic proliferation of this type of

---

[1] Jessie Bernard, *Women, Wives, and Mothers: Values and Options*
(Chicago: Aldine, 1975), p. 221; Henry Biller, *Paternal Deprivation*
(Lexington, Mass.: D.C. Heath, 1974).

[2] Mel Roman and William Haddad, *The Disposable Parent: The Case
for Joint Custody* (New York: Holt, Rinehart and Winston, 1978), p. 20;
Ira Victor and Win Ann Winkler, *Fathers and Custody* (New York:
Hawthorn Books, 1977), p. 28.

father far outweighs any increase in the number of nurturing new fathers.... Approximately one of every four children is growing up without a father in the home, more than twice as many as in 1960.[3]

Frank Furstenberg studied some of these fifteen million children and found that "more than half never visited their father's home in a typical year. Only one in five sleeps in a father's home in a typical month, while only one in six sees a father an average of once or more per week."[4]

Before analyzing the cultural and economic forces which lead to and maintain the father's *absence* from parenting, it is instructive to examine briefly what constitutes an appropriate *presence.* This measure of presence is essential to clarify what is meant by the many generalizations herein about fathering involvement, both factual and ethical.

FINDING BALANCE IN PARENTING

The interchangeable terms "active," "involved" and "present," when referring in this work to a father's level of participation in parenting, are positive valuations or affirmations based upon a set of criteria. These criteria fall into two categories: the *activities* of active parenting and the *attitudinal orientation* of active parents in weighing their own needs over against those of their children.

An appropriate presence for fathers involves engagement in a series of activities necessary to the growth of the child. The active father engages in and shares similarly in activities

---

3 David Blankenhorn, "Father who stays with family bucks major new trend," *Star Tribune,* Nov. 10, 1990.

4 Blankenhorn.

of parenting traditionally conducted only by mothers. He diapers infants. He bathes infants and young children, giving attention to both their safety and hygiene. Participating in clothing the children, he engages in selecting clothes, purchasing shoes and clothes, laundering and caring for them, dressing the younger children, and helping them to learn to dress themselves at an appropriate age.

His involvement in feeding his children includes planning their menu, preparing meals, purchasing food, and cleaning up the table, floor, kitchen and dishes after meals. If the infant is bottle-fed, he also engages in this activity, providing comfort and tactile stimulation as well as nourishment. Responsibility for night feedings is shared by the active father.

His interaction with infants includes lifting, carrying, patting, holding, rocking, cuddling, kissing and hugging. He establishes eye-to-eye contact with them, smiles, laughs, talks, sings and plays. With older children he talks, listens and participates in events with them toward the goal of establishing and maintaining a nurturing relationship.

In some ways these details and those which follow may appear to be trivial matters. Describing their significance in a normative fashion may appear to be moral casuistry. When these responsibilities are viewed together, however, it is evident that parenting involves a remarkable number of tasks which traditional fathers have *not* performed. Describing these activities is integral to a substantive definition of active parenting which can then be utilized in a more general discussion of a set of Christian ethical principles.

To be equally involved in parenting, fathers assume responsibility similar to mothers for the physical health of the children. They administer medication and take the children to the doctor, dentist and emergency room when appropriate. Attention is given by the active father to preventing accidents, avoiding unhealthy situations, teaching children preventive dental care and maintaining a balanced diet.

This father is present to his children in taking steps to provide for their emotional needs. He seeks to understand and facilitate their maturation through communication with them. By interacting to affirm the self-esteem of the children on a regular basis, he helps to create a relationship which they can depend upon and through which they can grow into their own independence.

The activities of caring for the emotional needs of children are less tangible and more difficult to describe. It is precisely in this area, however, that traditional fathers have been most reluctant and inadequately prepared to become involved. Even though nurturance cannot be as objectively described as other parenting activities, nevertheless it must not be overlooked or undervalued. It is essential to active fathering.

Discipline, when understood as meting out punishment, has been a part of even the traditional father's role. Other aspects of discipline are also shared by the active father, particularly the affirming and teaching of constructive behavior. In this way the child is aided in developing self-discipline.

This elucidation provides some concrete reference points for speaking about "active," "involved" and "present" fathers. Those fathers who do *not* engage in these parenting activities, or do so on a minimal basis, are referred to as traditional fathers or absent fathers.

Hereinafter, for brevity, the initials "ANF" will refer to the phrase "active nurturant fathering" and "ANF's" will refer to "active nurturant fathers."

This set of activities is given as a minimal standard for speaking of active fathers as opposed to absent fathers. The second category of criteria for defining an appropriate presence of fathers (and mothers) is not so much a standard as it is a set of limitations on how much parents' lives should be directed toward meeting the needs of their children.

In the traditional view of parenting, self-sacrifice by the parents (i.e., by the mother sacrificing at home and the father sacrificing at work) is regarded as absolutely necessary for the well-being of the child. The view is, perhaps, a reaction to the harshness of child labor and child neglect in working-income families of Nineteenth Century America.

A critical historical perspective enables us to see that child-centered families of the Twentieth Century are an antithesis to parent-centered families of the century before.[5] In the parent-centered authoritarian family, the children's lives were dominated by the needs of the family. Recreation, education or personal activities that hindered their work or reduced their earnings were considered frivolous. For these working-income families, parenting meant constant vigilance over children to see that they produced. Having many children and little income, the parents required the labor of the children for financial survival.[6]

In the child-centered approach, parents supposedly reap great joy from daily activities of parenting. Joy comes from sacrifice as well as from the intrinsic pleasures of caring for children. Parents enoble themselves by submitting to inconveniences, relinquishing their own personal dreams, and foregoing individual satisfactions all for the sake of the children. They show their love and prove their value as parents through some degree of martyrdom. Traditional mothers delay or forego careers or jobs to care for the

---

[5]Rhona Rapoport, Robert Rapoport and Ziona Strelitz with Stephen Kew, *Fathers, Mothers, and Society: Towards New Alliances* (New York: Basic Books, 1977), p. 14.

[6]Tamara Hareven, "The Family and Gender Roles in Historical Perspective," in Cater et. al., pp. 102-104.

children. Traditional fathers hang on to a secure income to provide for the family rather than change careers to find greater job satisfaction.

In the child-centered family, there are two presumptions about why parents do and should sacrifice themselves for the children. First, the satisfactions of parenting are regarded as adequate compensation for whatever sacrifice must be made by parents. Parents do and should sacrifice, supposedly, because they receive compensating satisfactions from parenting which foster their own well-being. Second, when sacrifices seem to be inordinately large, then the priority of the well-being of the children still requires that these sacrifices be made. Parents do and should sacrifice, according to this approach, because the child requires it for his/her well-being.

In the parent-centered authoritarian family the children sacrificed more of their hopes and satisfactions than the parents. In the child-centered family, the parents sacrificed more of their hopes and satisfactions than the children. Following in the wake of these two polarizations, a new synthesis is emerging.

This synthesis is the groundwork for a valuational premise which underlies both factual and ethical statements herein regarding active fathering (and mothering). Parents are appropriately present with their children when they are working toward a *balancing* of their own needs, satisfactions, and dreams with those of their children.

An ongoing goal of parents is finding an appropriate fit between their own needs and preoccupations and those of their children. It is neither presumed that the children's needs *always* come first, nor that the children should *always* be asked to adapt to the preoccupations of the parents.

Three related premises about parenting, which provide further clarification of an *appropriate presence*, underlie and support this new synthesis:

(1) Overmothering and overfathering (i.e., an exaggerated focus of parents toward doing *too much* to and for the child) can be detrimental to the child's well being.[7] A salient feature of an appropriate presence is the avoidance of overparenting by nurturing children progressively toward their own independence.

(2) Parenting is assumed to be one aspect of a father's life and of a mother's life, not their whole identity. Parents who are satisfied with other aspects of their lives are more apt (than those who are not satisfied) to be able to provide a relationship with their children which ensures proper attention, allows for independence and fosters the child's growth.[8]

(3) Parenting involves both joys *and* sorrows, pleasures *and* duties, accomplishments *and* frustrations. Emphasizing only the positive aspects of parenting *distorts* the character of the

---

[7] Kenneth Keniston, *The Uncommitted: Alienated Youth in American Society* (New York: Dell, 1965), pp. 309-310; Christopher Lasch, *The Culture of Narcissism* (New York: W.W. Norton Co., 1979), pp. 278ff.

[8] Rapoport, Rapoport, Strelitz, with Stephen Kew, p. 26; Lillian Breslow Rubin, *Worlds of Pain* (New York: Basic Books, Inc, 1976), pp. 169ff; Jean Stapleton and Richard Bright, *Equal Marriage* (Nashville, TN: Abingdon, 1976), p. 85.

daily involvement of most active parents with
their children.[9] A more balanced assessment of
parenting, rather than an idealized view, is
essential to the new synthesis.

Finding a healthy balance in the amount of time one
spends with their children is a concern for active nurturant
parents. At the height of popularity of the traditional family in
the 1950's, stay-at-home-with-the-kids mothers reacted with
horror at stories of child care in an Israeli kibbutz. It appeared
to these "overattentive mothers" (who saw their young
children as their only accomplishment) to be unconscionable
that pre-school children would spend the daytime in the care
of people other than their mothers. Today, dual-career families
take it for granted that someone else cares for the children
during a significant amount of time during the week as they
drop their pre-schoolers off at the day care center before work
and pick them up after work. Active nurturant fathers seek to
find some healthy balance in the amount of time they spend
with their children. This often results in some compromise
between the eight-hour day care and one person staying at
home all day. It usually involves the father in being at home
with pre-schoolers during some times that have traditionally
been the mother's responsibility.

Arlie Hochschild warned that parents who give too little
time to their children and who underestimate the needs of
children may be the other extreme that is being lived out by
some families now. When there gets to be too much work for
the family to handle, both parents can let the housekeeping go
without much damage. However, the children can suffer if the

---

[9]Ellen Peck, *The Baby Trap* (New York: Bernard Geis Associates,
1971), p. 12; Shirley Radl, *Mother's Day Is Over* (New York:
Charterhouse, 1973), p. 70.

parents let the needs of their children for nurturing go unmet.[10]

Finding a healthy balance of emotions in parenting is vital for both parents and the children. A "co-dependent" parent is one who feeds their own self-esteem parasitically off of the destruction of the child's self-esteem.[11] This parent is perfectionistic to an extreme and has high expectations of how the children should fulfill the parent's expectations. When the child does not live up to the high expectations of the parent, the parent becomes judgmental and angry. The parent attempts to live out their own dreams through the child. The parent's own failures and regrets fuel the fire of their criticism of the child. The parent attempts to put the child down and lifts himself up in the process---not unlike the co-dependent spouse of an alcoholic who frequently points out the failures of the alcoholic to them and tries to whip them into shape by chiseling away at their flaws while feeling better about themselves for not having the flaws that they point out to their spouse. The chiseling makes the behavior of the victim worse rather than more perfect. In trying to be an ANF, some fathers might become overactive in this way with their children. Fathering like this has been more devastating for some children than no father at all. I want to be sure that the reader understands that this kind of fathering is *not* the kind of fathering which I am advocating.

While some fathers can be "too hard on children" in this way, others can be too hard on themselves. Parenting is an inexact science. Sometimes the right course to follow is unclear. Doing the right thing in the height of crisis is not easy.

---

[10] Arlie Hochschild with Anne Machung, *The Second Shift* (New York: Avon Books), p. 230.

[11] Barbara Cottman Becnel, *The Co-dependent Parent* (Los Angeles, CA: Lowell House, 1990).

If fathers dwell upon their mistakes out of guilt, growth will not happen for them. If fathers can openly acknowledge the mistakes to themselves (if not to others) and face having done the wrong thing sometimes, they may be more free to change in the direction of more appropriate discipline, more approving affirmation or better communication the next time a similar testing moment occurs.

It can help a father to realize that even though he is not perfect (and should not be expected to be), that he is really a "good enough parent."[12] This basic feeling of being adequate is essential to being able to do a good job in parenting. It is the primary subject of the lessons that he has to offer his children and the primary gift he has to give to them: the awareness that they too are worthwhile and acceptable as they are (i.e., they are unconditionally loved). The best way for him to help them to learn this and feel it deep in their psyche is for him to show his own capacity for accepting himself and them.

A dominant theme in television depictions of fathers for the last thirty years has been that of the "inadequate" father. The main reason may be that on these situation comedies, adequate fathers would not be capable of amusing audiences. The shows succeeded in producing and sustaining audiences, but they also helped to create a low self image for fathers. It is human nature to live down to the level of a negative image that others have of us. The antidote to help today's ANF is to acquire and live up to an image of being a "good enough parent"---good enough to feel good about the job that he is doing, good enough to be respected and appreciated by his children, and good enough to take the same kind of pride in his child care as he does in his paid employment.

---

[12]Bruno Bettelheim, *A Good Enough Parent* (New York: Alfred A. Knopf, 1989).

Some fathers suffer and cease to be active and nurturant because their families are "too hard" on them. Fathers require tolerance and forgiveness from their families in order to sustain a nurturing relationship. If the family dwells upon the father's mistakes, out of unexpressed pain or unresolved anger toward him, the capacity for nurturing between the father and children may diminish. The children can close the door to his caring as well as he can shut them out. Forgiveness from others as well as themselves, can set fathers free to try again to get it right. Unconditional love is essential for the care and feeding of fathers too. If the family *refuses to* or neglects the emotional feeding of the father with nurturing love out of resentment of his shortcomings, the family may suffer even more down the road as the frustrations of the unloved father are visited upon the family that he considers to be "so ungrateful for all that he has done."

Forgiving love of father by the family requires their open expressing of grievances against him and then letting go of the anger through forgiveness and reconciliation. If they hold it in and hold it against him for years, they lose much and so does he. They can be partially responsible for the lack of love in the father-child (parent-parent) relationship in some ways if they self-righteously hang on to their grievances while refusing to express gratitude, unconditional love and affirmation of his good behavior. Of course, pre-schoolers do not bear the same load of responsibility for doing this as teenagers do. It must be asserted first that the father should be older and wiser and more mature and that he should lead by his good example. But the children have work to do in the relationship as well.

There is a proliferation of resources on *how* to be a good parent. Many are listed in the bibliography. While reading them and using some of their insights can be very helpful in developing parenting skills, reading all of them would certainly produce a mind in conflict about how to parent.

ANF's seek to maintain a balance between reading too much and reading nothing; between trying hard to improve and not trying at all; between attending every class offered on the subject (which may take them away from actually being with their children) and never taking a class.

It is now possible to explore with greater precision the cultural and economic forces which lead to and maintain some fathers' absence from parenting. How are the opportunities for men to nurture children limited by social, personal and institutional constraints? Why do men not utilize the opportunities that they do have for becoming actively involved in child care?

FINDING FATHERS AT WORK AND PLAY

For men in American culture, the most conspicuous achievements are centered in paid work (e.g., business, professions, politics, military and the arts). Economic success, or competitive occupational achievement, has become the highest standard by which males are judged as well as the one by which they have come to judge themselves as worthwhile or not.[13]

To succeed in their employment, men utilize great amounts of time and energy which usually results in both physical and psychological absence from their children. Because conditions related to work keep him occupied, "today's

---

[13]Robert Williams, "Achievement and Success," in Deborah David and Robert Brannon, eds., *The Forty-Nine Percent Majority: The Male Sex Role* (Reading, MA: Addison-Wesley Co., 1976), p. 107.

father has little opportunity to be with his children or even make his presence felt by them."[14]

The father frequently develops an intense relationship with a second "family" in the workplace, among colleagues who share in his achievements and "from whom he seems to get his greatest personal satisfaction."[15] These colleagues may become closer to him than his family and emotional distance may increase between the father and his children as well as between him and his spouse.

The workplace frequently overshadows family life as a source of the father's self-esteem, rather than sharing that place. As child psychologist Dr. Lawrence Brian explained, "A lot of guys use the office as a sanctuary. They feel successful, competent and in control at work but not necessarily at home."[16]

Most men feel that child care is a diversion from a man's "real" work---the exercise of paid work or a successful career. "Any man who not only says that he wishes he could spend more time with his children, but actually does so is suspected by his associates of not being properly ambitious."[17]

These feelings about work are, at least in part, internalizations of the conditions placed upon working fathers. Nearly all job advancement requires some form of outstanding performance evidenced by overtime work, results exceeding those of other employees (including the other two-thirds who

---

[14]Myron Brenton, *The American Male* (Greenwich, CT: Fawcett Publications, 1966), p. 120.

[15]Maureen Green, *Fathering* (New York: McGraw-Hill, 1976), pp. 8-9.

[16]Carol Krucoff, "Families: Fathers and the Big Business of Raising Children," *Washington Post*, May 18, 1979.

[17]Marc Feigen Fasteau, "Men as Parents," in David and Brannon, eds., p. 60.

are not fathers), or creative new ideas (that take time beyond the usual work schedule). This expectation by the employer, and the internalization of these pressures to perform by the employee, leave him in a constant state of anxiety about the job. If pressure to succeed causes him to concentrate on work long after he leaves the job-site and well in advance of his return there, it is little wonder that the needs of children are taken all too lightly.

For many fathers in middle management, commuting hours are long and business trips may be frequent. The workweek exceeds five days and forty hours. Changing jobs and moving long distances to relocate within the corporation are standard procedure. This is the way management positions are organized. Those who want to succeed must conform to the company procedures, which separate these fathers from their children. Women with children and only daytime assistance in caring for them cannot apply for these jobs. Fathers in middle management have usually relied upon their wives to care for the children and make their working style possible.[18]

For blue-collar jobs, overtime is often mandatory when offered, if only in subtle ways. In many workplaces, those who do not accept overtime when it is offered will jeopardize their chances of ever being offered overtime again. Furthermore, overtime is offered when the production schedule requires it, not when fathers are available to work without neglecting the needs of their children.

The nature of the work itself, not just the hours, may be destructive to a father's capacity to be present with his children emotionally when he *is* available physically. "The long hours men devote to work and to recovering from work

---

[18]Robert Seidenberg, *Corporate Wives---Corporate Casualties?* (Garden City, NY: Anchor Press, 1975), pp. 1-30.

are often taken from the untold stories, unthrown balls and uncuddled children left behind at home."[19]

Studs Terkel found that one of the most common complaints of working people was dissatisfaction with their working conditions and the effects these conditions had upon their lives overall:

> Significant numbers of American workers are dissatisfied with the quality of their working lives....To survive the day is triumph enough for the walking wounded among the great many of us....The scars, psychic as well as physical, brought home to the supper table and the TV set, may have touched malignantly, the soul of our society.[20]

One consequence of this dissatisfaction is that fathers frequently view the home as a space in which they should receive respect, attention and care. They come to the family with an attitude that they have sacrificed themselves on the job and for this they deserve nurturing from the family. They are not enabled by work to give respect, attention and patience to their children; rather, they expect it from their children. In fact, they may be hostile when it does not come.[21]

For the most part, in the American work world, the search for meaning, satisfaction and self-fulfillment, particularly between family members, is treated as a private matter for workers to develop in their free time outside of the workplace. Workers are paid to produce goods and services at the most efficient rate possible. Whatever negative influences the goals

---

[19] Arlie Hochschild with Anne Machung, p. xi.

[20] Studs Terkel, *Working* (New York: Avon Books, 1972), p. xiii.

[21] Richard Sennett and Jonathan Cobb, *The Hidden Injuries of Class* (New York: Random House, 1972), pp. 125-126, 140.

of production may have on the family's lifestyle are relatively inconsequential to the organizers of the workplace, unless these negative influences reduce the efficiency of production. Workers are paid to adjust to the needs of the workplace, and only through collective bargaining have workers been able to make the employer adjust to some of their needs.

At present, family life style is not a significant concern of labor organizers. Fathers generally have adapted their family life to the needs of their occupation. In adapting to the requirements of the job, fathers tend to have minimal control over their opportunities to be involved in child care when they may be needed most.

For a number of reasons, traditional fathers may utilize most of their non-working time in activities that do not include the family. They may become "seriously" absorbed in leisure activities. This "long arm of their leisure could intrude into the family as much as that of their job."[22]

If their job is not satisfying or if it produces anxiety, they may spend large amounts of time in recreation in an attempt to relieve their emotional tension. By watching sporting events, by playing athletic games or by golfing and fishing, they seek to recover from the stresses of deadlines, layoff threats and routinization of the workplace.

Fathers who spend very little of their non-working time with the family may have come to experience the presence of the children as just one more source of tension. By avoiding the family and escaping into recreation, they avoid one source of anxiety while relieving the tension produced by another (i.e., by work).

When fathers are interacting with their children, they may feel out of place and inadequate, believing that the

[22]Michael Young and Peter Willmot, *The Symmetrical Family* (New York: Penguin Books, 1973), p. 235.

difficulties that they experience in parenting are due exclusively to their lack of caring. Some of their frustrations may be due to their lack of training and motivation for the job of parenting. In this society where mothers are traditionally the experts in parenting, fathers may be quick to give up the task when they feel inadequate at it.

Irene Josselyn described the motives for fathers' retreat from the activities of parenting:

> Being frustrated in the attempt to find gratification of their fatherliness, and dissatisfied with the watered-down expression of themselves in the home (mothers' helpers or powerful ogres), (fathers) will continue to seek release by diverting their available free energy into channels in which they feel more adequate, with a resultant overinvestment in the gratification they attain from activities away from the home....[23]

As the workplace (or in some cases, recreation) becomes the primary source of the traditional father's self-esteem, the home becomes the major source of the traditional mother's self-esteem. She feels most confident, competent and in authority when engaged in nurturing the children.

Consequently, attempts of the father to take a major role in nurturing children, which is the main source of her self-esteem, are experienced as a threat to her. She feels that her space is being invaded and that her special talents will no longer be unique in the family. Perhaps she may even fear that she will not be worthwhile or needed.

These feelings were exemplified in a study where first-time expectant fathers wanted to share in the parental duties

---

[23]Irene Josselyn, "Cultural Forces, Motherliness and Fatherliness," *American Journal of Orthopsychiatry*, April 1965, p. 270.

"much more than their wives anticipate(d) or even permit(ted) once the child was born."[24] These mothers feared that they might have a much harder time validating themselves if the father also became an active parent. For mothers, this fear is heightened by the lack of opportunities for satisfying employment. Having little chance for personal satisfaction in employment, it is understandable that mothers would be reluctant to give up any substantial part of their primary source of satisfaction (i.e., child rearing).

The husband may be accepting of his spouse's working if she still manages to care for the children, but then resistant if her employment success gets in the way of his by requiring a substantial amount of his time and energy for child care. If he does not object to her working in principle, he may feel differently about her working at a full-time career and succeeding at it. Being the primary breadwinner has been his unique role. He may be reluctant to give up a significant part of this respected position which has been his primary source of self-esteem.

More detailed analysis of the disparity between men and women in paid employment is essential for understanding economic forces which lead to, result from and maintain disparity between men and women in their relative levels of involvement in parenting.

---

[24] Harold Feldman, "The First Child," Unpublished paper, quoted in Constantina Safilios-Rothschild, "Companionate Marriages and Sexual Inequality: Are They Compatible?, *Toward a Sociology of Women* (Lexington, MA: Xerox, 1972), p. 67.

FINDING THE DISPARITIES BETWEEN MEN AND WOMEN

Despite a dramatic rise in the labor force participation rates of women between 1940 and 1990, women are still segregated into categories of employment which are comprised mostly of female workers. Their income from these jobs is generally lower than those of men in a similar field. For example, while most doctors are men, most nurses are women. While most school administrators are men, most teachers are women. While most business managers are men, most clerical workers, servers of food and professional housekeepers are women.

Women's earnings for full-time, year-round work still are only three-fifths of the earnings of men.[25] But this statistic does not reflect the even greater disparity between women's and men's earnings overall. More women than men have part-time jobs and more men than women work full-time, year-round. Of those who work part-time, 64% are women. The full-time, year round work force is, on the other hand, 66% male.[26]

Even if women graduate from college, they still face barriers to employment success greater than those encountered by men, on the average. "The female college graduate can expect to earn less than 70% of the amount received by male graduates."[27] It is estimated that one in every five women college graduates is working in a clerical, semi-clerical or unskilled job.[28]

---

[25] Myra Strober, "Women and Men in the World of Work: Present and Future," in Cater, et. al., p. 120.

[26] Bobbi Wells Hargleroad, ed. "Women's Work is...": Resources on Working Women, p. 15.

[27] Hochschild with Machung, p. 249.

[28] Women Employed, Women in the Economy, p. 12.

Between 1955 and 1971, which covers a period from eight years before Betty Friedan's publication of *The Feminine Mystique* to eight years after, the rate of women's earnings to men's declined (i.e., the gap widened with women losing further ground rather than gaining).[29] This trend has continued in more recent years with women slipping further in economic power relative to men in the economy overall.

Women with infants receive little emotional or practical support to enable them to continue working. They may be temporarily out of the job market, in part, because they have few alternatives to staying at home with the child full time. Many working mothers have relied heavily upon relatives to assist in child care during working hours. But as more women enter the work force, these family members (e.g., sisters, mothers and grandmothers) are also at work. Child care centers do not come near meeting the needs for quality care at affordable costs.

In 1988, two-job families made up 58% of all married couples with children.[30] Women in these families have received lower pay, fewer fringe benefits, less job security and experienced less job satisfaction than their husbands.[31]

Many of these women have been working *and* doing the child care. Kathryn Walker studied the time budgets of 1,300 husband-wife families, concluding that the amount of time spent by husbands in household work and child care did *not* vary significantly by changes in the employment status of the mother. That is, working mothers did not receive more

---

[29]U.S. Department of Labor, Women's Bureau, "Fact Sheet on the Earnings Gap," 1972, p. 1.

[30]U.S. Department of Labor Statistics, *Employment and Earnings, Characteristics of Families: First Quarter* (Washington, D.C.: U.S. Department of Labor, 1988).

[31]Strober, p. 121.

assistance than non-working mothers.[32] She also found that almost all of the physical care of children was done by mothers, while fathers participated only in driving the children to and from activities and helping with homework. Working mothers had taken on a second role while working fathers had not.

Mothers have been pressured by public disapproval and economic inequality to remain the primary parent whether they work or not. The "feeling persists that a mother who creates a full life for herself outside the home may be cheating her children, if not her husband."[33] Fathers, on the other hand, have been pressured by public opinion and economics to remain the primary breadwinner and to stand at the periphery of parenting responsibilities related to physical care of the child.

Many fathers feel that the economic success of the family rests *primarily* upon their shoulders. Since they are the only wage earner in the traditional family or their opportunities for earning are better than those of the mother in dual-career families, it is an accurate perception of fathers to feel this pressure. When mothers do work, their wages are, on the average, lower than the father's.

Statistical analyses here have shown that men have higher paying jobs, more satisfying occupations and better opportunities to succeed and do succeed in the work world

---

[32]Kathryn Walker and Margaret Woods, "Time-Use Patterns for Household Work Related to Homemakers' Employment" (Talk presented to the 1970 National Agricultural Outlook Conference, Washington, D.C., Feb. 18, 1970), p. 5. See also Walker and Woods, *Time Use: A Measure of Household Production of Family Goods and Services* (Washington, D.C.: American Home Economics Association, 1976).

[33]Leonard Benson, *Fatherhood: A Sociological Perspective* (New York: Random House, 1968), p. 292.

more than mothers; consequently, they are under greater pressure to support the family financially.

This pressure is both personal, as experienced between individuals in the family, and structural, as a part of institutions which influence fathers' lives. As a personal phenomenon, pressure is experienced as acute anxiety about losing the job or not getting a promotion. As a structural phenomenon, pressure is exerted through a complex set of concrete conditions which limit, restrict and reward behavior that serves the interests of the institutions which exert such pressure.

To say that fathers are under pressure to succeed at work means that fathers feel acute anxiety which motivates them to invest heavily in their work. It might help them to succeed, but this anxiety might also prevent them from succeeding. Even though they may fail at work, their time and energy still is consumed by worry about the job which prevents them from being present to their children.,

To say that fathers are under pressure to succeed at work also means that since present institutional structures of discrimination against women make it more difficult for mothers to succeed financially at work, then fathers feel that they *must* make the most of their employment opportunities for the sake of the family. If either one of the two, the mother or the father, must be *less* involved in work so that the children's needs can be met, then the mother would be the family's usual choice on financial grounds. Her working time is worth less to the family because she earns less and cannot match her husband's earnings. Fathers are under pressure to become established in a well-paying job, to maintain the family income and to increase their earning power.

FINDING THE SOCIALIZATION FOR ABSENCE

Persons acquire their gender identity through socialization. From birth onward, males learn patterns of behavior which other people consider appropriate to males. These patterns are learned through social conditioning, molding, imitation, identification and direct instruction (i.e., modes of socialization). Despite the common attitude of those who take traditional family roles for granted or assume that they are an intrinsic part of being human, the appropriateness of these gender roles is determined by *people* in a social, cultural, economic and historical context. In the case of socialization for fathering, the traditional view of fathering has been the predominant model toward which males have been socialized.

Men do *not* nurture children, in part, because they have been socialized *away from* nurturing activity with children. Fathers have been *restricted* by modes of socialization from participating actively in child care. They also have come to restrict themselves from active parenting as a result of internalizing the restrictions of the society.

Traditional sex-role allocations are legitimated by a series of beliefs about parenting which constitute a mythology that is passed on to others. The content of a myth of motherhood and of a corollary image of fatherhood reflects the inequality between men and women in the economy and the family. Propagation of these myths perpetuates such inequality. To refuse to adhere to the sex-role model of parenting which these myths support is to risk shame and guilt.

The myth is multifaceted and contains variations on several themes. Every normal woman is born with an instinct for mothering; fathers have neither the instinct for parenting nor the physiology necessary for nurturing children. Children require a mother's constant care; a father's care is not an adequate substitute for the mother's attention. Any woman who does not show evidence of intense involvement with her children is neglecting them; any father who *is* involved with his children is unmasculine, taking risks with the emotional health and proper sex-role development of his children, competing with his wife in her role or being vindictive toward his ex-wife (if divorced).[34]

Socialization against ANF is not as overt and prevalent in 1991 as it was in 1971. In order to get some perspective on the traditional viewpoints which affected the maturation of males who are young fathers today, it is helpful to examine relevant past sources and literature on parenting education to see what attitudes about fathering were prevalent in the culture during the early years of these men's lives. In this manner the socialization of today's young fathers may be examined.

In growing up, males have been socialized most effectively by their own fathers. In speaking of men in their twenties, Stephen Koch wrote:

> Who, among those fiery sons, with their vague and blasted eyes, really connected with his father; who even knew, let alone admired, what the father did in that invisible city of his? Fatherhood meant delivering or not delivering, checks. It meant not being around, or being unwelcome when around. It meant shouting, or that soul-crushing silence most deeply instilled in the soul of any red-blooded American boy: Dad mute behind his newspaper. Dad losing an argument. Dad standing watering the law, wooden as a dead post---while inside

[34] Ann Oakley, *Woman's Work: The Housewife, Past and Present* (New York: Vintage Books, 1974), pp. 156-221.

the house lived that real life in which he didn't count. Fatherhood, and to that degree, manhood, meant being feared, or ignored, or despised, or pitied, or hated.[35]

Young fathers of today were influenced negatively since early childhood by television programs in developing their images of fatherhood. From a study of television images of fathers, it can be concluded that there was an exaggerated representation of *inadequate* fathers in programs which were viewed during childhood by men who are in their thirties and forties today. A sample audience observed the fathers in selected programs to be "less adequate, competent, effective, wise, strong, decisive, consistent and predictable" than their own images of good fathers.[36]

Bruno Bettelheim provided scientific weight to the traditional assumption with this advice:

> Today's father is often advised to participate in infant care as much as the mother does...(but) this is empty advice for man is moral, economic, political (and therefore should stick to using his natural capacities for paid employment as a way of being a good parent).[37]

John Bowlby's research on maternal deprivation served as a major authoritative work which influenced social attitudes

---

[35] Stephen Koch, "The Guilty Sex: How American Men Became Irrelevant," *Esquire*, July 1975.

[36] June Foster, "Comparison of an Ideal Father Image with Selected Television Father Images," *Journal of Marriage and the Family*, August 1964, pp. 353-355.

[37] Bruno Bettelheim, "Fathers Shouldn't Try to be Mothers," *Parents' Magazine*, October 1956, pp. 124-125.

about parenting throughout the 1950's and 1960's. He concluded that a child's development is "almost always retarded---physically, intellectually and socially" when the mother is not caring for the child.[38] The father's role in infancy is to earn money so that the mother can be constantly with the infant and to help the mother "maintain that harmonious contented mood in the aura of which the infant thrives."[39]

Child psychologist Haim Ginott discouraged ANF through this warning:

> In the modern family... many men find themselves involved in mothering activities, such as feeding, diapering and bathing a baby. Though some men may welcome these new opportunities for closer contact with their infants, there is the danger that the baby may end up with two mothers rather than a mother and a father.[40]

These few sources provide only an example of how the traditional viewpoint on fathering dominated literature on parenting between 1945 and 1980 (the period in which fathers of today received much of their socialization about fathering). Reviews of more technical studies in sociology and psychology identify the way in which the traditional viewpoint

---

[38]John Bowlby, *Child Care and the Growth of Love* (New York: Penguin Books, 1965), p. 21.

[39]Bowlby, *Maternal Care and Mental Health* (New York: Schocken Books, 1967), p. 13.

[40]Haim Ginott, *Between Parent and Child* (New York: Macmillan, 1975), pp. 168-169.

had also become the dominant paradigm in research on fathering and masculinity and femininity.[41]

In a study of divorced fathers, nearly all of the fathers interviewed admitted to one common failing in their relationships with their children. They found themselves better prepared for the physical aspects of parenting--- shopping, cooking, cleaning, taking the child to the doctor--- than for dealing with the child's emotional needs.[42] Being unprepared to deal with the emotions of children, most fathers are reluctant to take an active role in meeting these needs of their children.

Fathers are also reluctant to deal with children's emotions because they are generally not prepared to deal with and understand their own emotions. Men are socialized to repress and control their feelings, perhaps because this has been the dominant mode of operation in the workplace.

This common problem also relates to the reasons why men do not generally perceive what rewards are possible in caring for children. Marc Fasteau explained:

> The rewards of caring for a child are real, but essentially personal, hard to measure or hang on to. This is not the kind of experience men are taught to value. It does not lead to power, wealth or high status. As we have seen, the male stereotype pushes men into seeking

---

[41]Robert Fein, "Research on Fathering: Social Policy and an Emergent Perspective,"*Journal of Social Issues*, Vol. 34, No. 1 (1978), pp. 122-135; Joseph Pleck, "The Psychology of Sex Roles: Traditional and New Views," in Cater, et. al., pp. 181-199; John Nash, "The Father in Contemporary Culture and Current Psychological Literature," *Child Development*, Vol. 36 (1965), pp. 262-266.

[42]Georgia Dullea, "Divorced Fathers: Who Are the Happiest?" *New York Times*, October 18, 1977.

their sense of self-esteem almost exclusively in achievement measured by objective, usually competitive standards.[43]

Boys do not learn from their fathers how to be nurturing because their fathers are absent. When fathers are controlling, frequently punishing, and/or silent, the child does not feel nurtured nor experience what nurturing is from his father. While boys may learn what nurturing is from their mothers, they also learn that it is not a father's place to nurture. As adults, men later tend to play out the roles they learned from their own fathers.

Inequality in the roles men and women play in the family and paid employment has been perpetuated by the socialization of males to perform the breadwinner role while avoiding the responsibilities of active parent. This inequality has also been perpetuated by the socialization of females to be the primary parent while avoiding success in paid employment. Socialization toward traditional roles both reflects and reproduces the conditions of inequality between men and women, mothers and fathers.

---

[43]Marc Feigen Fasteau, "Men as Parents," in *The Forty-Nine Percent Majority*, ed. Deborah David and Robert Brannon (Reading, MA: Addison-Wesley, 1976). p. 63.

CHAPTER THREE

A MORAL AGRUMENT FOR ANF

In direct opposition to the moral argument I propose for
active fathering is the patriarchal argument for the increased
participation of fathers in family life. The proponents of this
position have pleaded the case that fathers should fulfill
traditional family roles and that they should do so more
frequently. They have argued for male control of the family;
not nurturing by fathers; not daily meeting of the child's
physical needs by fathers; not sharing child-care
responsibilities equally between fathers and mothers; not
promoting equality in economic and social power between
spouses.

Proponents of the patriarchal argument have delineated
the father's responsibilities as exercising authority, disciplining
the children, supporting the mother in her care-taking roles,
teaching the children about the world outside the home, and
inculcating morality in the children. This position rests upon
the assumption that men and women are, by nature, very
different and that women are suited best to caring for the

children while men are most appropriately fit for other functions in the family.

In a 1951 book appealing to fathers, O. Spurgeon English exhorted them to assume their "rightful place" in the family:

> Plainly this nation needs father in the arm chair at the head of the table again, carving the roast, disciplining the children, keeping the peace, settling the disputes, loving his wife but reserving the pants for his own use, serving as an example for sons to emulate and daughters to seek in husbands of their own....Father is essential. Homes require him. Mothers need him. Children must have him to round out their development.[1]

Throughout the book, English commends fathers to become more involved in certain limited areas of parenting, but he does not deal with issues of equality in parenting or paid employment. Rather, he assumes that the different roles in child care and paid employment are justified.

One of the more emphatic patriarchal stances grows out of the Mormon tradition, as evidenced in Ed Pinegar's book, *Fatherhood*.[2] As he summarizes, "the thrust of (his) book has been to help us as fathers to awaken to our responsibilities and our blessings as true patriarchs in the home."[3]

For Pinegar, *The Book of Mormon* proclaims that fathers are placed at the head of the family by God, and therefore, fathers must live up to this responsibility. For father to be uninvolved in the traditional role of patriarch is tantamount to

---

[1]O. Spurgeon English, *Fathers are Parents Too* (London: Allen & Unwin, 1951), p. xi.

[2]Ed Pinegar, *Fatherhood* (Salt Lake City: Deseret, 1976).

[3]Pinegar, p. 72.

disobedience of God's will. The mother's role is to care for the children most of the time and serve her husband as a "mate supporting and sustaining and allowing him to be the true leader and patriarch of the family."[4]

Gordon MacDonald's book, *The Effective Father*, draws upon biblical descriptions and commandments, "which leave no questions about who is to be the head of the home and the family."[5] For MacDonald, the Bible presents a normative view which tells "exactly what God wanted the family to be."[6] What follows is an endorsement of traditional family roles as "*the* Christian family."

Proponents of the patriarchal argument reinforce traditional roles through their insistence upon males heading the family. Fathers are assumed to have special capacities for patriarchal behavior and women are assumed to have special capacities for nurturing behavior. This is clearly *not* my argument for active involvement by fathers in parenting.

In the previous chapter, ANF does not simply refer to more quantity of traditional fathering activities. It is a normative term to be used in referring to involvement in the full range of parenting activities previously described as an "appropriate presence." Furthermore, ANF is that phenomenon which occurs in the context of relative equality between the father and the mother, not in the context of a large imbalance of career and parenting involvement between the two parents.

No single approach to moral theorizing adequately serves in the attempt to give a rational assessment of the ethical situation dealt with herein. Stressing competition between various approaches for the best theory would be rather

---

[4]Pinegar, p. 73.

[5]Gordon MacDonald, *The Effective Father* (Wheaton, Ill: Tyndale House, 1977), p. 16.

[6]MacDonald, p. 17.

pointless if a "co-ordination" of approaches would help to
provide a more accurate analysis of the multifaceted character
of the moral issues at stake.[7]

In the approaches to moral theory which I have
considered relevant to reasoning about ANF, no single
approach is adequate. With Lawrence Becker, I have concluded
that instead of utilizing one ethical theory, "effort is much
better spent in trying to co-ordinate various theoretical results
and in investigating the way in which theoretical results...enter
into practical affairs," that is, into the moral issues regarding
ANF.[8] While Becker considers this a co-ordination of theories,
William Boyce and Larry Jensen defend the legitimacy of
utilizing "mixed theories" of morality.[9]

Four types of moral theory are coordinated in this
argument for ANF. They supplement each other in providing a
balance of various approaches to the moral action in question:
ANF. Four moral perspectives are necessary rather than one
because of the complexity of the issues, the variety of rational
disciplines involved (theological ethics, moral philosophy,
psychology, sociology, physiology, etc.), and the strengths and
weakness of each perspective.

First, the case is made for the justification of ANF as an act
of love commensurate with the Gospel imperative to love one
another. In an agapeistic approach, such as that utilized here,
morally desirable action is that which expresses the *love*
commended by the Gospel. This justification is inadequate
without reference to other considerations, like the

---

[7]Lawrence Becker, *On Justifying Moral Judgments* (New York:
Humanities Press, 1973), pp. 17, 193.

[8]Becker, p. 17.

[9]Becker, p. 17; Boyce and Jensen, *Moral Reasoning* (Lincoln:
University of Nebraska Press, 1978), pp. 46, 59.

consequences of the action, the spirit in which it is carried out and the specific obligations of persons to others.

This approach seldom stands alone even in the theorizing of those who profess to rely solely upon religious belief for their moral imperatives. For example, Lyman Abbott based his claims for the moral rightness of the sex-role differentiated family upon the Gospel, yet he clearly drew many of his conclusions from observations of his contemporary culture. Abbott concealed the means by which he arrived at conclusions about moral good in family life and did not present explicit moral arguments other than the claim that the Gospel required such action.

The acknowledged and appropriate utilization of other moral approaches and social research methods is invaluable in establishing rational criteria for the determination of which actions may be most loving in human relations and which actions are destructive. From Christian tradition and scripture we may affirm the commitment to love one another, but in each age we must ask again what is loving, what is not, and how to balance obligations between competing claims.

Second, ANF is justified from a deontological perspective, which involves a focus upon why persons have a moral obligation or duty to perform such action. In this approach attention is given to the obligations persons have toward each other---to assure equal rights and responsibilities, to promote mutual fulfillment, and to treat others fairly.

While the obligation needs to be recognized, particularly by absent fathers who do not fulfill it, it is more efficacious to emphasize a positive moral motivation toward nurturant activity. An overemphasis upon duty would tend to negate the spirit of love and engender resentment in personal relations between fathers and their children and between husbands and their wives.

Third, a positive moral motivation toward nurturant activity is commended in an ethics of virtue. In this theoretical approach, attention is given to the cultivation of *habits* or dispositions toward acting morally. Persons who have developed a nurturant disposition are better able to experience self-fulfillment in nurturing. They are *willingly* drawn toward caring for the child as a source of satisfaction rather than being pushed against their will to perform a duty.

Fourth, the case is argued for the justification of ANF on teleological grounds (i.e., on the basis of the consequences which result from such action). Among social researchers who have studied fathering this type of justification is commonly utilized, but the moral character of the argument is seldom acknowledged.

If the consequences produced by ANF could be shown by social research to be more beneficial to children and parents than detrimental and also more beneficial and less detrimental than the alternatives, then ANF would be morally justified on teleological grounds.

ANF AS UNCONDITIONAL LOVE BY FATHERS

The moral argument for ANF that follows originates from a starting point which is the grounding of the argument. In this case, it is a theological starting point. From this point forward an increasing number of rules, virtues and consequences will be elaborated upon. If one were to work backward from the rules, virtues and consequences of ANF seeking the "non-arbitrary stop to reason-giving" for ANF, one would find this to be the point at which reason-giving began.[10] It is the most basic reason why ANF *ought* to be performed.

---

[10]Becker, p. 64.

It seems appropriate for a Christian ethicist to make the theological grounding clear from the beginning. To add it as an afterthought would be to trivialize its significance. Conversely, to place it at the end as if to rescue with divine sanction whatever points had become untenable on rational grounds, would be an illegitimate use of the justification which I propose.

"You shall love your neighbor as yourself" (i.e., the love commandment) serves as the theological and ethical grounding for all subsidiary principles and rules which are proposed herein to justify ANF. To say this is not to say that ANF is automatically or immediately deduced from the love commandment. Rather, love is the grounding of rules concerning ANF "not by its nature alone, but by its nature together with the facts about the world in which it is seeking to fulfill itself."[11]

For Christians, the belief that love of neighbor is the appropriate grateful response to God's love (especially made known in Jesus) remains central to Christian morality. It requires no other justification. It is the moral grounding upon which Christian ethical reasoning stands, or rather it is that on which it moves.

Only those aspects of love will be suggested here which are most relevant to the argument for ANF. The remaining and longer part of the argument for ANF involves the attempt to embody the love commandment, giving specificity and clarity to the meaning and work of love between persons who come face to face and who influence each other's lives through institutional connections.

---

[11]William Frankena, "Love and Principle in Christian Ethics." *Perspectives on Morality: Essays by William Frankena* (Notre Dame: University of Notre Dame Press, 1976), p. 82.

Love without regard for the doing of justice between persons in a family is sentimentality. Love (i.e., agape expressed in nurturing children and in promoting equality between spouses) and justice (i.e., fairness, equality between men and women, equal treatment, etc.) are not purported to be identical in this application concerning ANF, though they are integrally related at some points. Gene Outka's distinction is instructive here:

> While agape and justice are distinguished conceptually, they nonetheless overlap in some cases, and whenever they do, agape may require more but never less than justice does, in both self-other and other-other relations.[12]

> To contend that agape and equalitarian justice are deeply conjoined in at least part of their extension is not to say that they are interchangeable. Agape is normally taken as a more inclusive standard in that it applies in situations where justice has far less direct relevance.[13]

In one type of case an overworking father cuts back on his working load to spend more time in caring for his child primarily so that his spouse may also continue in her career development. He does so out of regard for issues of justice. Because he wishes to be fair with her, he attempts to acquire skills in nurturance, limits his work and commits more time to parenting activities. His act of promoting equality between himself and his spouse is an act of love motivated by a concern for justice.

---

[12]Gene Outka, *Agape: An Ethical Analysis* (New Have: Yale University Press, 1972), p. 80.

[13]Outka, *Agape*, pp. 309-310.

A father who claims he loves his spouse but refuses to share in child care and insists that his wife not work, despite her expressed wishes to the contrary on both points, denies opportunities for equality between them. His form of "love" is an expression of sentimentality which is inadequate to be called agape because it denies justice.

When a father promotes the well-being of his child from a desire to interact positively with the child's needs, he is acting more from love than for justice (though justice is also being fulfilled). Coordination of love and justice is essential to the moral argument for ANF and is further explored in the following sections of this chapter.

ANF AS EQUALITY BETWEEN MEN AND WOMEN

Equality has been accepted by a respectable minority of ethicists as a primary criterion for a just distribution between persons.[14] Distributive Justice for both men and women requires equality of results in the distribution of good and evil between them.[15]

Among the social goods and evils which are mediated through social systems, three categories encompass most distributive considerations relevant to this case. First, there is the socially acquired power to determine one's own direction and activity. This is one's relative degree of freedom as opposed to one's degree of domination at the hands of

---

[14]S.I. Benn and T.S. Peters, *Social Principles and the Democratic State* (London: Allen & Unwin, 1959), p. 109; Frankena, *Ethics* (Englewood Cliffs, NJ: Prentice-Hall, 1973), pp. 48-52.

[15]Frankena, *Ethics*, p. 50; Constantina Safilios-Rothschild, *Women and Social Policy* (Englewood Cliffs, N.J.: Prentice-Hall, 1974), p. 7.

others.[16] Second, there is that participation in culture and society which enables one as a determiner of social value to have a positive sense of belonging and self esteem. The opposite of this social good is the negative experience of marginality felt by those whose lives and values are determined by others, Third, there are socially determined decisions which assure or deny access of persons to life-sustaining employment and economic resources as well as to activities which provide meaning and satisfaction.

Anything approximating near equal distribution of these goods and evils is not possible as long as fathers do not participate actively in caring for their young (i.e., as long as ANF is not a reality in families and in society at large). This judgment is shared by a large and growing number of social scientists and critics. ANF is considered to be a necessary, though not a sufficient, condition to provide for equal distribution of positive and negative results between men and women.

Social research has been utilized to verify this hypothesis so frequently that it has become a widely accepted conclusion.[17] It is presented as a hypothesis, that is, in principle, verifiable by evidence. While the judgment is not value-free, neither is it given simply as a moral judgment in this context. Though influenced by value perspectives, it is primarily a judgment based upon available social science data.

If ANF is necessary to the realization of a more equal distribution between men and women (as social scientists have judged that it is); and if equal distribution between men and women is morally required by principles of distributive justice

---

[16]Gibson Winter, *Elements for a Social Ethic: The Role of Social Science in Public Policy* (New York: Macmillan, 1966), p. 223.

[17]James Levine, *Who Will Raise the Children? New Options for Fathers and (Mothers)* (New York: J.B. LIppincott, 1976), p. 149.

(as ethicists have asserted); and if distributive justice is morally required by the love commandment (as Christian ethicists have agreed); then ANF is morally required by the love commandment in which Christian obligation is grounded.

A further necessary condition of justice is that similar cases be treated similarly.[18] Differential treatment (i.e., preferred or discriminatory treatment) of men and women has been legitimated by some legislators and employers on the rational basis that men and women are substantially different in their capacities for success in paid employment.[19] In Chapter One, this claim was refuted. Men and women are similar enough so that dissimilar treatment which further reduces opportunities for women's employment success and work satisfaction is unjust treatment.

While the denial of equal pay for equal work is obviously inequality of treatment, so also is the segregation of women into categories of employment where wages, benefits and satisfactions are lower.[20] By being treated differently from men in hiring, paying and promoting, women are being denied equality of opportunity and also equality of results in distribution. Justice requires equality of treatment when such treatment leads to equality of results in distribution.

However, if dissimilar treatment in a particular case would help to produce a more equal distribution between men and women as a result of the dissimilar treatment by compensating for present inequalities, then such treatment

---

[18]Frankena, *Ethics*, p. 49.

[19]Janice Fanning Madden, "Discrimination---A Manifestation of Male Market Power?" in Cynthia Lloyd, ed. *Sex, Discrimination and the Division of Labor* (New York: Columbia University Press, 1975), pp. 157-158.

[20]Madden, p. 169.

would be morally justifiable.[21] Dissimilar treatment would be justifiable in a particular case if it could be demonstrated that the treatment would result in more equal distribution.[22] This is the moral ground correctly given for affirmative action programs and other compensatory programs.[23]

Who ought to be held responsible for promoting such equality? When should persons be excused from responsibility? Who or what systems should be held accountable for the distribution of positive and negative results between men and women?

Those institutions affecting families and society through employing workers and regulating other employers are responsible for promoting equality. In a negative sense, they are also to be held accountable, morally and legally, for discriminatory practices, gender bias and working conditions which perpetuate inequality between men and women. Responsibility for the imposition of legal sanctions generally rests with governments and regulating agencies.[24] Organized labor and individual workers may also be a positive or negative agent influencing the relative degree of equality in the society and families.

Since the obligation to foster equality is also an obligation to promote ANF, institutions have a moral responsibility to alter procedures, policies and attitudes which prevent ANF (and consequently, equality) and to develop ways to promote ANF. Inasmuch as the legal obligation to equality is widely applied to institutions by government regulations and

---

[21]Madden, p. 169.

[22]Frankena, *Ethics,* p. 52.

[23]Madden, p. 160.

[24]Eleanor Brantley Schwartz, *The Sex Barrier in Business* (Atlanta: Georgia State University, Bureau of Business and Economic Research, 1971), pp. 29-59.

sanctions, some of the institutional supports for ANF might also justifiably become legal obligations. Therefore, the work world should be required by government to provide parental leave time for caring for sick children as well as for the adjustment during the birth or adoption of a child, particularly because these are the times that inequality between the parents is most at issue. Mothers risk their jobs by taking time off and the family cannot afford to have fathers share equally in the family work. Inequality is perpetuated by the lack of opportunities for fathers to take time off from work to care for the children.

Parents have a moral obligation to do justice vis-a-vis their spouse by acting in ways which promote equality and reduce disparity between them in parenting and paid employment. This love between the parents which is expressed in the mutual promoting of the well-being of the other in family and work overlaps with justice. Because of love, they may give more to each than justice requires but they should not give less.

Discussions of deontological theories do not usually clarify whether a person has a duty to promote his/her own equality, but in the case of marital and parental relationships it is not so problematical to give an affirmative answer. If promoting one's own equality promotes the equality of the other, and if denying one's own equality denies the equality of the other; then one is obligated to promote one's equality. Because each affects the other, a father is obligated to promote his own equality and a mother is obligated to promote her own equality because in doing so each promotes the equality of the other as well as their own.

For example, if a mother does not seek equality for herself by preparing for and obtaining satisfying employment, she may also be limiting her husband's (the father's) opportunities for equality (e.g. to be similarly satisfied in his employment and in actively nurturing his children). However, it could be said that she is legitimately excused from moral responsibility to share equally in breadwinning under certain circumstances. It would be unfair to suggest that a mother has a moral responsibility to share equally in paid employment if, in fact, there were no satisfying, well-paying jobs available. To require her, in a moral system, to take on added stress through alienating work would do little to improve her life. It would also create greater inequality if her husband were satisfactorily employed, and still greater if he were not sharing equally in child care.

It should be clear by now that fathering, and even equality between parents, cannot be treated merely as an individual matter involving only private choices which do not affect the larger society or others' lives. To persons who do not view these as *social* issues, this moral argument may come as a shock. One must remember the shock expressed by some who said "You mean to tell me that I can't beat my wife!" or "What business is it of anyone else's whether I keep slaves!" Theories of moral obligation are forever breaking in upon social custom and offending those who defend the prevailing status quo against this inbreaking of a higher ethical standard.

In ascribing responsibility for seeking equality to individual mothers and fathers, one must ask how far it is possible for these persons to overcome barriers to equality. By a concerted effort, some persons may be able to move a long way toward equality. At the other end of the spectrum, some persons may be controlled so much by institutions and economics that they have no alternatives but to play out their lives within the boundaries set for them by others. Somewhere in between these extremes of free choice and powerlessness stand a great number of people whose circumstances may defy analysis. Only they themselves may be able to ascertain how much freedom they have to change in the direction of greater equality.

It is unreasonable to suggest that a father is personally responsible for his absence from parenting activities (and for the unequal division of family labor which results) if his employer requires extended work-related travel, the family budget from a single paycheck cannot withstand a change in his employment, and there are few alternatives in the job market anyway.

While he may not be entirely controlled by forces outside himself, his power to change the circumstances is severely limited. In such a case, some major responsibility for the inequality rests upon others, particularly those in the institutions affecting his employment who control his travel, work hours and conditions of work.

It is reasonable to suggest that a father is personally under a moral obligation to ANF if it is within his power to affect such changes that would promote equality both for himself and his spouse. Individuals may also be morally obligated to promote the equality of others and ANF.

Placing emphasis upon the guilt of individual mothers and fathers for not promoting equality between them is an unproductive emphasis. By compounding the problems of parenting through imputing guilt, this approach may lead to a reaction opposite from the intended goal. Rather than produce a constructive change in behavior, emphasis upon guilt seems likely to produce a hardening of attitudes in those threatened by challenges to their assuming of traditional roles.[25]

Through the advice found in recent child care literature, parents are already made to feel a great deal of guilt over how they care for their children or fail to. At the same time,

---

[25] William Chafe, *Women and Equality: Changing Patterns in American Culture* (New York: Oxford University Press, 1977), p. 168.

parents tend to blame themselves for economics-related problems that are frequently beyond their control.[26] Bringing more guilt by imputing personal responsibility may only lead toward greater inertia on the part of those being judged rather than lead toward equality.[27]   Even if equality and ANF were furthered by such sanctioning, the person who parents and works primarily out of guilt has little chance to receive the satisfaction and sense of self esteem that may otherwise be experienced in these activities. In order to avoid an over-emphasis on moral obligation, a shift in perspective will be helpful. By coordinating the deontological approach with an ethics of virtue, the emphasis may be directed in a more positive way.

Moral Philosopher Lawrence Becker commends such a shift when faced with the limitations of a deontological approach:

> It can be argued with considerable force that, at least in some cases, a good deal of what we want to say about the morality of human conduct is grossly distorted by haggling over the balance of goods and bads on the one hand, and by the messy business of assigning responsibility, considering excuses, and deciding whether, and if so, how to intervene in a (person's) affairs on the other. There is at times a certain loss of nobility in such practices---a loss we often want to

---

[26]Kenneth Keniston and Carnegie Council on Children, *All Our Children: The American Family Under Pressure* (New York: Carnegie Corporation of New York), 1977), p. 4.

[27]Walter Kaufmann, *Without Guilt and Justice* (New York: Peter H. Wyden, Inc., 1973). pp. 114-137.

express by insisting on shifting the focus of the discussion....[28]

William Frankena also laid theoretical groundwork for this coordination of approaches:

> I propose therefore that we regard the morality of duty and principles and the morality of virtues or traits of character not as rival kinds of morality between which we must choose, but as two complementary aspects of the same morality.[29]

ANF AS NURTURANCE WITH CHILDREN

An ethics of virtue is complementary to an ethics of obligation in providing for an adequate understanding of the spirit in which moral obligation may be fulfilled. A moral virtue, when learned and adopted, fosters in persons a disposition that both helps in deciding what to do and in what spirit an act can be done.

If the obligation to do justice stood alone as the moral justification for ANF, there would be too great an emphasis upon the external performance of a duty and too little concern for the motivation or spirit in which ANF occurs. One who is acting purely out of obligation experiences a loss of self in giving over one's actions to another's need, while one who is acting out of a disposition to act so (i.e., a desire to do x) experiences a self-fulfillment and satisfaction in doing x. In daily life it seems that the persons we most respect tend to act morally less from a sense of obligation than from disposition

---

[28] Becker, p. 14.

[29] Frankena, p. 5.

and traits of character, or virtues, cultivated in them such that they find self-fulfillment in acting morally as they do.[30]

Two virtues are correlated with the principle of justice and are needed to supplement the deontological approach. An ethics of virtue emphasizes the motivation needed by persons to support ANF as well as the motivations of active nurturant fathers. First, the virtue of justice is a disposition to act, not merely out of a sense of being obligated, but from a desire to express the good of justice in itself. This disposition to treat others equally, to support others in their search for equality, and to act in ways which secure just relations between self and others, is what we mean by the virtue of justice. It is derived from and morally justified by the principle of obligation to justice. One major difference between duties and virtues is in the spirit of performance.

The second virtue is that of nurturance. A contested issue in literature on parenting has been whether the disposition to nurture is innate, acquired through learning, or both. The traditional mythology, often repeated by the experts, is that mothers are born with an instinct for nurturing.[31] Others have suggested that fathers also "possessed the basic nurturant disposition---the 'fathering instinct.'"[32] A third, and the one that I find to be the most acceptable, perspective explains that both physiology and social learning affect the development of a nurturant disposition.[33]

---

[30]H.A. Prichard, *Moral Obligation* (New York: Oxford University Press, 1958), p. 12.

[31]Warren Farrell, *The Liberated Man* (New York: J.B. Lippincott, 1973), p. 121.

[32]Henry Biller, *Father Power* (Garden City, NY: Anchor Books, 1975), p. 13.

[33]James Harrison, "A Critical Evaluation....," p. 229; Eleanor Maccoby and C. Jacklin, p. 219; Alice Rossi, "A Biosocial Perspective on

Aristotle theorized that "virtues are implanted in us neither by nature nor contrary to nature; we are by nature equipped with the ability to receive them, and habit brings this ability to completion and its fulfillment."[34] Applying this theory to the matter at hand, it could be said that a person may utilize (by habit) the capabilities of the body (e.g. hormones, senses and emotions) to develop a nurturant disposition.

Nurturing, as an expression of virtue, is that moral act in which a father (or mother) facilitates the growth of his (or her) child because of the intrinsic value of the relationship with the child. This disposition arises from the parent's emotional bonding and physical engrossment with the child.

The parent is physically engrossed (i.e., disposed to care for the child by an emotional bond) when a significant number of the following feelings recur with some regularity:

(1) Pleasure in looking at the child.
(2) Desire for and pleasure in *appropriate* physical contact with the child.
(3) Awareness and appreciation of the child's physical and emotional characteristics.
(4) Wonder at the uniqueness and precious quality of the child's life.
(5) Attraction of one's attention toward the child.
(6) Elation over the presence of the child.

Parenting," in Rossi et. al., ed., *The family* (New York: W.W. Norton & Co., 1977), pp. 1-31; Craig Rypma, "Biological Bases of the Paternal Response," *The Family Coordinator*, October 1976, p. 235.

[34]Ostwald, Martin, Trans. Aristotle, *Nichomachean Ethics* by Aristotle (New York: Bobbs-Merrill), p. 33.

(7) Increased sense of self-esteem based upon the child's well-being.[35]

The terms "engrossment" and "emotional bonding" denote a disposition toward the child whereby the parent perceives the child as prominent and significant. The parent is interested in and cares about the well-being of the child in spite of the child's behavior. In general, the parent has increased recurring feelings of self-esteem and competency because of the child.[36] This is not to deny, however, that children are not always well behaved, parents are not always happy with their children's behavior, and that parents do not feel ambivalent about parenting in general or toward the child at various times in particular.

Activity which expresses the virtue of nurturance includes being emotionally close with the child, being accepting of him/her, being supportive of the child's efforts, and being affectionate verbally and physically.[37] In that nurturing is helping children to grow into their own independence, it also involves teaching self-discipline, granting emotional distance, and letting go of parental control when appropriate.

Nurturance is justified as morally right for both parents by the deontic principle of justice as equality and the obligation to ANF which follows from that principle. Reason-giving for cultivation of this virtue is, at its most basic level, grounded in the love commandment. In developing a nurturant disposition and embodying this virtue in nurturing

---

[35]My reworking of a definition based upon observations recorded by Martin Greenberg and Norma Morris, "Engrossment: The Newborn's Impact Upon the Father," *American Journal of Orthopsychiatry*, Vol. 44, No. 4, July 1974, pp. 522-524.

[36]Greenberg and Morris, p. 529.

[37]Biller, *Father Power*, pp. 139-140.

children, a father pursues a moral good which expresses the love of neighbor as oneself.

ANF AS CAUSE WITH EFFECTS

One must also ask whether ANF does, in fact, result in happier, more satisfied and more fulfilled children and parents. In this teleological argument, the criterion for what is regarded as morally right is the value of that which is brought into being. An act is right if it produces more good than bad and if it produces more good and less bad than any other alternative.[38]

The positive values brought into being in this case are satisfaction, fulfillment and high self-esteem. The negative alternative values are the negatives of deep dissatisfaction, depression and low self-esteem. Those for whom and among whom this balance of good over bad is produced are the child, the mother and the father (self). The act which is being justified by the good which it produces is ANF (i.e., in the context of equal sharing of parenting and breadwinning).

ANF could be justified as morally right if greater good than evil were produced, if this distribution of good were the most equitable for both parents and the child (greatest good for the greatest number), and if ANF were to produce more good and less evil than any alternative available.

There are few studies which really help to answer questions about the consequences of ANF in the context of relatively equal responsibility for work and parenting. Most family studies have dealt with circumstances of disparity

---

[38]Frankena, *Ethics*, pp. 14-15.

between spouses, not relative equality.[39] In those which address the issues, however, very supportive evidence is presented for a teleological justification of ANF.

In a longitudinal study of 400 university-educated couples, those marriages in which there was greater equality between spouses were characterized by higher marital *satisfaction* than those in which there was an imbalance of career success between husband and wife. In marriages where men outdistanced women in career success there was a greater incidence of isolation, separation of interests and lack of communication.[40]

In research on dual-career couples with children, those fathers and mothers who were symmetrical (i.e., shared equally) in careers and parenting were found to have a higher level of *enjoyment* of everyday activities than couples in which both spouses were career oriented, or both family oriented, or one of the couple family oriented and the other career oriented. This enjoyment was associated with high marital *satisfaction*.[41]

In a study of adjustment and satisfaction among college males, the most well-adjusted were also those who reported at least a moderate degree of nurturance and availability from their fathers. The most poorly adjusted had fathers who were either present too little or were not very nurturant when at

---

[39]Robert Fein, "Research on Fathering: Social Policy and an Emergent Perspective," *Journal of Social Issues*, Vol. 34, No. 1 (1978), pp. 122-135.

[40]Jan Dizard, *Social Change in the Family* (Chicago: Community and Family Study Center, University of Chicago, 1968), pp. 73-76.

[41]Rhona Rapoport and Robert Rapoport, *Dual Career Families Re-examined: New Integrations of Work and Family* (New York Harper & Row, 1976), p, 332.

home. ANF promoted the *satisfaction* and *adjustment* of the child, particularly in later years.[42]

Comparing grades and achievement test scores of children with high father presence to those of low father presence, Henry Biller and Robert Blanchard concluded that involved fathers can help the children's school work and non-involved fathers can negatively affect school performance. This area of the child's life was a major source of self-esteem or anxiety. By helping in this area, active nurturant fathers promoted *self-esteem* and overall *satisfaction* with life for the child.[43]

Fathers who care for their infants are less likely to become child molesters. "Whether the child is the father's or someone else's, when a man is involved in the physical care of his child before age 3, there is a dramatic reduction in the probability that the man will be involved later in life in sexual abuse of children in general as well as his own."[44]

Frank Pedersen found that the more actively involved a six-month old baby has been with the father, the higher that baby's scores on mental and motor development tests have been.[45] Ross Parke found that the more fathers were involved in the everyday repetitive aspects of caring with infants (such as bathing, feeding, dressing and diapering) the more socially

---

[42]Mark Reuter and Henry Biller, "Perceived Paternal Nurturance---Availability and Personality Adjustment Among College Males," *Journal of Consultative and Clinical Psychology*, Vol. 40 (1973), pp. 339-342.

[43]Henry Biller, "Father Availability and Academic Performance Among Third Grade Boys," *Developmental Psychology*, 4 (1971), pp. 301-305.

[44]Kyle Pruett, *The Nurturing Father* (New York: Warner Books), 1989.

[45]Frank Pedersen, et. al. "Infant Development in Father Absent Families," *Journal of Genetic Psychology*, 135 (1979), pp. 51-61.

responsive the babies were and the better able they were in handling stressful situations.[46]

Norma Radin concluded from a study that ANF contributed to better social adjustment and competence, to the child's perception that they were masters of their fate, and to a higher mental age on verbal intelligence tests.[47] Another study showed that ANF resulted in more empathetic children (i.e., more caring).[48] Another study showed that preschoolers of active nurturant fathers achieved higher test scores.[49] These good results which are brought into being by ANF also morally justify ANF as preferable to less involved fathering.

Interviews with 129 divorced fathers of children aged 3 to 7 produced evidence that those fathers who "share(d) child custody equally" with their former wife were *happier* in their parenting role and experienced *more satisfaction* as parents than full-custody fathers or weekend fathers. They had much

---

[46]Ross Parke, "Perspectives on Father-Infant Development" in *Handbook of Infant Development*, J.D. Osofsky, ed. (New York: Wiley), 1979.

[47]Norma Radin and Graeme Russell, "Increased Father Participation and Child Development Outcomes," in M.E. Lamb, ed., *Nontraditional Families: Parenting and Child Development*, (Hillsdale, NJ: Erlbaum), 1982, pp. 191-218.

[48]A. Sagi, "Antecedents and Consequences of Various Degrees of Paternal Involvement in Child-Rearing: The Israeli Project," in Lamb, ed. *Nontraditional Families*, pp. 216-231.

[49]Carolyn Cowan and Philip A. Cowan, "Men's Involvement in Parenthood: Identifying the Antecedents and Understanding the Barriers," in P. Berman and F.A Pedersen, eds., *Father's Transition to Parenthood* (Hillsdale, NJ: Erlbaum), 1986.

greater regard for the rights of their former spouse, who also experienced relatively higher *satisfaction* in parenting.[50]

In a longitudinal study of children whose parents shared more equally in the child's care, the shared custody facilitated the child's adjustment to the divorce and helped to promote the child's *happiness*.[51] By comparison, the "disinterested father left behind a legacy of depression and damaged self-esteem" for the child and a heavy burden for the custodial parent.[52]

The moral approaches in this chapter present a relatively harmonious argument for ANF. By constructing the argument as it is, I have sought to bring these theories into a mutually supportive role. In most cases, the moral conclusions of these theories coincide rather than contradict each other, but in some circumstances the approaches will be in conflict.

For the sake of brevity and clarity, I have presented the positive case for ANF while refraining from discussion of exceptional cases in which shared parenting would not be morally justified. Such an approach has been adopted in order to provide what has been lacking most in moral discussions on fathering---a holistic moral argument which includes concerns for love *and* justice, intrinsic good *and* consequences, duty *and* satisfaction.

---

[50]Kristine Rosenthal and Harry Keshet, *Fathers without Partners: A Study of Fathers and the Family After Marital Separation* (Totowa, NJ: Rowman and Littlefield, 1980), p. 65; James Levine, "Parents' Passages," *Psychology Today*, November 1980, p. 112; Georgia Dullea, "Divorced Fathers: Who Are the Happiest?", *New York Times*, October 17, 1977.

[51]Judith Wallerstein and Joan Kelly, "California's Children of Divorce," *Psychology Today*, January 1980, pp. 71, 76.

[52]Wallerstein and Kelly, pp. 71-72.

While no hard and fast rules can alleviate the moral responsibility of persons for choosing a course of action when these theories conflict, two examples of such conflict follow to give some indication of how one might utilize these approaches and develop a wider discussion of the points of conflict.

If reliable evidence were produced to show that ANF causes adjustment problems for men not adequately prepared for parenting, this evidence could be cited to reject ANF on teleological grounds. However, in such a case, the other theories would enable us to argue that ANF is morally right as an act of justice, as an act of love of one's neighbor, and as expression of the virtue of nurturance. Some temporary adjustment problems, dissatisfactions and frustrations may be morally acceptable in order to fulfill the obligation to equality. In the long run, the goal of greater mutual satisfaction might also justify a short-term period of dissatisfaction. The competing priority of the well-being of the mother and child might justify some temporary dissatisfaction (e.g., curtailment of career plans) by the father.

On the other hand, if the consequences of ANF in a particular case were found to be detrimental to the child (e.g. emotional and physical damage at the hands of an abusive father), then equal parenting time by the mother and father could not be morally justified, The obligation to equal parenting as a fulfillment of the obligation to justice and equality would not morally override the negative consequences to the child. In this case, it could also be said that the parenting of an abusive father is not characterized, on the whole, by the virtue of nurturance, nor is it really an expression of neighbor love. It would also hinder rather than help the mother's career in such a way that equality between them in paid employment would not be promoted either.

The society must continue to grow in its conscience regarding the needs of fathers, mothers and children. Family

life today is *not* a private matter alone. Employers have long
exploited the family's capacity for nurturing the overworked
male and financially supporting the underpaid female. It is
time for more employers to accept their fair share of the
responsibility for supporting the well being of the people who
produce the profits of the corporation by their labor. Justice
requires it, but the self-interest of the employer is more likely
to produce future change in the direction of family support
benefits. In Chapter Six, this issue will be addressed at greater
length.

If the moral judgment for ANF presented here were to
become widely accepted, the prospects for social change in this
direction would be greatly improved over the present
circumstances in which widespread traditional beliefs about
fathering undergird the resistance to change. Attempting to
bring about a shift in what is understood to be morally
justified is one essential part of any movement toward
transformation. Chapter Four provides motivating images that
may help individual fathers to learn the habits and acquire the
mindset of a nurturing disposition.

CHAPTER FOUR

MOTIVATING MYTHS FOR ANF

Those who want to change their behavior and adopt ANF need further understanding of what it entails, what spirit is required to succeed at it and what complications are involved. They need some helpful images to give an overview of the philosophy behind the activities of ANF.

Those who are already active nurturant fathers could benefit by images that help to motivate them to understand the importance of what they are doing. Such images could help to generate enthusiasm for the task. Myths, metaphors and theology can clarify the significance of the commitment of ANF and give direction when the purpose of daily routine seems painful or pointless.

The first section ("The Myth of Equality") describes a hypothetical family engaged in shared parenting. The second section ("The Myth of Wholeness") provides a psychological interpretation of the wholeness that is produced by ANF. The third section ("The Myth of God's Love") creates a theology for ANF. The fourth section ("The Myth of Fierce Love") reweaves an ancient tale for the purpose of helping men to discover the power to be nurturing with their children. These additional distinct pieces of the puzzle are part of a whole which is designed to work together to motivate men to be ANF's.

THE MYTH OF EQUALITY

Equality can be said to be a "myth" because it may be as rare as unicorns. Those who live out this myth live in a fantasyland that many others will never have the opportunity to experience because of the many barriers that stand in the way of ANF.

Having such a myth may help one to strive for the ideal image. Achieving that goal with any degree of perfection is very difficult in the current social situation where few supports and great resistance make individual choice in the matter irrelevant for many. Nevertheless, it is important to have a clear picture of what that goal would look like in action. In order to clarify that goal, so as not to confuse it with alternative and less egalitarian approximations of shared parenting, I will develop a mythological image of the egalitarian family. This myth of equality serves as a model, an ideal or a goal to inspire those who would endorse, encourage and adopt ANF.

This image is mythological because it is not a description of a dominant trend that is happening, though I affirm that it ought to be. Regrettably, there are more factors moving the society toward fatherless families than there are moving men toward ANF. That means that these motivational images are even more important than if ANF were a dominant trend that would just happen with little or no resistance.

A mythological image of an egalitarian family will help to provide more substance to our mutual understanding of what

ANF is and is not. The myth will help others to know what ANF ought to be. It will provide some clarity for those seeking to fulfill goals of equality in families. It can serve as a measure against which families can evaluate their own behavior to ascertain whether they are very liberated in their thinking or whether they are doing a simple rearrangement of sex-role stereotyped behavior.

A cautionary note is due, however. This is not the only possible image for equality. Some issues may not be treated adequately in this myth. Some of the details presented in this myth may be only one way of arranging for equality in the family.

Although taking turns may appear unequal if viewed over a short period of time, it *can* be equal if viewed over a longer period. If a father or mother stays at home for a few months while the other parent is working full-time, finishing school, etc., and later the other parent stays at home while the first goes back to work full-time; there would be equal sharing over a long period of time even though during a given week there would be an imbalance of paid work and family work in comparing the two.

This myth is not timeless. Next year new issues may arise that have not yet entered the discussion of fairness in family and work balancing by the egalitarian family. However unfinished the picture of ideals of equality may be, one must begin to paint the picture. Like an oil painting, additional layers and details may be laid on in additional brush strokes in the future.

Let's call this mythological family the "Fair" family. It includes Fay, the 34 year-old mother; Ray, the 34 year-old dad; Jay, the 8 year-old son; and May, the 6-month-old daughter.

Ray and Fay have just finished a 6-month parental leave from their jobs. They were paid full salary and received full benefits while working less than full time. Their employers viewed this leave as well spent, since they did not have to hire someone else to fill their jobs and it would encourage high productivity, staff stability and good will among these employees.

Fay does caseload work as a counselor with a counseling service. She takes counseling appointments at her convenience as long as she works the required number of hours. While on leave she was required to work sixty-percent of the full-time hours. Ray works for a computer software firm. When working full time, his hours are flexible: he has to work 7 hours on weekdays some time between 7 a.m. and 7 p.m. While on paid paternal leave, he worked four hours a day in this flexible manner. Ray and Fay chose leave arrangements from several options available to them from their employers. They felt it was the best way for them to adjust to the new baby, to have an adjustment period for negotiating sharing work and family joys and options, to share child care after the birth, to balance work and family life, to avoid losing any ground at work and to maintain their income level when they needed it most to cover costs for the baby.

Today is the first day after they have both returned to work full time (with flexible hours). This morning Ray is home while Fay is at work. She left the house before May woke up crying for a feeding at 6:30. Ray changed May's diaper, then fed May with a bottle of mother's milk that Fay prepared the night before. After feeding the baby, Ray gave her a bath. He encouraged Jay, who is 8, to join in making faces and cooing sounds. Ray told Jay stories about funny things he did as a baby. They looked at a few pictures together and laughed. Ray was sensitive to the Jay's need to feel important at this time when the new baby was getting so much attention.

May went down for a nap. Ray fixed breakfast, packed a lunch for Jay, and then wrestled a bit with Jay on the floor as they watched for the school bus to pull up out front. Now Ray picked up the pace and rushed about doing laundry, washing dishes and cleaning like a basketball player making big plays. Ray thought about how this may not appear to some guys like important stuff to be doing, but he felt it was really vital to the well being of his family and himself. He enjoyed it and felt competent much like he did at work. He considered this work to be the fundamentals like those in basketball (which he plays three times a week for fun and to stay in shape): passing, running, blocking out, playing defense, and rebounding. They were not as glamorous as scoring the winning basket, but they made all they difference in whether the team won together (i.e., whether the family was satisfied with their life together). He beat the buzzer with a final sprint of housework, finishing with a few precious minutes for reading the paper before May woke up again.

Around noon, Fay arrived home to a lunch that Ray had fixed. They ate together and talked. It wasn't always easy to schedule May's naptime so that they could eat together and talk, but it worked today. After lunch, Ray went off to work. He fielded questions and provided assistance to clients. He enjoyed the variety of tasks and was less tired when he could find such balance in his day. It helped that he didn't stay in either place or at one kind of task for too long.

Around five o'clock Ray picked up Jay from Cub Scouts and went home to dinner that Fay had prepared. Ray cooked more stir-fried vegetables and rice. Fay did more variations on the chicken and potatoes theme. They worked hard at being sure they would each cook meals that the family liked. They shared equally in planning meals and cooking. Sometimes they did a meal together and at other times they took turns. It took some negotiating to get there but they had developed a rhythm and appreciation for each other's cooking. Mutual *gratitude* was high. When neither felt like doing the work, they would take a break and simplify it a bit with microwave cooking or eating out.

Tomorrow Ray would be taking the baby to the pediatrician to ask a few questions about a skin rash she had developed. He was concerned about it. Fay thought it would heal with some non-prescription ointment, but Ray wanted to be sure and it was time for a checkup anyway. Jay would be out of school for a vacation day and Ray had a light afternoon of work planned at the office so that Jay could come to his office for a couple hours. Dad's work with computers was very impressive to Jay. He got to play some games on one computer while Ray worked on another.

Jay is Ray's son from a previous marriage. Ray shares custody with Jay's mother. Half of the week Jay lives with Ray and the other half he lives with his mother a few miles away. Ray was very close to Jay from the beginning. When he was born, Jay remained in the same birthing room with his parents for three days. Ray slept there too and cared for Jay around the clock with Jay's mother. Ray had learned a lot about nurturing babies and doing the basics by watching both his mother and his father take care of his sister and brother when he was young. Now he just did what seemed to come naturally for him.

When May was born, Fay was not reluctant to see Ray as competent as a caregiver with the newborn infant. She did not have a need to be the "expert" and "in charge" of parenting. She realized that if parenting and housework were her domain, she would be doing more than her share of the worrying and the work. If she asked Ray to "help" her in the housework and parenting, Ray would view it as *exceptional* when he did that work. Equality was possible for them because they agreed together that breadwinning, billpaying, childrearing, caregiving, cooking and cleaning were neither *his* nor *her* work but joys and responsibilities to be shared equally. They also expressed their gratitude to each other frequently for doing the work that each new the value of very well from their own experience of doing that work.

They both looked at their careers as a source of fulfillment to be held in balance with the needs of the family. Both are *primary* parents. Ray does not "babysit" the children for Fay. Ray is not just "taking care" of the children until Fay gets back. Like Fay, he is a "caregiver" and not just a "caretaker" for the moment.

Ray and Fay have worked out a schedule for a typical week that provides for them to spend amounts of time at work and at home that are equal with each other. They each have a few unique talents and jobs they do: he does the plumbing, she does the sewing. They assure equality in other jobs by alternating responsibility between them. They share the laundry, taking out the trash, vacuuming, cleaning, doing dishes, doing the yardwork, etc. Work at home does not become burdensome for either of them because they share it and have a balance in the kinds of work they do in the family. Sometimes they work side by side. The sharing is not calculated exactly because they have a high level of trust and reliability. Each does their fair share willingly. They have both lowered their standards of cleanliness during the busiest times. Perhaps because they have been used to autonomy at work, neither criticizes the family work of the other. They do, however, encourage each other a lot by signs of appreciation and affection as well as reciprocated labor when it is clear that a lot of work was done by the other.

This arrangement has been widely viewed as a myth because so many women have longed for it and so few have found it. So many sociologists have documented its arrival in some rare cases but few have found it in a form that comes very close to equality. In order for this myth to become a more widely spread reality, more men and women will have to adopt this ideal. Caution is suggested here, however. It is one thing to hold an ideal in one's hopes and quite another to live it out in reality.

A woman who holds such hopes in a marriage where equality is not likely to happen, may be very dissatisfied and depressed. She may abandon such hopes to preserve peace in the relationship. She may abandon the relationship to search for realization of the dream. It would not be unusual for a woman to have this dream. Many women have had such hopes for a long time. But if great numbers of men were to begin having such a dream of what it takes to find satisfaction in family life and were to start doing what it takes to make it happen, then a significant change will have taken place in the society.

Therefore, it is strategically vital that a clear picture of an egalitarian ideal be shared, advertised, taught, narrated, repeated and disseminated so that future generations of fathers may know the image well and grow to want it like current and past generations of men have wanted to be powerful, successful and rich. If this myth begins to sell better than it has in the past among men, the next generation of men may find real happiness and deep satisfaction in the fairness lived out both at home and at work.

THE MYTH OF WHOLENESS

Having a motivating ideal, metaphor or mythical image can be especially necessary and helpful to fathers who did not have active nurturant fathers for role models in their own childhood. One father expressed this point in lamenting, "the lack of previous role models affects me at the level of motivation, not the level of skill acquisition."[1] A good myth bears truth in a symbolic way. It provides an image that has the power to motivate behavior.

A myth of wholeness can be a motivating image for active nurturant fathers. The person who is whole has free use of the capacities for thought, feeling and action. While purveyors of traditional gender-role stereotypes espouse the view that men and women have very different capacities, practitioners of the image of human wholeness assert that men and women share these capacities in common. However, this does not mean that men and women have to accomplish things the same way. "Androgyny" implies alikeness of men and women, but "wholeness" implies that even though men and women, on the average, may tend to do things differently, they share in working at similar goals, tasks and responsibilities within the family and society. For example, it would not contradict the concept of "wholeness" if most active fathers tended to play and wrestle with infants more while most active mothers tended to sit and talk to their infants (as some researchers have concluded).[2] Whole men and whole women may live out their relative wholeness in different ways. The differences between men and women in a group, however, may be greater than the differences between men as a group and women as a group. A greater wholeness happens as men and women move beyond dysfunctional symbiosis of traditional roles that kept them both half-human, incomplete and mutually defective.

Among the motivations for ANF is the drive to satisfy the need for balance in life---balance between work and family,

---

[1] Harry Brod, "Fathering: New Styles and Old Problems," in Carole Kort and Ronnie Friedland, eds., *The Father's Book* (Boston: G.K. Hall & Co., 1986), p. 122.

[2] Kyle Pruett, *The Nurturing Father: Journey Toward the Complete Man* (New York: Warner Books, 1987).

balance between achieving and being, balance between history-making and nurturing. Such balance (or "wholeness") is experienced as more fulfilling than career-centered or child-centered lives. When men are deprived of the opportunity to exercise some basic skills of ANF, these skills atrophy. In order to find wholeness, fathers need to work at developing these skills further. Traditional mothers may have lost or failed to develop many skills that could bring deep satisfaction and creativity to the lives of others through paid employment. Wholeness for them could be found in building up and using a wide repertoire of ways to exert their creativity in the work world.

Balance helps fathers to appreciate both work and family to a greater extent than when too much emphasis is placed on one or the other. Giving one's life and soul away to the "company store" may no longer be as necessary or fulfilling as it was for previous generations. Two incomes have become more necessary to survive, but families have also been finding ways to adjust their needs downward so that parents do not have to work overtime hours or push beyond the 40-hour work week. Active nurturant fathers have adjusted their work commitments to make time for family joys and responsibilities and thereby balanced their lives.

Wholeness is also the gift that ANF's can give to their children. Dorothy Dinnerstein addressed this issue profoundly in *The Mermaid and The Minotaur*.[3] She analyzed how "mother-raised children" exhibit several debilitating pyschological dysfunctions that would not be as likely to occur if both mothers and fathers shared equally in the care of infants and pre-schoolers (especially the "pre-articulate and

---

[3] Dorothy Dinnerstein, *The Mermaid and the Minotaur: Sexual Arrangements and Human Malaise* (New York: Harper & Row, 1976).

pre-rational"[4]). Active nurturant fathering is vital to facilitating the wholeness of the next generation.

I want to expand upon Dinnerstein's use of the mythological images of the mermaid and the minotaur as they relate to this discussion of "wholeness." The mermaid is half woman and half fish. She lives in the "underwater world from which our life comes and in which we cannot live."[5] Being a fish below the waist, she cannot get out of the limited environment that traps her (the water). The modern counterpart to the mermaid is a woman who has been created and reinforced, or restricted to feel, that her only appropriate source of satisfaction must be caring for a succession of young children at home. She has been created by socialization to stay put and has been prevented from venturing into the work world. From her realm she lures people in by her attractiveness and empathic nurturing. She understands well what others need and think, but does not have the opportunity to use that in exerting her will in the world. She has a longing to be fully human and thus capable of full human love. Being trapped makes her resent where she is. Being trapped by overwork in her role makes it difficult for her to appreciate the joys of nurturing as much as she could if she did not have to be so overly consumed with it. She could be more free to experience love of the children instead of constant struggles that come in the face of overfamiliarity and *her* fatigue as well as that of the children.

She wants to get out of the sea and be active in the world, but she cannot do so because of the limitations imposed upon her. She longs for wholeness that would come with the opportunity to balance work and family. She needs for the

---

[4]Dinnerstein, p. 201.

[5]Dinnerstein, p. 5.

father to share equally in child care and housework so that she and he can both be free to be whole persons.

The ancient mythical minotaur is also only half-human. While his body from the neck down is human, his head is that of a bull. Today's minotaur, the bull-headed absent father storms about in the world without much consciousness of empathic nurturing at work in his family relations. The mythical minotaur is fearsome, gigantic and eternally infantile. He represents mindless, greedy power, and he insatiably devours human flesh (disregarding the well being of others on his way to the top). His modern counterpart in the absent father also devours people thoughtlessly. He has not developed the empathic capacity to see people from their own perspective and treat them with compassion. He pursues his career aspirations at the expense of his family's happiness. He is as bullish with his family as he is at work, allowing his work and his will to overrun the needs and wills of others. His competing activity on the job and/or at recreation take him away from the place and style of being that is necessary for nurturing his children well.

These characters are mythological in the sense that they are metaphorical explanations for a complex set of realities. The mermaid and the minotaur provide a simple and more memorable reference to the complex dynamics of destructiveness of the traditional roles and to the deformed results of the traditional arrangements.

Wholeness is a myth in two ways. First, it may be said to be "just a myth" (i.e., unreal) because there is so little wholeness in our present situation where there are so few ANF's. Second, "wholeness" is a concept that helps to explain more simply and with a single specific image (like a mythological character) what happens when fathers are active in caregiving with their children. It happens for the fathers and mothers as well as the children.

Wholeness is a mythical reference to the ultimate goal that may not be completely realized by anyone. ANF's experience a greater degree of wholeness (than traditional fathers) as do the children they care for; and the mothers who are also liberated. And yet there is always the possibility of more complete wholeness. Because most fathers today work out of and over against their relatively traditional upbringing, there is likely to be recurring regression to a more traditional mindset and behavior pattern.

Arlie Hochschild documented the way in which some fathers espouse an egalitarian gender ideology but subvert that ideology with a gender strategy that is working in the opposite direction.[6] While some men believe that they *ought* to feel like being an ANF, this is not how they really feel. Consequently, they do things that, in reality, do not add up to ANF on a regular basis. The wholeness of ANF is "just a myth" for some; a reality for a few others; and a mixed bag of partially fulfilled goals and missed opportunities for most at this point in history. This does not have to be the case, however.

In her search for what it would take to facilitate wholeness, Dinnerstein develops a critique of what is wrong with the traditional arrangement from the perspective of the infant's psychological development. She argues that mother-raised children have been stunted in their growth. As adults, these children raised by mothers in the absence of their fathers in early life are half human beasts. They represent partial humanity---not full humanity (wholeness). They are incomplete beings; part animal and part human.

As infants they have not had the opportunity to experience men in the same way that they have experienced

---

[6]Arlie Hochschild with Anne Machung, *The Second Shift* (New York: Avon Books, 1989), pp. 11-21.

women. Early infancy is controlled by mother and that control involved great ambivalence for the child. The infant feels a great deal of ambivalence about the one who cares for its basic needs. The caregiver is pleasantly identified and loved as the source of pleasure but also she is rejected and hated as the one who does not stop the hurt, or does not grant pleasure or does not give it quickly enough. This vacillation between love and hate toward the one the infant perceives to be the source of pleasure and pain stays oriented toward the "hand that rocks the cradle."[7] The infant does not see the mother as simply another agent outside itself who is not totally responsible for the pleasure and pain the infant feels. The infant sees the mother as the direct producer of good and bad feelings within the child. She is blamed and held totally responsible. That is why she becomes the object of the infant's rage and tears.

The major source of the infant's pain is located within: hunger, physical pain and discomfort. The major source of the infant's pleasure is also within: pleasures of the senses and the capacity of the brain to generate good feelings about the world. But life also involves the actions of others. The mother will have to withhold some things that the child desires and give others that the child does not want. Later the mother will have to separate from the child for its own growth. The child will react with strong negative feelings toward the mother when these things happen. It is a fact of life and love as much as dying is a part of being human. The infant sees the caregiver as the controller of all these things and as the one who is to be held responsible for how the infant feels. The caregiver may be seen as a despot who seems to the infant not to care at all about what the infant wants.

That is not unlike the belief of some that God is to be held responsible for the good and bad that happens in the world.

---

[7] Dinnerstein, p. 175.

When things go badly, such a believer expresses rage toward God or rejects God. When things go badly for the infant, it expresses rage toward the caregiver or rejects the caregiver. When things go well, the caregiver and God are worshipped. That is a burden that neither mothers nor God should have to bear. Neither mothers nor God have manipulated things for the purposes that the infant and believer have assumed. The psychological wholeness of the adult and believer will both depend upon how well they will be able to take responsibility for the things they do to create and sustain happiness as well as for the trouble and pain they cause for themselves and others. Their degree of wholeness will also depend upon their developed capacity for relating to others as outside their feelings rather than as producers of their feelings. Wholeness is taking responsibility for having self-generated the mix of feelings, for satisfying one's own emotional needs, and for being able to help others do the same.

When the mother is the only one doing this caregiving with the infant, then the infant comes to associate mothers/women with the deep feelings of ambivalence. If fathers also gave such caregiving, infants would have similar feelings about fathers/men, but infants would be more likely to separate the ambivalence from what they view as female or male. They would be more free to identify the feelings of ambivalence as characteristic of all aspects of life and relationships.

When fathers are relatively absent from caregiving with infants, they remain separated from the infant in a way that the cradle rocker does not. The infant sees the distant father as outside the self. Because he is more distant from the infant, he can be perceived with a mixture of feelings that are not nearly as intense as those the infant has about the mother. The intimate mother is so close that the infant perceives its own pain as her doing and blames her (and later, women in general). It perceives its own pleasure as her doing and worships her as a goddess. Both reactions are too extreme and too heavy a load for mothers to bear. Under these circumstances, mothers are not allowed to be human. They are either devils or goddesses. Having this approach to mother/women (and its corollary distortion of fathers/men) still operating in adulthood is very dysfunctional for many areas of life including sexuality, parenting and dealing with one's own feelings as well as the actions of others. ANF is essential to set mothers and infants free from this malaise.

ANF's, like active mothers, must also face rejection from their young child sometimes when the child is expressing the negative side of their ambivalence about being cared for and being so painfully dependent. These fathers who may experience pain in these moments, may take some consolation in realizing that this drama is preparing the child for a healthier psychological life as an adult. It is not to be taken as a personal rejection of the father as worthless. The rejection is most likely to come when the father is doing a good job that frustrates the child's will to do otherwise. The child is discovering that it is not just mothers/women who frustrate their desires. It is not just fathers/men who frustrate their desires. Neither fathers/men nor mothers/women are the appropriate object for their anger. It is life itself that fills them with ambivalence. It is their own reaction to the world that causes most of the pain. On the pleasure side, it is not just mothers/women that can give them pleasure or just fathers/men that can help them to feel good. It is life itself and their own capacities for joy that can fill them with satisfaction and enjoyment. Upon discovering this, they can be free to make their own happiness rather than be totally dependent upon someone else for happiness. Shared parenting could help children to contain both the intense positive and intense negative feelings inside themselves where they belong rather than projecting all responsibility for good and bad feelings onto mothers/women as they do in traditional families.

Dinnerstein argues that ANF is essential for men's growth toward wholeness:

> (as long as the traditional arrangement prevails) "woman does not share man's right to have (character traits that make her less than perfectly parental) without loss of human stature, and man does not share woman's obligation to work at mastering them, at shielding others from their consequences. Woman never will have this right, nor man this obligation, until male imperfection begins to impinge on all of us when we are tiny and helpless, so that it becomes as culpable as female imperfection....Only then will the harm women do be recognized as their familiar harm we all do to ourselves, not strange harm inflicted by some outside agent. And only then will men really start to take seriously the problem of curbing, taming, their own destructiveness."[8]

THE MYTH OF GOD'S LOVE

This section of the chapter is an exploration of some awakenings to how God's love can empower ANF's. Faith experiences can be powerful motivators. Faith experience does not motivate everyone, however. Statistically, men as a group are moving further and further away from participation in religious institutions. But this does not necessarily mean that men are abandoning religious experience. For those who have

---

[8]Dinnerstein, p. 238.

ears to hear, I will provide some images of faith that I find empowering for ANF. They stand in some contrast to the conservative religious underpinnings for the traditional family that was critiqued in Chapter One.

Jesus affirmed the value of children in the face of other priorities when he welcomed little children to come and sit on his lap. He reminded the Disciples that the children were indeed precious and worthy of the time and attention of adults and God (Mark 10:10-16). Jesus lifted up the unconditional love of a father when he told a story about God's love as like that of a Dad who celebrated upon the return of his prodigal son (Luke 15:11-32). Jesus lifted up the love of a father when he spoke of the love of God as like that of a Dad who knows how and is willing to give "good gifts" to his children. "What father would give a serpent when his child asks for a fish, or a stone when he asks for bread?" (Matthew 7:7-11).

Where did Jesus acquire such nurturing habits with children? We have no indication that he was married or had children who would have given him opportunities to practice nurturing habits. He must have learned from Joseph and Mary and his siblings.

Risking the accusation of historical anachronism, I have deduced that Joseph was an ANF who had a very positive influence upon Jesus' view of fathers and God. Jesus must have received these "good gifts" from Joseph to speak so well of the gifts that fathers give to their children. Jesus must have experienced unconditional love from Joseph that was like the love of God. Jesus must have witnessed a father's active nurturing behavior in his home to have turned the religious emphasis in his land away from a judgmental God to a loving-father-God.

Jesus and Joseph must have worked side by side as carpenters for years---a closeness that is hardly likely for fathers and sons today. Part of the absence of fathers today is due in no small part to the Industrial Revolution which took fathers away from home to work in factories and mines. The closeness that Joseph and Jesus must have had as carpenters in the First Century is not easily recaptured by fathers today.

As a father, Joseph might be a good role model for today. He did not run away in fear when God called him to stand by this pregnant woman who was bearing a child not his own. This is a good model for the multitudes of young men who have participated in the creation of a human being and then left the single mother to care for it. Taking responsibility for one's procreative actions may require some courageous actions. Joseph could be a model for the young men who are weighing the alternatives. Joseph stood by Mary and faced whatever embarrassment it involved in order to care for this child of God. What will fathers do today for the children they know that they helped to conceive?

Later Joseph faced hardship to save his son from being killed when he took the baby Jesus to Egypt. In Jerusalem, Joseph must have had a clientele that ordered and purchased his carpentry work. Should he stay with this clientele that could support his family and himself? Should he take the child to Egypt to save him from certain death? Today, we call this a dilemma between the competing arenas of work and family. Today, fathers face the dilemma of whether to move with the company's order of his transfer or to walk from the company and find different employment in order to protect the family from great stress and disruption. Joseph made a tough decision that modern fathers may learn from. Love for one's family sometimes requires that the career be placed on the back burner in order to meet other needs of the family.

Judging by the results in Jesus, Joseph (and Mary) must have been (a) good mentor(s) in the home where much of the religious learning and worship took place in that day. Jesus must have learned his compassion from a family that was accepting of others, that was healing, that was unconditionally loving, that was affirming, that was encouraging, that was nurturant, that was inclusive of men and women. What Jesus did and said that turned the religious world upside down from judgment to grace must have been formed in his family where most religious education and worship took place in that day.

Beyond this rudimentary consideration, we should not seek specific direction in scripture to instruct modern fathers in *exactly how* to nurture or in what activities to be involved in caregiving with children. Our values have come a long way from the patriarchy of the First Century. To expect the full range of activities (that I have described as ANF) in that time *would be* anachronistic. Instead, some theological ethics from the scriptures can be applied to our current situation.

The unconditional love of God is the most basic grounding I have for seeking to be an ANF. When I am most fully aware of God's love for me, I am most capable of sharing that love with others. I am better prepared to help my children to know that love because I have been there repeatedly in communion with God receiving affirmation and strength. For me, faith is a journey with many awakenings along the way when I come to a more complete realization of how miraculous love is and how grateful I am for that love of God. I am able to nurture my children because I have been nurtured; because I am grateful for that nurturing; and because my gratitude moves me to let that love overflow in me for others and the God who has nurtured me.

A father must first be able to affirm his own unconditional acceptability in order to be capable and willing to nurture children. Nurturing involves a lot of emotionally neutral activities in caregiving but many *are* emotionally and spiritually charged with elements of answering the child's most basic question: am I loved? The father who knows from his own childhood and adult experiences how painful it feels to wonder about this question, and how wonderful it feels to arrive at a positive affirmation; has the most basic knowledge and motivation necessary for being an ANF. He can put this vital information and empathic capacity to work for him and his children as he seeks to understand, to love and to help them grow and develop. A parent's appropriate answer to the question ("Do you love me?") when it is posed by the child in the form of attention-getting misbehavior may first involve a short scolding or "time out" before a gentle hugging and reassurance of unconditional love. It may involve saying "no" to inappropriate requests with a gentle explanation and provision of love in other forms. Whatever else the father communicates, it is imperative for the well-being of the child that he communicates *unconditional love* for the child.

Fathers must have learned about this unconditional love somewhere when they were young. It may have come from their mothers, their fathers or another caregiver. If they learned it from their mothers but not from their fathers, they may grow up knowing what nurturing is but feel somewhere deep inside that it is "women's work." While men can learn many of the elements of nurturing behavior from many sources, it is especially important that they experience their fathers exhibiting this nurturing behavior. In some exceptional cases, ANF's have been able to learn a lot of nurturing from what their own fathers did not do. They have been motivated by a feeling that their own childhood lacked their father's nurturing and now they want to make up for it in their own ANF. Approaching their upbringing from a critical perspective, they have learned what an ANF should do by observing what was *not* nurturing in their fathers. Even so, they have to learn it from someone and feel it somewhere in life. Perhaps some men are also able to teach themselves through therapy, or by their own ingenuity, or in a good adult relationship. The habits of nurturing are learnable. In order for one to be able to learn nurturing behavior, it is vital to have a solid emotional grounding. One needs to have a healthy sense of self-esteem (emotional wholeness) to live out what one knows in their heads to be nurturing behavior. Religious experience is the most firm grounding for healthy self-esteem that must be understood more as a *gift* to humanity than a *grade* for being a good person.

Human love has much to teach us about Divine love and vice versa. A deeper awareness of the value and dynamics of both may provide firmer grounding for an ANF. In the present, men can learn to draw upon their own emotional reservoir of positive images from their childhood when nurturing took place. They may also dip into the negative pool for awareness of what behaviors led to their feeling shortchanged in the amount of nurturing their experienced with their fathers.

My personal reservoir of feeling memories that I draw upon for recalling the deeply felt nurturing I experienced with my Dad frequently guides me. In my relationship with my Dad, I have discovered much about the love of God that is an integral part of me. I have felt deep security partly because Dad was there for me when I needed financial help or emotional support. I have known God's comforting love from back rubs Dad gave me and delicious food he cooked. I have known the joys of companionship as Dad and I went to sports events together. I have been empowered for life and love most basically by Dad's total acceptance and encouraging affirmation of my work and his hesitancy to lay any judgments on me. I learned of the tender love of God at work as my Dad visited with his mother frequently through her long decline with Parkinson's Disease, as he remained close with his brothers and sister, and as he has visited with strangers like they were long-time friends.

I have felt the comfort of being held by God as Dad and I wrestled playfully on the floor. Such closeness reminds me of the wrestling between Jacob and God. It formed a bond between them whereby the father gave his blessing to the son. In that wrestling with my Dad I first felt the *blessing*. As we moved beyond the wrestling stage of our relationship, he has continued to give me that blessing in countless emotional ways.

Recently, my fifteen-year-old son wanted to test his strength against me. He has grown taller than I. He is maturing and our ways of expressing affection are going through some transformations. We symbolically marked a point of growth and change in the relationship as he pinned me easily in wrestling. It was like Jacob wrestling until the break of dawn and prevailing. The father could now give some kind of *blessing* as they acknowledged together that he had arrived at the threshold of manhood.

Young women may mark such a time as the onset of menstruation or another event, but many young men may point to the day that they could prevail in wrestling Dad. This may not be limited to boys. My daughter likes to wrestle too. She is very athletic and eight years from now she will probably be able to prevail against me too. Many cultures have a tradition of giving the blessing to the child. Wrestling has been a rite of passage for me in a culture that no longer hunts. However the blessing rite takes place, nurturing requires a long-term reality in which the child experiences the blessing of the parents. This involves the experience of the unconditional love of the parent, the endorsement of the child's existence, and the affirmation of who this person is becoming. Fathers must learn how to extend that blessing to their children. It is a spiritual gift that fathers have received and gratitude for this gift must be allowed to motivate them to pass it on to their children.

God's forgiving grace has been embodied for me in Dad's response to my mischievous moments, "You know what you did was wrong. You have already suffered enough. Go. You have learned your lesson." Dad modelled good work habits and fulfillment in working that helped me to focus not just on God's comfort but also on God's calling me to work for others and to enjoy it thoroughly. Somewhat like God affirming the creation on the seventh day, Dad would rise early, whistling a beautiful melody and enjoying the sun shining and birds singing. The depth of gratitude for life that is so basic to my joy in living came as a gift of God that I learned in imitating my Dad.

In the negative pool, there was an uneasy reluctance by my Dad to disclose his feelings on many subjects. Mom would tell us what he was thinking or feeling. Because I felt distant from him at times as a child and wondered whether he loved me, I have a deep appreciation for the need of my children to hear my reassurance of them, my self-disclosing explanations for my moods, and my sharing of some frustrations, hopes and dreams. My Dad either got much better at expressing his feelings or I just got better at reading them in recent years. Now he continues to teach me how to be a good father by the way he affirms and accepts me.

My mom helped me to know how to talk about feelings. She opened herself up to me freely as a child. My Uncle Bob was open emotionally in his conversations with me and I saw in him that men could do that too. My Aunt Wilma was one who affirmed what I did. I needed that appreciation of my good actions. Her affirmation helped me toward entering the ministry. A reservoir of feeling memories like these helps me to nurture my children. As I remember how I felt when these people cared, I have greater awareness of the value of what I am trying to do in caring for and with my children.

There are other reservoirs from which to drink for the feelings of nurturing. In the moving conclusion to the stage version of *The Grapes of Wrath* on Broadway recently, a young woman delivers a still-born child, who died from malnutrition and the suffering inflicted upon its mother by strike breakers, union busters and abusive farm bosses. The dead infant is placed in a box and floated down the river rather than buried so that maybe the corpse will be found and the horror of it will awaken the conscience of the world to this suffering of a people. As the box was released, I saw it as an image like the baby Moses being sent out upon the waters so that a savior might be raised up to deliver the people. The event also mirrored the image of Mary, the mother of Jesus, who saw her own child die at the hands of persecution.

The saving nature of the event followed as the mother came upon a dying black man. He had not had anything to nourish his frail body for six days. With her breast, swollen with milk for her dead infant, she nursed this dying man back to life. I experienced an awareness of the profundity of the love of God and of a parent in this act. I sobbed tears of great sadness for human injustice that were balanced by overwhelming joy as I felt deeply that the love of God was indeed *like that* in a world like this. The child's death, like Jesus' death would raise the consciousness of the world. The mother's loss, like Mary's loss, would find meaning in the saving of life. The mother's milk like the milk of God's compassion would resurrect the dead.

This image of God as the nursing mother has not been affirmed very much in our patriarchal culture today or in the one which is represented in the Bible. One of the most basic impediments to adopting an image of God as nursing mother has been male envy of the female power to lactate and feed from the breast (as well as to conceive and bear children). Because it is such a wonderful miracle and profound power, men have done much throughout history to assure that it was not given the recognition and affirmation that it deserves. In the only times that it has been affirmed, there has also been heavy economic suppression of women (i.e., the pedestal syndrome).

Sometimes the old images become cliche's and they lose their life-giving power. For some who have had bad experiences with their fathers, the image of God as a father never had any life-giving power. I experienced both of my parents as nurturing. So both mother and father images of God have great power to communicate the experience of God's love for me. At this time in history, I do not use the father image very much because there is a need to bring some balance into a church that is in the process of being healed of its bias in favor of men and male images of God (as well as the preservation of male power).

This age calls for inclusive and non-gender specific images of God, in part, because we want to affirm that men and women can and should be nurturing; that women and men can and should be self-reliant; that there are admirable human qualities that are not just masculine or feminine (as previously thought). However, there is also a deep-seated human need for an embodied God who is not abstract or distant---a God who is incarnate or in the flesh. My religious experience has become more abundant and satisfying as I have come to know a God of *both* genders as well as beyond gender; a God who *is* a body (both male and female) and who is also not *just* a body but more.

I want to commend the image of God as nursing mother and "flesh it out" with tools of theology, psychology and experience for those of us who find it life-giving. I believe that this image can enhance the understanding of the nurturing we have received and continue to receive from God. At least four biblical passages refer to the image of a nursing mother. The Psalmist in 131:2 suggests that God has been like a nursing mother and that the believer's soul has been quieted and calmed "like a child at it's mother's breast."9 In Numbers 11:12, Moses sarcastically asks if he is supposed to be like a mother who gave birth to a child and now carries it at her breast as it sucks on the way to the Promised Land---the land of *milk* and honey. This points toward the image of God as the one who really bore them like a mother and nurses them on the way to the Promised Land. In Isaiah 49:15, there is a statement that the nursing mother would not forget her child or fail to have compassion for it. God's love is like that. She will not fail to have compassion for those born of her love. Isaiah 66:10-13 suggests that we might have faith in order to "suck and be satisfied with her (Jerusalem's and God's) consoling breasts; that you may drink deeply with delight" and verse 12 continues "and you shall suck, you shall be carried upon her hip, and dandled upon her knees. As one whom his mother comforts, so will I comfort you" (says the Lord).10

Why is this image so empowering for me? It is our first comforting experience of life as an infant after the trauma of birth. In our mother's arms and at our mother's breast, we were first comforted by the softness and tender caresses. The first delicious taste of life was her sweet milk. From the milk, we received the antibodies that would protect us against disease. This is indeed an empowering image. It is our nourishing and life-giving source. This action, that is symbolic of our ultimate comfort and consolation from God, is embodied in the love and touch of our mother. It is a defense against spiritual illness and a balm for emotional wounds.

One might think that this is an image for women only to appreciate. One might assume that it is an affirmation of women that leaves out men. I believe that it is an image that

---

9*Holy Bible,* Revised Standard Version (New York: Thomas Nelson & Sons, 1952).

10*Holy Bible.*

helps men to recall what being nurtured feels like in the emotions, the spirit and the body. If men don't know how it feels, they won't know how to share it with their children.

While human fathers do not have the biological equipment to breast-feed children and not all mothers can and do breast-feed, there are other activities that can help to provide the vital touch that creates bonding and emotional nourishment for the infant. I cuddled my infants close in my arms as they sucked from a bottle. At other times, they sucked comfort from my little finger. Men can learn much at a deep level from making this image come alive in their emotional reservoir that they draw upon for the motivations to be ANF's.

After telling the Disciples to let these infants come to be blessed by him and not to hinder them, Jesus says, "whoever does not receive the (love) of God like an (infant) shall not receive it."[11] An infant receives love and affection first and very profoundly in a nursing posture. How appropriate then to metaphorize God's love as the nursing of the new creation which has been borne out of the womb of God. How appropriate then to metaphorize the believer as receiving the gracefilled love of God like an infant, quieted at its mother's breast.

Fathers who come up against the wall (like a marathon runner), and feel their emotional resources depleted by the demands of parenting might look to their faith images for some consolation and empowerment. Those who have reached this point know all too well that spiritual empowerment for fathering is absolutely necessary!

When men become frustrated with themselves and their children, there is great advice in Philippians 4:4-14. Let me paraphrase it here in language more specifically related to ANF:

---

[11]*Holy Bible, Luke* 18:17.

Be patient and put up with a lot. Have no anxiety about anything that your children may do but pray about it. Give thanks for what *is* good. "The peace of God, which passes all understanding, will keep your hearts and minds in Christ Jesus." Instead of dwelling upon your grievances with your children, give thanks for them and dwell on what *is* good and beautiful about them. Learn to be content and accept whatever happens without regret for what might have been. Face the enjoyable moments and the challenges with the same spirit of joy in God who strengthens you.[12]

When I get off the track suggested by Philippians, it helps me to look at my children's birth pictures with the words "I love Jessica" and "I love Jonathan" next to them. I look at a picture of me when I was two years old and realize that I got to be happy and healthy today, in part, because somebody loved me and was patient and nurturing with me when I was young.

I also look at a cross that my son colored when he was three years old which says "I love you!" (a reminder of God's love and Jon's). I look at a card on which my daughter drew a picture of herself with a wide smile and a balloon with a heart in it and the words "I love you, Dad! Have a good day! Love, Jessica." These are among the many images that motivate me to be more nurturing and more actively engaged in caregiving with my children. They remind me of the love I share with them. They remind me of God's unconditional love for me and them. They sing to me the tune of God's love and remind me of the rhythm of nurturing when my memory fails. Then

---

[12]*Holy Bible.*

gratitude returns in full force and love overflows again. Then "Daddy" is back!

THE MYTH OF FIERCE LOVE

In Robert Bly's book, *Iron John: A Book About Men,* he recovers an ancient myth with midrash-like interpretation (i.e., throwing other sacred stories and human experience up against the text to shed light on what would be veiled for most of us). Bly writes that myths have been a place where human beings have stored knowledge that lay outside the instinctual system.[13] Some birds and animals have nurturing instincts that direct them in how to care for their young. Perhaps there is some element of instinct in what men feel and know about caring for their young. Craig Rypma has studied this hypothesis and found indicators to substantiate such a view.[14] But most of what men need in the way of motivation and knowledge for ANF is likely to be learned. Passing on myths has long been a way of passing on knowledge and wisdom. The story bears power as the teller and hearer identify with the characters and feel the roles as if they were their own. In taking on these roles in their lives, they find motivation and power for living out the dreams, quests, tasks and meaning of the myth. The father who is bored by parenting and does not see what is at stake for him and his family, tends to stay away. But the father who sees the vital importance of his fathering and who approaches it with imagination, enthusiasm and depth of understanding; brings far more to his family and gets

---

[13] Robert Bly, *Iron John: A Book About Men* (Reading, MA: Addison-Wesley Publishing Co., 1990), p. xi.

[14] Craig Rypma, "Biological Bases of the Paternal Response," *The Family Coordinator,* October 1976, pp. 335-340.

far more out of fathering because of this approach. Motivating myths can help fathers to set the stage in their hearts and minds for wonderful fathering moments (in stark contrast to just "babysitting" the kids for mom).

Myths can be passed on from generation to generation with flexibility to accommodate the new truth in an ancient form. Bly calls them a "reservoir where we keep new ways of responding that we can adopt when the conventional and current ways wear out."[15]

More important than what the story of Iron John meant at the time is what the story can mean for the full development of men now. Women have been working on this recovery of mythic power for women's full development for years and Bly provides great insight into a way in which men can find mythic power for fathering.

I want to emphasize men's nurturing as an act of courage. Nurturing a child may take great courage and incredible exertion of energy. Fathering is a series of activities that are carried out within a larger context. This context is the mindset that a father has about what he is trying to accomplish for himself, his wife and their children. The predominant image of a parent that ought to be larger than all other images is that of helping the child to know that they are loved and valued. This requires generous helpings of unconditional love and attentive affirmation of the child's good behavior along with helpful direction away from destructive behavior. This is no job for the faint-hearted. That may be the most critical source of the problem: fathers need help in acquiring courage to be equally and actively involved in nurturing their children.

My understanding of why so many fathers are distant, absent and abusive is that they are unwilling to face the pain of being as vulnerable as active parents must become. Absent

---

[15]Bly, p. ix.

fathers, workaholic fathers and abusive fathers stay away from their children to avoid getting hurt. Men are running from pain. If they open up their feelings enough to be very compassionate with their children, fathers are bound to get hurt. They don't want to feel that pain. So, they remain distant by overworking, yelling and leaving. The overwhelming emotional needs of the children and the vulnerability of the work of parenting frightens many fathers away. If they do stick around, somebody is going to have to pay emotionally for the pain they feel.

In light of this reality, one must recognize that nurturing is not a passive quality. Nurturing is repeating *courageous* acts of love in the face of vulnerability to getting hurt. When one invests that much energy in someone else, one is open to greater pain, but also greater joy. Nurturing is continuing to love and give gentle discipline when a child is saying "I hate you" to try to get his own way. Nurturing is continuing compassionate caregiving with a child when a child tells her divorced and single father that she loves mom best in order to make him try harder to please her with gifts, treats and entertainment. Nurturing is investing years of a father's life in caring with a child who decides at age fifteen that running away from home is the answer to his emotional pain.

Nurturing takes strength and courage that many men cannot muster. Perhaps because men have feared the vulnerability that goes with actively caring with children, they have put such caregiving down as "woman's work" or put it on a pedestal as requiring a "woman's touch." Ironically, many men have viewed the job of parenting as a "soft job" while knowing in their hearts that it is a challenge that they themselves cannot bear to face.

Normal people are not so courageous and they require a variety of resources to bolster their courage to be good parents. The myth of Iron John can be a story of empowerment that enables fathers to do a difficult job with great joy in spite of the pain that may come with it. If fathers can identify with the characters and live out the roles, they can find guidance for creating the meaningful mindset that is an invaluable resource for everyday fathering activity.

I will take liberty in reappropriating the story, though I believe my use is not very far off from the original purpose of the myth.   Updating the meaning for us today is not anachronistic. It is the work of each generation to bring the old truth in the story alive again in the contemporary context. I focus more specifically on how the characters are enlightened to affirm the love of ANF as one very important form of compassion and vitality.

The story for men and women can be interpreted to be about enlightenment in general. For fathers today I see it as a potential vehicle for visualizing the mindset that it takes to be an ANF. It is a story with power for those who can enter into its images and take on the energy of the characters. If this story is "taken slowly into the body," it can give breath and life to the bearer.[16] Like a tale that one repeats to remember who they are and why they are here, the tale of Iron John can empower men to be ANF's.

Traces of some form of the Wild Man myth go as far back as prehistoric times and cave paintings. Throughout the centuries, it has been adapted to tell the story of the times. Some central issues have remained the same while the reference to the contemporary context of the point of the story has been updated. I find the story to be empowering for fathers when inserting some key issues for ANF into the places where they fit in the ancient myth. Here is my brief reappropriation of the story for the specific purpose of encouraging and empowering men to adopt the myth in their

---

[16]Bly, p. ix.

motivations for ANF. Much of the credit for translating and modernizing the myth with insights about men and fathering goes to Robert Bly. I recommend your reading *Iron John* to see the story in full and Bly's commentary on the myth. The criticism anyone might wish to offer for this interpretation of the myth that follows can fall on me. My additions to the story are in parenthesis. My abbreviated, paraphrased and altered version of Bly's translation follows:

Once upon a time, a King (active nurturant father) lived near a wild forest (worldly attractions that lure fathers away from caregiving with their children). After several hunters disappeared there (became absent fathers), the King sent a volunteer (ethicist or researcher) to explore (to figure out why fathers were not using their abilities and energy to care for their children).

Hiding (like an absent father) under the water in a deep pool (immersed in political and economic power different from the power to be an ANF) was a Wild Man (one capable of passion and compassion in nurturing but not actually using his skills to be the ANF that he should be). He was captured and imprisoned in the King's castle so that people (fathers) could venture into the forest (work world, recreational world, etc.) and return again (to active parenting without getting swallowed up by other priorities).

As long as the Wild Man was imprisoned, however, there was a lack of fierce love in the land that was essential (for good parenting). The King's Son, who was eight years old then, played with a golden ball (acquiring the capacity to be nurturing), but it rolled into the Wild Man's cage. In order to get it back, the boy had to steal the key from under his mother's pillow (seizing his autonomy to become nurturing with others besides his mother). In doing so, the boy pinched his finger (experienced the vulnerability and pain that sometimes comes with caregiving). The boy set Wild Man free (enabling the fierce energy of love to flow) and left home on his shoulders (was empowered to nurture people beyond his parents by his mentor who gave him fierce love).

Wild Man then brought the boy to a spring with water that turned things into gold (empowered them by loving them). Wild Man told him to be sure that nothing contaminated the spring (destroyed the fierce loving spirit). The boy contaminated it himself (being human and imperfect in his love), but he got some of the gold (capacity for fierce loving) on his hair (it became a part of him) and his wounded finger (becoming strong in his compassion for others because of the pain he had known). So the Wild Man sent him out (reminding him that his love was not perfect) to go and experience poverty (in order to acquire deep awareness of just how incredibly important fierce love is for people). Iron John told him to call whenever he needed the energy of fierce love (and then he could get strength to be nurturing from God/spiritual sources especially when loving was not easy).

Another King's daughter (who knew love because of her father's nurturing behavior) saw this fierce love in the boy and threw him some golden apples (her love which was possible because of the love her father gave her) and they were married (nurtured each other and shared equally in work and parenting).

Another King (ANF) came to the wedding and announced that he was Iron John, who had been turned into a Wild Man (a man of fierce love and capable of actively engaging in parenting but not actually doing the job he was called to do because of the way he used his energy wildly without caring with his children), but who was now freed (able to do the job of ANF) because the boy who had befriended him had shown him by their relationship that he could find great fulfillment in channeling his fierce love into caring (for his own children).

All the treasures of Iron John (spiritual, physical, emotional vitality for loving) would belong to this man- -the King's son (now a father himself who had been taught by his father about how to be a caregiver and who had been empowered with the Wild Man's fierce love). Iron John helped the boy to acquire fierce love and the boy had helped Iron John (to discover that children were indeed fit recipients for such love as well as caregivers themselves). Each had become empowered (to be ANF's by the nurturing relationship that developed between them).[17]

This myth is life-giving for one who identifies with the characters. Adult men may identify with the Wild Man because they know fierce love and use it in other parts of their lives but not in relating with their children. Young boys may identify with the boy because they have not yet discovered

---

[17]My adaptation of Robert Bly's translation of the story by Jacob and Wilhelm Grimm in *Grimms Marchen* (Zurich: Manesse Verlag, 1946).

the fierce love in themselves that they could have for their future children. They may know how it feels for a girl friend but not for a child of theirs. Even though they know something about doing the tasks of caring for an infant/child, they have not yet discovered the depths and heights of love in their hearts that will be necessary for long-term commitment, quality and quantity time, and patience in their parenting.

CHAPTER FIVE

REBIRTH FOR ANF

No one is born a good parent. It takes preparation and training to be a good parent. While men and women may learn information about child rearing with relative ease and speed, the desire and disposition to nurture do not come overnight or by a simple act of the will. The habits of nurturing a child may be promoted and valued or denied and blocked by socialization and structures of society.

To produce significant change in the general attitudes of the society and the attitudes of individual fathers about ANF, the basic process which influences these attitudes must be transformed. To prepare fathers for ANF, the most crucial moments for this preparation must be understood and utilized. To provide continuing support for fathers as active parents, the most significant barriers must be overcome and superseded by policies and attitudes which facilitate a father's continued active engagement in the care of his children.

It is an undeniable fact that women are physically able to bear children and that men are not. However, men *can* nurture children. This point was explored in Chapter One. Ann

Oakley expressed the traditional assumption in terms of a faulty syllogism:

> Only women can give birth.
> Only women look after children.
> Therefore only women can look after children.[1]

To the contrary, men can "look after children" if they learn how and acquire a disposition toward nurturing. This is true of women as well, who are not born with the ability to parent. However, one must ask whether men and women are equally inclined to learn nurturing behavior or equally disposed to persevere as active parents.

Alice Rossi explored a number of social and pyschological factors pertaining to the reproductive and endocrine systems involved in childbirth, pregnancy and breast-feeding, which seem to facilitate most women's learning of skills in child nurture and predispose more women than men toward nurturing activity.[2] Her research does not require a conclusion, however, that women, therefore, *should* be the ones to do most of the child care. Nor does she insist that this fact alone explains why women in the society are more often the primary parent than men. Rather, she concludes from such evidence:

> Unless these biosocial factors are confronted, allowed for, and if desired, compensated for, the current press toward sexual equality in marriage and the workplace and shared child-rearing may show the same episodic

---

[1] Ann Oakley, *Women Confined: Towards a Sociology of Childbirth* (New York: Schocken Books, 1980), p. 80.

[2] Alice Rossi, "A Biosocial Perspective on Parenting," in Alice Rossi et. al., eds., *The Family* (New York: W.W. Norton, 1978), pp. 1-31.

history that so many social experiments have demonstrated in the past.[3]

In terms of social policy to promote ANF, she advises:

> If a society wishes to create shared parental roles it must...institutionalize the means for providing men with compensatory exposure and training in infant and child care in order to close the gap produced by the physiological experience of pregnancy, birth and nursing. Without such compensatory training of males, females will show added dimensions of intensity to their bonds with children.[4]

The depth of the bonding between a father and his child may be increased by the exercise of various habits in parenting which social policies and practices may facilitate. Martin Greenberg and Norman Morris studied the newborn's impact upon the father and developed the concept of "engrossment" to explain how parents become positively attached to their infant. They theorized from observations that the development of engrossment (i.e., the feeling of preoccupation, absorption and interest in the child) is beneficial, if not essential, to fostering ANF.[5]

In some primitive cultures, the father was thought to be effectively engaged in childbirth by the practice of "couvade." The father would remain in bed during the time of delivery and for days thereafter. During childbirth, he would mimic the labor, express feelings of pain, and go through the motions of

---

[3]Rossi, p. 2.

[4]Rossi, p. 18.

[5]Greenberg and Morris, "Engrossment: The Newborn's Impact Upon the Father," p. 527.

giving birth to the infant as if it were coming from his own body.[6] A modern counterpart is the participation of expectant fathers in classes and exercises in prepared childbirth and in being actively involved in emotional aspects of the birth with the mother.[7]

While fathers are not able to participate in the pregnancy in the same way that mothers are, fathers can begin to get into the act when mothers do. They can begin to get a feel for the positive and challenging aspects of parenting. Fathers can begin exercising skills in support and understanding that are beyond what may have been required of them before. Fathers can get in touch with their own feelings of wonder at the kicking fetus.

While Frank Pedersen concluded that the father's support of the mother helped her in being more effective in feeding the baby,[8] it is conversely true that the mother's support of the father can greatly enhance the father's nurturing ability and effectiveness. Criticism from the mother can undermine the effectiveness of the father and reduce his interest and willingness to be an ANF. A mutually supportive relationship between the parents in which there is a mutual exchange of *gifts and gratitude* can help to set up the conditions for ANF rather than begrudging performance of a few obligatory tasks by the father.

6J. Miller, "Fathers in the Delivery Room," *Child and Family,* 3 (1964), p. 4.

7Nathan Hal, *The Birth of a Family: The New Role of the Father in Childbirth* (New York: Anchor Press, 1979).

8F.A. Pedersen, B.J. Anderson and R.L. Cain, "An Approach to Understanding Linkages Between Parent-Infant and Spouse Relationships" (paper presented at the "Society for Research in Child Development," New Orleans, March 1977).

Some expectant fathers have displayed the Couvade Syndrome. Couvade is derived from the French word "couver," meaning to "hatch or brood over the eggs in the nest."[9] The syndrome is a set of symptoms by the father that coincide with the time of the pregnancy. He suffers from loss of appetite, nausea and backaches. While some may point to this as a way to show support for the mother, I am skeptical because it may take more away from the father's ability to support the mother. It might be an unconscious attempt by a father who feels abandoned because of the attention going to his pregnant wife and because of the loss in nurturing he may feel at this time. It may be the result of anxieties about added responsibilities. The syndrome may have been dysfunctional to some families and helpful to others. If physical and graphic ways of identifying with the mother is helping her to feel support and helping the father to get involved, then there is nothing inappropriate about it. However, if couvade-like symptoms appear and they are driving the father away from ANF and the mother is feeling neglected, a father should get help in dealing with the feelings behind them.

Joanna Gladieux found that fathers who turned to their parents and friends for support in this stressful time when they too needed a little more reassurance found higher satisfaction and were able to be more supportive of the mother.[10]

---

[9]W.H. Trethowan and M.F. Conolon, "The Couvade Syndrome," *British Journal of Psychiatry*, 1965, 111, pp. 57-66.

[10]J.D. Gladieux, "Pregnancy---The Transition to Parenthood: Satisfaction with the Pregnancy Experience as a Function of Sex-role Conceptions, Marital Relationship and Social Network," in W.B. Miller and L.F. Newman, eds., *The First Child and Family Formation* (Chapel Hill, NC: Carolina Population Center, 1978), p. 292.

Another study documented the link between the mother's emotional well being as supported by the father and the infant's lower irritability. Supportive fathers help to sustain greater serenity for mothers and this is passed on to the infant with less irritability and greater ability to recover from upset.[11] Conversely, mothers who are supportive of new fathers in their caring with the infant can also contribute to the emotional well being of the child and the satisfaction level of the father.

A father's support of the mother and his interest in pregnancy has been found to be positively related to how much he holds the baby in the first six weeks of life and to whether he will attend to the baby when it cries.[12] The implications for ANF are that fathers should be involved as early as possible to maximize the possibilities for their continued involvement later on. It starts with his sharing the decision to have the baby, continues through pregnancy with his interest and support of the mother and culminates in the birth experience. The development of ANF habits and disposition should begin here and not later. Patterns of non-involvement that develop during pregnancy establish a pattern that is not easily changed after the child is born.

The importance of a father's participation in childbirth experiences and parenting during early infancy is accentuated by the wide influence this period has upon the later relationship between the father and the child. For instance, T. Berry Brazelton observed that fathers absent from their

---

[11]F.K. Grossman, et. al. *Pregnancy, Birth and Parenthood* (San Francisco: Jossey Bass, 1980).

[12]D.R. Entwisle and S.G. Doering, *The First Birth* (Baltimore: Johns Hopkins, 1981).

newborn infants during the early months had difficulty showing affection for the child.[13]

Henry Biller postulated from studies of paternal deprivation that "the earlier the father can feel involved with the infant, the more likely will a strong father-child attachment develop."[14] The child's attachment to the father facilitates the father's engrossment with the child and vice versa. Frank Pederson and Kenneth Robson found that the more the father cared for, stimulated and was involved with the baby, the more this infant responded with attachment behavior.[15] Greenberg and Morris observed that the greater and the earlier physical contact and nurturing takes place between the father and the infant, the more likely it is that engrossment will occur.[16]

Further evidence clarifies the importance of this transition period for the development of ANF as opposed to father absence. In a study of couples who recently became parents, Ross Parke concluded that "the birth of a baby seems to bring even egalitarian parents back to traditional roles....There was a marked return to the customary division of labor for a variety of functions, from decision-making to baby care and housework."[17]

In analyzing the transition of a married couple from being spouses to becoming parents, Alice Rossi has noted the plight

---

[13]T. Barry Brazelton, "What Makes a Good Father," *Redbook*, June 1970.

[14]Henry Biller, *Paternal Deprivation* (Lexington, MA: D.C. Heath, 1974), p. 163.

[15]Frank Pederson and Kenneth Robson, "Father Participation in Infancy," *American Journal of Orthopsychiatry*, April 1969, p. 472.

[16]Greenberg and Morris, "Engrossment," p. 527.

[17]Ross Parke and Douglas Sawin, "Fathering: It's a Major Role," *Psychology Today*, November 1977, p. 111.

of many mothers who have come to assume the role of primary parent without shared responsibility from their husbands:

> For many women the personal outcome of experience in the parent role is not a higher level of maturation but the negative outcome of a depressed sense of self-worth, if not actual personality deterioration....The possibility must be faced, and at some point researched, that women lose ground in personal development and self-esteem during the early and middle years of adulthood (with the onset of parenting), whereas men gain ground in these respects during the same years.[18]

Ellen Goodman explored the "worry gap" in families that shared parenting. Even mothers who thought that they were egalitarian took more responsibility for figuring out what is needed and what is missing in the care of a child and fathers left it to her. ANF's should pick up their share of *concern*. Mothers may lay too much guilt upon themselves, but fathers have tended to ignore the needs of the children. Two busy career spouses can choose to let the housework slide when each feels it is the other's job, but caregiving with children demands attention. Mothers tend to pick up the slack while fathers tend to ignore it. It takes a nurturing eye to see when the children need attention and time. Teaching this skill "may be as hard as training someone to see dirt on the windowsill."[19] The training must begin very early when the infant and father are developing patterns of interaction. If the

---

[18]Rossi, "Transition to Parenthood," in C, Greenblatt, et. al., eds. *The Marriage Game* (New York: Random House, 1974), p. 109.

[19]Ellen Goodman, "Dads should forget gifts of perfume and build bridges to span the worry-gap," *St. Paul Pioneer Press*, May 1990.

father learns to take the responsibility for picking up on the child's cues, then he will be establishing a pattern for future active nurturing attentiveness.

The transition to parenthood is a sensitive and critical period during which a father's degree of involvement in parenting is highly susceptible to influence in either direction (i.e., toward greater or lesser involvement). Policies which promote ANF at this critical period can be expected to have more significant influence than at any later stage of a father's life.[20]

With fathers who are ambivalent toward their newborns at first, early contact "may be sufficient to push these fathers over the the threshold, resulting in the release of engrossment."[21] If parents nurture the infant more or less equally during this period, the infant will become attached to both of them and be more likely to hold the father's interest.[22] This attachment in the early development of the father-and-child relationship is more likely than at any other time to sustain involvement throughout later years.[23] This should not be taken as a discouragement to fathers who find later in the child's development that they want to start getting more involved. It may mean that it is a little harder than if they had started earlier and that their good intentions may not last as long as if they had started ANF in the beginning. It may mean that they will have to work that much harder to make it happen and to keep it up.

---

[20]Greenberg and Morris, p. 529

[21]Greenberg and Morris, p. 527.

[22]Marc Feigen Fasteau, *The Male Machine* (New York: McGraw-Hill Co., 1974), p. 201.

[23]Levine, *Who Will Raise the Children?*, p. 31.

OVERCOMING ALIENATION FROM
THE PROCESS OF REPRODUCTION

To support ANF, critique and reform must be directed at the period of transition to parenthood which involves childbirth. This experience is vital for the development of a father's will and disposition to take equal responsibility for parenting activities. If barriers to ANF at this stage are superseded by support systems, fathers will be more inclined, better prepared and more positively encouraged to share equally in parenting.

Practices of hospitals, obstetricians and the workplace have frequently alienated men from the process of reproduction.[24] Even though most hospitals have developed some programs for prepared childbirth and father participation, there continues to be an emphasis upon the medical aspects and the need for institutional order that limits family participation.

The mother, father and infant are separated from each other by walls, procedures, schedules and staff members doing their job. The first important moments during which a father may become attached to and engrossed with his infant may be taken away from him. Natural childbirth has also been "colonized" by hospitals seeking to attract customers. Each designs a program and parents can choose between hospitals, but parents still have relatively little freedom within that program.

A shift to birthing rooms rather than the sterile delivery rooms has enhanced the participation of fathers in the delivery and consequently enhanced the likelihood of later

---

[24]Joel Richman, W. Goldthorp and C. Simmons, "Fathers in Labour," *New Society.* October 16, 1975, p. 145.

ANF. These rooms are the next best thing to being at home. They look more like a bedroom and nursery than an operating room. The best for active nurturant fathering are those that allow the father and the infant to remain there around the clock.

In 1972, fathers were permitted in the delivery room in only twenty-seven percent of U.S. hospitals surveyed. In 1974, the American College of Obstetricians and Gynecologists endorsed the father's presence during labor. By 1980, eighty percent of American hospitals admitted fathers.[25] In 1990 several Twin Cities (Minnesota) hospitals widely advertised that they had the most warm and homelike atmosphere for births.

Some fathers have been encouraged by the obstetricians to help in the delivery. When my daughter, Jessica, was born, the obstetrician came into the room only at the crucial time of the delivery. A nurse talked to us occasionally with reassurance, but for the most part we did it as a team with medical participation only for a brief period of time during the actual delivery, checkup and placenta delivery. I was encouraged to cut the umbilical cord, to help clean my daughter up and to hold her immediately after the birth (as was her mother). This took place in a birthing room where I also slept for two nights in the hospital before we all went home together. We did the feeding, bathing, comforting and diapering. In those precious moments so much happened to connect me with my daughter and to prepare the stage for a lifetime of nurturing.

Fathers who participated in a study of those who helped in the delivery were twice as likely to be involved in the daily care of their infants. They were spending an hour or more

---

[25]Parke, *Fathers* (Cambridge, MA: Harvard University Press, 1981), p. 20.

with their babies daily, compared to fathers who had not participated in the delivery.[26]

There has long been an assumption that fathers could not be present in the delivery room during Caesarean births because of the danger of infection. This has not proved to be as prohibitive a concern as previously thought and fathers are increasingly being allowed to be present during Caesarean deliveries.[27]

Fathers who were present during Caesarean births were even more likely than fathers present at births delivered vaginally to be highly involved in regular care and feeding of infants when they got home.[28] This probably took place more frequently because the mothers were not ready to take on these responsibilities as readily as other mothers. The need to get involved right away helped the father to get an active start and to develop a pattern of ANF.

A Swedish study found that fathers who had the opportunity to feed and diaper the baby in the hospital did more of this care three months later as well.[29] Patterns are developed early. Hospitals can help to develop active patterns or inactive patterns. The future of fathers' involvement can be enhanced with the cooperation of hospitals. It is a contribution

---

[26]M. Levine and R. Block, unpublished study cited by Parke, *Fathers*, p. 24.

[27]Parke, *Fathers*, p. 25.

[28]F. Pedersen, M.T. Zaslow, R.L. Cain and B.J. Andersen, "Caesarean Birth: The Importance of a Family Perspective" (paper presented at the International Conference on Infant Studies, New Haven, CT, April 1980).

[29]J. Lind, "Observations After Delivery of Communications between Mother-Infant-Father" (paper presented at the International Congress of Pediatrics, Buenos Aires, October, 1974).

that hospitals can make to the health and well-being of families long after they leave the hospital.

There is no automatic correlation between prepared childbirth and fathers' involvement, however. In a study by Robert Fein, there was considerable variation among the fathers in caring involvement with infants later on.[30] In another study, "several lamaze fathers indicated that they had expected to be more involved with the care of infants than they actually were. They mentioned their own demanding work schedules and/or their wives' breast-feeding as reasons for the discrepancy between expected and actual care time."[31] These fathers felt poorly prepared for the rest of parenting activity which came after the initial stages of childbirth were ending.

A receptive time for teaching a father about infant care and nurturing is immediately after the birth. Then he is fascinated with the new infant and probably a bit concerned about how he will care for this baby. His interest in learning about ANF peaks at this point. Ross Parke showed fathers a videotape on infants and caretaking skills. It helped them to learn more, to be more involved in caretaking activities, and to do so for a longer time after the birth.[32] This is not the only time that fathers may learn active patterns of involvement, however. At each stage of development there are new things for fathers to learn and opportunities for emotional ties to develop.[33]

---

[30] Robert Fein, "Men's Entrance to Parenthood," *The Family Coordinator,* October 1976, p. 347.

[31] Fein, "Men's Entrance to Parenthood," p. 346.

[32] Ross Parke, *Fathers* (Cambridge, MA: Harvard University Press, 1981), p. 112.

[33] Ross Parke, *Fathers* , p. 112.

In another study, eight weekly classes were held to teach fathers how to read and respond to infant signals appropriately. Compared to a control group, fathers increased their interactions with their infants. They held them more, were more likely to smile at them, and to talk in response to the baby's behavior. In short, the education had a significant impact upon the father's level of involvement.[34]

Philip Zelazo and his colleagues showed that classes in play skills can help fathers to improve their interactions with their infants. The infants of these tutored fathers showed increased interest in their fathers as a result of the learned skills. Improving skills made for a closer relationship between father and infant.[35]

In spite of such parenting education, fathers will still learn by their mistakes in some cases. As one father lamented, "It is too bad that you have to learn to be a father on someone as precious to you as your own children."[36] More parenting education could help fathers to be more involved by alleviating the anxiety about making mistakes as a parent. A lack of confidence comes from a lack of experience and training for the job. More training could raise the level of confidence and the predisposition to do the job.

Because there are limits to how much people can learn from books and the experience of others, males would be better prepared for ANF if they had some first-hand

---

[34] Jane Dickie and S. Carnahan Gerber, "Training in Social Competence: The Effect of Mothers, Fathers and Infants," *Child Development*, 1980, 51, pp. 1248-1251.

[35] P. R. Zelazo, M. Kotelchuck, L. Barber and J. David, "Fathers and Sons: An Experimental Facilitation of Attachment Behaviors," unpublished paper cited in Ross Parke, *Fathers*, p. 113.

[36] Joel Thingvall, "Fatherhood a tough job but immensely gratifying," *St. Paul Pioneer Press*, June 19, 1987.

experience with babies to go along with hearing and reading about parenting experiences, participating in workshops and coursework about ANF. For one of the most important jobs in life, fathers have few opportunities for job training and don't take advantage of those. Their careers require endless updating of skills and continuing education. Their family work is just as complex, but most fathers do not take any continuing education courses in parenting skills and issues. If fathers were better prepared for their job as parents, their performance level would be higher and their satisfaction level would increase so that fathering would be more self-rewarding and more self-sustaining.

GOING BEYOND REPRODUCING TRADITIONAL ROLES

A social policy to promote ANF must also address the socialization barrier. Traditional sex-role socialization against ANF inhibits most men. They have not been emotionally prepared, sufficiently motivated or adequately supported to become ANF's.

The traditional division of family labor has been perpetuated by the process of socialization. Children are often prepared by molding, teaching and experience to internalize and assume the same imbalance of social and economic power as that held by their parents and the society in general.[37] Therefore, what the parents and other people in the society *do* may be the most significant teacher, even more significant than what they *say* about sharing parenting.

Some creative resocialization is required to prepare male children for ANF. Partly because schools and teachers play

---

[37]Gloria Morris Nemerowicz, *Children's Perceptions of Gender and Work Roles* (New York: Praeger Publishers, 1979), p. 162.

such an instrumental role in children's development, the most extensive studies of sex-role socialization have been conducted in the formal educational setting.[38] Critical research on the effectiveness of strategies to reduce sex-role stereotyping in schools has provided helpful direction for policy to promote ANF.[39]

The role of curriculum and classroom procedures in encouraging or inhibiting sex-role stereotyping was explored in a six-week curriculum research project involving twenty-four teachers at three grade levels. Utilizing several instructional methods, "it became clear that the teachers were the vital links in promoting non-sexist attitudes in the children in this short-term intervention (program)."[40] The amount of children's attitude change in the direction of non-stereotyping closely correlated with the teacher's skills in implementing the curriculum."[41]

Because of the rather large significance teachers carry in the lives of school-age children, they have a substantial role in creating or undoing traditional roles. "Even the influences of peer groups can be mediated by the teacher's classroom interaction" since teachers control the bases of reinforcement in the classroom.[42]

Having a male or female instructor was found to be an insignificant variable in the program effectiveness. Both men and women were able to use the curriculum effectively to

---

[38]P. Lee and N. Gropper, "Sex-Role Culture and Educational Practice," *Harvard Educational Practice,* 44 (1974), pp. 369-410.

[39]M. Guttenberg and H. Bray, "Teachers as Mediators of Sex-Role Standards," in Alice Sargent, *Beyond Sex Roles* (St. Paul, MN: West Publishing, 1977), pp. 395-411.

[40]Guttenberg and Bray, p. 406.

[41]Guttenberg and Bray, p. 408.

[42]Guttenberg and Bray, p. 409.

undo the sex-stereotyping of boys and girls. Given some training in methodology, a willing and creative teacher could dramatically open up children's sex-stereotypes even in a six-week curriculum.[43] Perhaps the most important perspective children can gain from this type of intervention program is the ability to think critically about traditional role prescriptions.

Carol Joffe studied a nursery school which carried out a policy to avoid imposition of sex-stereotypes.[44] Despite the attempts by the school staff, effectiveness was limited because there were no male teachers; there was subtle stereotyping that had not yet been eliminated from the curriculum; no fathers were involved in the after-school part of the program; and the families continued traditional roles at home.[45]

Males cannot be effectively socialized toward ANF by the school if traditional roles continue at home. The socialization of children within families where there is an unequal balance of power between the parents predisposes these children to an easy acceptance of injustice between men and women.[46] Furthermore, such experience leads them to recreate the same relationships to power in establishing their own personal identities. In order to aid children in developing a sense of equality and fairness in male/female relations, changes in the parents' power relations are essential.

Socialization and education at school and in the home can prepare males for ANF. If boys are helped to experience, accept and work through their own emotions and understand

---

[43]Guttenberg and Bray, p. 408.

[44]Carole Joffe, "Sex Role Socialization and the Nursery School: As the Twig Is Bent," in John Petras, ed. *Sex: Male/ Gender:Masculine* (Port Washington, NY: Alfred Publishing Co., 1975), pp. 104-119.

[45]Joffe, p. 117.

[46]James Harrison, "A Critical Evaluation....," p. 258.

the feelings of others, they will be better prepared to deal with the emotions of tomorrow's children. If they are aided as children in developing a respect for the emotional life of others, they may be less terrified as adult males by the free-flowing emotions of children. If males of all ages are socialized and educated to perceive the rewards and satisfactions of intimacy, they will be better prepared to nurture children and more inclined to seek opportunities for ANF.[47]

INITIATING STRATEGIES FOR CHANGE

John Scanzoni has outlined three strategies of transformation that might be utilized by men and women to accomplish changes in the direction of ANF. These are referred to as the strategies of "self interest," "altruism" and "conflict."[48] Results seem to be most positive when all three are utilized, with each being applied in appropriate circumstances.[49]

In the self-interest strategy an appeal is made to fathers that they recognize how ANF can be personally fulfilling. The case may be argued to fathers that balancing their lives between work and parenting, being an ANF, and supporting their spouse's career development are really in their own best interest. This was the perspective taken in some arguments appearing in the early to mid 1970's.[50] Mothers may use this

---

[47]Sargent, p. 12.

[48]John Scanzoni, "Strategies for Changing Male Family Roles: Research and Practice Implications," *The Family Coordinator*, October 1970, pp. 435-442.

[49]J. Rubin and B. Brown, *The Social Psychology of Bargaining and Negotiation* (New York: Academix, 1975).

[50]Warren Farrell, *The Liberated Man* (New York: Bantam, 1973), pp. 133-134; Fasteau, p. 98.

strategy in bringing their spouses to an awareness of what personal benefits may be gained in parenting more and being a little less work centered.

Robert Fein commended this perspective in writing, "Men are finding that contact with children leads them back to themselves, allowing them to integrate their childlike selves with their grownup selves."[51]   In speaking of their motivation to change, Fein emphasized the self interest of men:

> Growing awareness of the "sandpaper existence" of many American men (the pervasive loneliness, the frantic competition, the prevalence of ulcers and heart attack, the premature dying) propels some to seek new ways to order the structure and meaning of their daily lives.[52]

In closing this statement, Fein shifted the approach slightly to include the altruistic strategy: "Relationships between men and young children, long awaited homecomings, may lead toward a more caring society."[53] In this approach, other-centered values have been presented to morally justify ANF. The altruistic strategy is an appeal made to fathers that they should be ANF's because it is right, fair, just, good and moral. This has been "the dominant theme that runs through the literature on changes in male sex roles."[54]

Men and women may press this strategy by presenting moral arguments, publicly and in conversation, to support ANF. Many people need to be persuaded that it is morally right for mothers and fathers to share work and parenting

---

[51]Fein, "Men and Young Children," p. 61.

[52]Fein, "Men and Young Children," p. 62.

[53]Fein, "Men and Young Children," p. 62.

[54]Scanzoni, "Strategies," p. 436.

more equally. Developing a sense of moral virtue and also of moral obligation toward ANF may help men to become more ANF's. This strategy may help to overcome the quasi-moral prescriptions which keep men from parenting.

A third strategy, conflict, stems from an awareness that unless the subordinate group (women) presses for greater male involvement in child rearing and their own opportunity in the work world, this desired justice is not likely to come about.[55] Men have generally not regarded equal parenting as desirable in the way that many women have. At present, men are unlikely to want to reduce their work commitments thereby relinquishing some of the power they hold by virtue of work and the satisfactions they find in work. Women, who are presently less rewarded for employment than men and are more frequently overloaded with two roles than men, are also, therefore, more likely to be the ones to press for changes in the family and work roles.

At the microsocial level, conflict and negotiation have resulted in some positive changes toward greater justice between men and women in employment. Some women are able now to negotiate with men on a relatively more equal basis at a personal level.[56]

By utilizing this improved power within families to negotiate, women may be able to bring their spouses to make the necessary changes that will result in ANF. The two parents may be able to come to a better balance in the well-being of both parents by creating a more equal distribution of parenting and work responsibilities between them.

Arlie Hochschild's study on the "second shift" documented strategies of active renegotiation and passive negotiation. The

---

[55]Scanzoni, "Strategies," p. 437; E. Walster and G. Walster, "Equity and Social Justice," *The Journal of Social Issues*, 31 (1975), pp. 21-44.

[56]Scanzoni, "Strategies," p. 439.

former involved making long lists and schedules and insisting that they "cannot go on like this." Passive negotiation meant playing dumb, feigning incompetence, getting sick, and other means of indirectly inducing fathers to do the work. Fathers have been doing their share of passive resistance too: playing dumb about child care and acting incompetent in the basic skills. While many women now feel that they are allowed to ask for help, they still have to *ask* and it is still only "help" in most cases. That is a long way from men presuming that it is also their role to be an active nurturant parent.[57]

Hochschild illustrated some aspects and potential costs of the "sharing showdown." That is her term for a woman renegotiating with her husband for him to take on more of the child care and housework. Sometimes it works for a while. Sometimes it is ignored by the father. Sometimes it is abandoned by the woman after she withdraws or modifies the request out of realistic fear that she will lose this man if she pushes him any further toward sharing. The fear of divorce leads some to stop asking for help. When life "out there" looks frightening, a woman may try to stay warm inside an unequal marriage and do the second shift herself. While improvements in women's paid work push in the direction of men doing more parenting work, the "wage gap between men and women and the rising divorce rate work in the opposite direction."[58]

As men become more aware of the benefits to themselves, they may become the initiators of negotiation toward ANF more frequently. As more fathers become convinced of the moral rightness of ANF, more may initiate changes toward ANF without the necessity of personal conflict initiated by women to achieve such ends. Couples may then be able to come to a

---

[57] Arlie Hochschild with Anne Machung, *The Second Shift* (New York: Avon Books, 1989), p. 258.

[58] Hochschild and Machung, p. 253.

consensus about changes toward ANF without risking marital dissolution as much as is presently the case.

CHAPTER SIX

DO WORK INNOVATIONS PROMOTE ANF?

Efforts in the United States to promote equality between men and women in the workplace and to encourage ANF have been disjointed compared to those in Sweden.[1] Since 1968, when a report on the Status of Women was presented to the United Nations Economic and Social Council,[2] Swedish government policy has been directed toward promoting equality partly by supporting ANF:

The aim of a *long-term* "program for women" must be that every individual, irrespective of sex, shall have the same practical opportunities, not only for education and employment, but also in principle the same

---

[1] Sheila Kamerman and Alfred J. Kahn, *Family Policy: Government and Families in Fourteen Countries* (New York: Columbia University Press, 1978), pp. 29, 472.

[2] Maj-Britt Sandlund, "The Status of Women in Sweden: Report to the United Nations 1968," in Edmund Dahlstrom, ed., *The Changing Roles of Men and Women* (Boston: Beacon Press, 1971), pp. 209-302.

responsibility for his or her own maintenance as well as a shared responsibility for the upbringing of children and the upkeep of the home. Eventually to achieve complete equality of these rights and obligations, a radical change in deep-rooted traditions and attitudes must be taken by the community to encourage a change in the roles played by both. The view that women ought to be economically supported by marriage must be effectively refuted---also in the legislative field---as this view is a direct obstacle to the economic independence of women and their ability to compete on equal terms in the labour market. Similarly, the husband's traditional obligation to support his wife must be modified to constitute a responsibility, shared with her, for the support of the children. This concern for the children should also be manifested in a greater degree of participation in the supervision and care of the children on the husband's part.[3]

According to research data in the United States, some innovations in employment policies and measures to improve the status of women, which have been presumed to be conducive to the wider adoption of ANF, have not, in fact, produced the expected results. While these policies have benefitted some people for other reasons, only minimal progress has been made toward ANF in the United States because of them alone. This chapter is an analysis of these findings with a view toward understanding the practical problems and theoretical issues that must be worked through if social policy to promote ANF is to become more effective.

---

[3]Sandlund, p. 215.

DO PART-TIME JOBS PROMOTE ANF?

Arguing that many full-time jobs do not provide adequate opportunities for ANF when the children are pre-school age, some advocates of ANF have proposed the creation of more part-time positions in the labor market.[4] For this situation, part-time (hereafter referred to as PT) is defined as less than 35 hours per week.

Carol Schwartz Greenwald, one of the leading proponents of PT, based her case for these jobs on the benefits that have accrued to employers who tried it. She argued that offering PT is a drawing card for corporations competing for the best employees. In seeking to persuade employers to take the initiative in creating PT positions, she cited studies showing greater productivity as well as lower unit costs due to the rapid and dramatic decreases in absenteeism, turnover, recruiting activity and overtime pay.[5]

Permanent PT jobs, at best, would provide the same fringe benefits as full-time but on a pro-rated basis. Years of PT work would be "credited toward seniority, promotion, tenure and salary adjustments in the same way as years of full-time work."[6] Part-time positions would be created in all

---

[4] Jessie Bernard, *The Future of Marriage* (New York: Bantam, 1972), pp. 277-297; Maureen Green, *Fathering* (New York: McGraw-Hill, 1976), pp. 213-214; Kenneth Keniston, *All Our Children: The American Family Under Pressure* (New York: Harcourt, Brace, Jovanovich, 1977), p. 123.

[5] Carol Schwartz Greenwald, "Working Mothers: The Need for More Part-Time Jobs," *New England Economic Review*, September-October, 1972, p. 21.

[6] Safilios-Rothschild, *Women and Social Policy* (Englewood Cliffs, NJ: Prentice-Hall, 1974), p. 21.

categories of employment, not only the least skilled. Without these conditions of permanent PT, few fathers would be induced toward utilizing PT. The economic sacrifices of moving from full-time to PT would be too great.[7]

Among the fathers that James Levine interviewed across the country was a corporate executive who changed to PT when overwork interfered with his fathering.[8] He was the model of a career-oriented man who devoted his life to his career. After his child was born, this devotion became more of a problem than something to admire. The relationship between himself and his wife deteriorated. He was bearing down harder than ever in his work. His wife felt isolated, unfulfilled and overcome by the demands of sole responsibility for child care.

After coming to terms with this situation in an intense confrontation, they each agreed through negotiation to make some major changes. He cut back his work to three days and she began working PT. They took a temporary reduction in family income and knowingly reduced his opportunities for career advancement. As he commented on this matter, "If you want to share in the child care as I am doing, you won't be president of the company."[9] The tradeoffs were considered acceptable by them in order to provide for more mutual fulfillment by sharing parenting and paid employment.

Another form of PT, called "job sharing," has been utilized to facilitate ANF. This work innovation involves the splitting of the total workload, salary and benefits of one full-time job

---

[7]Safilios-Rothschild, p. 21.

[8]Levine, *Who Will Raise the Children?*, pp. 56-61.

[9]Levine, *Who Will Raise the Children?*, p. 61.

between two people.[10] While some spouses have chosen to share the same position, others have preferred to work with someone other than their spouse.

Shared positions, at best, would also be created in all types of employment and would not be limited to categories of work which provide only low status, low wages, few benefits and little job security.[11] Hypothetically, by enabling both mothers and fathers to work shorter hours without inordinate economic and career sacrifices, this work innovation could help to promote shared responsibility for parenting.[12] In personal accounts about their experience in joint employment, several participants noted that their major motivation to share a job was the need to find a more mutually fulfilling balance, for both themselves and their spouses, between work and parenting.[13]

Two interviewees in Levine's study, were able to share equally in parenting because they each held half-time appointments at a college as professors. In acquiring these appointments, they had to challenge the institutional practices geared toward maintaining full-time as the predominant pattern of employment.[14]

They each applied for a position on the faculty, were equally qualified, and the Dean wanted to hire both of them. At first, the Dean thought of offering the man an assistant

---

[10]William Arkin and Lynne R. Dobrofsky, "Job Sharing," in Rhona and Robert Rapoport with Janice Bumstead, ed, *Working Couples* (New York: Harper Colophon Books, 1978), p. 122; et. al.

[11]Arkin and Dobrofsky, p. 122.

[12]Erik Gronseth, "Work Sharing: A Norwegian Example," in Rapoport and Rapoport with Janice Bumstead, ed., *Working Couples*, p. 111.

[13]Levine, *Who Will Raise the Children?*, pp. 62-73.

[14]Levine, *Who Will Raise the Children?*, pp. 68-70.

professorship and his wife a research associate position at much lower pay and status. But the Dean's wife suggested that since they were equally qualified, he might offer them one appointment to be held jointly. When this proposal was first presented formally, the administration turned it down because they were afraid that it would not work, it had never been done before, and the trustees probably would not go along with it. Eventually, with pressure from the Dean, the college hired them both on an equal, half-time basis. Later, after this experiment proved quite satisfactory for everyone concerned, similar opportunities for job sharing were offered to others.[15]

Another study included a couple who shared a job that they created.[16] They have viewed their integration of family and career as similar to the cottage industry or farm family of the period prior to the Industrial Revolution. They are partners in an architectural practice which they conduct from their home. This arrangement has enabled them to have control over their working space, working hours and the amount of work they do. In part, their choice of projects and amount of work has been determined by the time they have available in relation to the needs of their children.

By working at home, they have maintained a flexibility for putting aside their work in order to provide parenting when needed or desired. By working in business as equal partners, they have supported each other's career pursuits. By managing their own work, they have more control over factors which affect their availability for parenting.

There is no doubt that some fathers have succeeded in obtaining PT and have utilized this arrangement toward ANF.

---

[15]Levine, *Who Will Raise the Children?*, p.73.

[16]Rhona and Robert Rapoport, *Dual-Career Families Re-examined: New Integrations of Work and Family* (New York: Harper and Row, 1976), pp. 97-150.

On the other hand, it must be seriously questioned whether the creation of more PT jobs has, in fact, resulted in significantly more ANF. In dealing with the latter issue, the problems of a strategy to support ANF through the creation of more PT positions are explored.

Although the PT work force has been growing larger, fathers have *not* been a significant part of this growth in PT. These jobs have been filled mostly by women and school-age youth. The growth in PT positions has been due primarily to the increased numbers of women and youth who have been seeking less than full-time employment while spending the rest of their time dealing with school and family needs.[17]

Fathers have not been affected by the increase of part-time jobs because this increase has been limited to relatively unskilled and lower paying categories of employment in which the number of fathers has been small by proportion.[18] In those positions where more fathers than mothers are presently employed, e.g. higher managerial and skilled labor, employers are much less likely to permit PT.[19] Because PT is easily available to mothers, on the one hand, and difficult for fathers to obtain, on the other, even greater pressure is being exerted in the direction of mothers taking care of children instead of fathers.

A major barrier in attempts to increase PT for men has been the problem of overcoming the traditional views of management. Because administrators have assumed that men are the primary economic providers for families and that they

---

[17]William Deutermann, Jr. and Scott Brown, "Voluntary Part-Time Workers: A Growing Part of the Labor Force," *Monthly Labor Review,* No. 6 (1978), pp. 1-6.

[18]John D. Owen, "Why Part-Time Workers Tend to be in Low Wage Jobs," *Monthly Labor Review,* Vol. 101, No. 6, June 1978, p. 13.

[19]Deutermann, p. 8.

ought to remain so, they have either been reluctant to hire men for shared jobs or they have pushed for a hierarchical division of tasks within the shared job. The woman's salary and responsibilities are set lower than the man's in some shared appointments.

Those who seek PT have frequently been stigmatized as lacking in occupational commitment or motivation.[20] Men have been very reluctant to risk a loss of career satisfaction or status. If they work less than full-time in a job market that is predominantly full-time, it is likely that advancement would be slower, benefits would be reduced and status would remain lower. Presently, tradeoffs are somewhat extreme. Less than full-time work requires more sacrifice than it should and this reality inhibits many fathers from wanting to work less than full-time. The loss of family income is greater if the father cuts back than if the mother cuts back in these circumstances where women are paid less. That pressures the family to keep the father at his job while the mother takes time off from her job. Her time off then reduces her opportunity for job advancement later on. The economic considerations within the family move him away from home and keep her there.

The common experience of feeling unfairly underpaid in the shared job has deterred many from taking this option. Some employers consider it good business to get "two for the price of one" and some advocates have used this argument to convince employers that the arrangement is in their best interest,[21] but fathers are not likely to seek out these jobs and settle for half the pay if it means working only a few hours less.

---

[20] Arkin and Dobrofsky, p. 131.

[21] Nancy Jo Von Lackum and John P. Von Lackum, III, *Clergy Couples: A Report on Clergy Couples and the Ecumenical Clergy Couple Consultation* (New York: National Council of Churches, 1979), p. 26.

Since 1962, several organizations have been formed to promote PT job options for *women* who want to combine work and active parenting. However, no agencies have been doing the same for men.[22] Given the low involvement of fathers in PT, it is clear that the potential of PT work to facilitate ANF has not been widely realized. In fact, by making PT more readily available for women, the PT movement has put even greater pressure on fathers to stay at work and let the PT working mother do the parenting.

DOES FLEXITIME PROMOTE ANF?

Flexitime (hereinafter FT) is a work innovation which allows workers to choose when to begin and end work each day. While a wide variety of schedule options have been experimented with, most have conformed to a basic pattern. Generally, employees can arrive and depart at their own discretion as long as they put in eight hours and are at work during "core" times of the day when everyone must be present.[23]

Control Data Corporation instituted the first American FT plan in a private corporation in the Minneapolis plant in 1972.[24] That same year the Bureau of Indian Affairs had the first program in federal government offices.[25] By 1978, those on FT included twenty-thousand federal employees (10

---

[22]Levine, *Who Will Raise the Children?*, p. 67.

[23]Halcyone Bohen and Anamaria Viveros-Long, *Balancing Jobs and Family Life: Do Flexible Work Schedules Help?* (Philadelphia: Temple University Press, 1981), p. 16.

[24]Bohen and Viveros-Long, p. 16.

[25]Bohen and Viveros-Long, p. 63.

percent of the civilian work force)[26] and 2.5 million employees in the private sector.[27]

Evaluations of FT have been very positive on some criteria. Management surveys show employees have been almost universally enthusiastic about the plan.[28] A General Accounting Office survey of thirty government organizations on FT (133,000 people) revealed less tardiness, less absenteeism, less short-term leave taken, higher morale due to more job satisfaction, easier commuting and easier child care arrangements. Job satisfaction was improved primarily because employees were given "more freedom to control their work situation and to assume responsibility for their own actions."[29]

The need for flexitime in the family was indicated in two studies of conflict between work and family. A 1987 study of a Minneapolis firm with 1,200 employees, found that more than 70% of the fathers under age 35 reported serious concerns about work-family conflict with wives. And 60% said that these conflicts affected their goals and plans.[30] A 1987 study looked at 1600 employees in two corporations, finding that 36% of the fathers and 37% of the mothers reported a lot of stress in balancing work and family life.[31]

---

[26] Stanley Nollen and Virginia Hilder Martin, *Alternative Work Schedules, Part 1: Flexitime* (New York: AMCOM, a Division of American Managements Association, 1978).

[27] Bohen and Viveros-Long, p. 16.

[28] Bohen and Viveros-Long, p. 64.

[29] U.S. Comptroller General, *Benefits from Flexible Work Schedules---Legal Limitations Remain* (Report to Congress; EPCD-78-62), (Washington D.C.: General Accounting Office, 1977), p. 11.

[30] Carol Kleiman, "Daddies may also need fast track to parenting," *St. Paul Pioneer Press* , July 16, 1989.

[31] Kleiman, "Daddies."

Two surveys of employees at DuPont Co., showed an increased desire by men to work flexible hours. Between 1985 and 1988, these men increased in number by 18%. The percentage of men who said that they would like more flexible hours during the transition period after birth of their child also jumped significantly from 11% in 1985 to 30% in 1988.[32]

Investigating the assumption that flexitime would be beneficial to a worker's family life, the Family Impact Seminar, a non-governmental independent organization, conducted the first systematic study comparing flexitime workers with those on standard schedules.[33] This study (FIS) focused on the impact of social policies on families.

Among FT workers at the Maritime Administration studied by FIS, half reported less job-home interference than standard time employees and liked FT both for work and parenting reasons. In general measures, "flexitime appears to have benefits for family life."[34]

In interviews, several fathers whose wives were not employed emphasized the advantages of FT as more opportunity for meals with the family, time with children, less strain and tension and more time for recreation (both individual and family oriented).[35] According to survey data, these men, who were on FT and whose wives were not employed, did spend more time on family than standard time fathers whose wives were also not employed. For these fathers, flexitime did make a difference in their level of involvement in child care. "A slightly greater degree of control

---

[32]Pamela Reynolds, "The Daddy Track," *St. Paul Pioneer Press,* March 25, 1989.

[33]Bohen and Viveros-Long, p. 63.

[34]Bohen and Viveros-Long, p. 146.

[35]Bohen and Viveros-Long, p. 142.

over their time help(ed) a lot."[36] This group of fathers also experienced less stress as a result and that contributed to a better relationship with their children.

However, contrary to idealistic expectations and bold claims for all that FT could accomplish, the FIS study produced more realistic and somewhat shocking findings for ANF advocates. When more specific measures were applied to ascertain whether FT resulted in more family work (in terms of hours) for fathers and greater equity between fathers and mothers in sharing family work, FT was found to have *no* perceptible influence. As a group, fathers did not spend significantly more time on child care than fathers on standard time.[37]

A father, who is also a lawyer, spoke about his imbalance between work and family despite the flexible hours he worked:

In the law firm you have latitude about when you put in the hours but not about how many there are....the pleas that your family gives you are not so clear and obvious. And the penalties aren't quite so immediate (as paid work).[38]

Interviews with small groups of survey respondents suggested that "as desirable as flexible work schedules are for most people, other factors are far more influential" in making equity possible, or in thwarting ANF. Far more important than schedules of work are sex-role expectations (i.e.,

---

[36]Bohen and Viveros-Long, p. 196.

[37]Bohen and Viveros-Long, p. 135.

[38]Bohen and Viveros-Long, pp. 158-160.

responsibilities prescribed by others and felt by parents) and work expectations (i.e., external and internal work demands).[39]

This is not to discount the potential of FT for helping some fathers to become more actively involved in the lives of their children. Fathers whose wives were not employed did become more involved in child care because of FT. Furthermore, "flexitime may be an important first step towards altering the traditions in which work roles and work organizations have been defined and structured as if the family did not exist."[40]

If opportunities for FT are greater for mothers than fathers, a negative effect is more likely to result. If a mother is working FT when her husband is working a regular schedule, the mother is even more likely to perform most child care tasks than if both work FT or if both work regular schedules. The utilization of FT by mothers and not fathers further tips the balance of family work onto her side.

A system of scheduling that could, in some cases, facilitate greater equity between mothers and fathers in child care responsibilities may, instead, serve sometimes as a support to the status quo of the traditional division of labor in families.[41]

DOES PARENTAL LEAVE PROMOTE ANF?

Parental leave has finally become a popular political cause in the 1990's. As this book goes to press in 1991, Congress is still struggling with The Family and Medical Leave Act. A similar bill suffered a 1990 veto by President Bush. Whether

---

[39]Bohen and Viveros-Long, p. 197.

[40]Bohen and Viveros-Long, p. 202.

[41]Bohen and Viveros-Long, pp. 132-134.

sufficient votes to override a veto can be garnered remains to be seen at this time. The leave allows for unpaid, job-protected time off to care for a newborn, adopted child, or sick child. Between 1988 and 1989, three national surveys showed that a majority of the U.S. public supported the idea of establishing federal requirements for employers to allow parental leave, and recently seventy-nine percent favored a national parental leave bill.[42] Some state laws already provide parental leave.

Theoretically, fathers who have the opportunity to be free of work for more adequate time to care for and bond with their newborn would be getting encouragement to be ANF's. Theoretically, fathers who could take time off from work to care for a sick child would have greater opportunity to become ANF's. Some parental leave for fathers has been offered in the U.S. and one might assume that a significant trend is moving fathers quickly into using paternal leave to become ANF's. Is parental leave having that effect in the U.S.?

There has not actually been a large number of parental leave programs in existence. In 1990, paid or unpaid parental leave was offered by only 5% of the 837 major U.S. employers surveyed by Hewitt Associates. Less than half even offered maternity leave for women.[43] Only about 40% of all businesses, large and small included, even offered women unpaid, job-protected leave to care for a newborn or newly adopted child.[44]

---

[42]Luanne Nyberg, "You Should Know," *Newsletter of the Children's Defense Fund---Minnesota* (St. Paul, MN, August 1989), citing Ethel Klein, "Public Opinion Polls, Family Policy and Analysis," (New York: Columbia University Press, 1989).

[43]Lynda McDonnell, "The Work-Family Equation," *St. Paul Pioneer Press*, Nov. 26, 1990.

[44]Pat Schroeder, "A promise of parental leave is pro-family," *St. Paul Pioneer Press*, April 6, 1990.

Businesses in Minnesota, Wisconsin and two other states with parental-leave legislation had little trouble or expense in fulfilling the requirements. This suggests that the greatest fears of opponents to parental leave legislation (that it will cost too much) are not founded in fact. Sixteen percent of the employers did not provide parental leave before the state laws were passed and 13% of those who did granted less than six weeks' leave, so the legislation had a positive impact and changed practices of some employers not yet offering leave.[45]

In a June, 1991 survey of 30 Minnesota businesses, 47 percent of the employers said that employees who are fathers took parental leave at some time to care for their children. Nearly 70 percent reported that fathers have taken parental leave following the birth or adoption of a child. The average leave lasted one to two weeks, with some as long as three months. A 1990 Minnesota law allowed employees to use sick leave to attend school conferences, care for sick children or be home after the birth or adoption of a child.[46]

At American Telephone and Telegraph the ratio of women to men who took family leave rose from 400 to 1 a decade ago to 50 to 1 today.[47]   One might expect a slowly increasing ratio as more men learn about the option and see their male coworkers taking parental leave. While there is a pattern of increasing percentages of men taking parental leave, there is still an inadequate amount of change in the direction of ANF. Why are so few men taking parental leave?

---

[45] "Study finds few parental-leave problems," *St. Paul Pioneer Press,* May 23, 1991.

[46] R.A. Zaldivar, "Businesses adjusting to dad's needs: parental leave policies permit time with kids," *St. Paul Pioneer Press,* June 15, 1991, p. 9A.

[47] Cindy Skrzycki, "More men trying to juggle career, family," *St. Paul Pioneer Press,* Dec. 30, 1990.

The most significant reason is that the leave is usually unpaid. At the time the father needs to care for his newborn, he cannot afford to have his pay dropped because the family needs that income to pay for the increasing expenses of having a baby. Continuing pay during the leave is necessary to give any significant encouragement for ANF. Minnesota law enables fathers to use their paid sick leave time. That provides greater encouragement but places hardship on any fathers who may need the time for an illness.

Even paid leave may not be sufficient incentive if the employer has a negative attitude about the father's taking leave. Fathers are not likely to take leave if the employer does some of the following: comments on the high cost of bringing in temporary help to do his job; jokes about his wanting to take time off for this purpose; questions his commitment to the job; reminds him about how much harder he will have to work when he gets back; hints at the insecurity of his job there; or comments about how good it was in the "good old days" when "women were women and men were men."

James Levine, Director of the Fatherhood Project at the Families and Work Institute in New York, pointed out that while a company may provide parental leave, coworkers and management may say things that make the father who actually tries to take the leave feel like a "wimp."[48] The father may then decide that he would rather just do his parenting work quietly and face the stress in his home life personally without public ridicule than face the stress that it adds to the

---

[48]Carol Lacey, "More dads today facing 'Mommy Track' detours," *St. Paul Pioneer Press*, Dec. 30, 1990.

workplace. "Fathers often find it easier to tell the boss a little lie than to ask for time to handle a domestic duty."[49]

Levine added in his lecture to men and women gathered during lunch break from work in downtown St. Paul, that fathers may find their allies in places that they do not expect. Female supervisors are not more likely to be supportive of paternity leave just because they are female. Some women have chosen to work instead of parent. They are not real likely to encourage men to use options that would allow them to do both. Those who tend to be more supportive in management, whether men or women supervisors, are those who have children themselves and who understand the importance of the father being there.

Making the leave available is not enough. Corporations must also give encouragement to those who take leave. Catalyst showed that 114 companies offered unpaid leave to new fathers. When they were asked what amount of time they thought was reasonable for father to take off, 41% said that men should not take any time off.[50] Putting it on the books is one thing, supporting those who do it is another. Support is what is needed for men to use the opportunity. If the corporation does not endorse it openly and views fathers who take leave as less committed on the job, then fathers will not take parental leave in great numbers. The cost is just too high for them to justify it. When risking a financial loss appears to be a move that could hurt the family, men are not likely to take parental leave. Rather than risk hurting their child by

---

[49]R.A. Zaldivar, "Businesses adjusting to dad's needs: parental leave policies permit time with kids," *St. Paul Pioneer Press*, June 15, 1991, p. 9A.

[50]Cindy Skrzycki, "More men trying to juggle career, family," *St. Paul Pioneer Press*, Dec. 30, 1990.

reducing their potential for earnings, they stay on the job and view being at home as a luxury the family cannot afford.

Offering unpaid parental leave for mothers is good. However, offering paid maternity and paternity leave with a support system to encourage fathers to use it and make the most of it is really what is needed to give incentive to men to be ANF's.

What employer would want to do that? The employer who wants to keep good employees from transferring to another company would. The employer who wants to reduce the costs that are incurred with employee turnover would. The employer who wants to raise productivity by maintaining good morale among employes would.

The employer who wants to recruit the best employees would. A survey of 200 human resources managers found that "two-thirds named family-supportive services and flexible hours as the two most important tools for recruiting workers in the future."[51] The Los Angeles Water and Power Department studied the family conflicts of its employees and concluded that absenteeism and turnover was costing the department $1 million a year. They created a family services program that included child care, special services for expectant parents, family support groups, a library and a "fathering" program. Under the fathering program, fathers can use company beepers for family needs, can take kids on company-sponsored outings, and can attend learning and support groups for fathers.[52] This is the kind of substantive support that fathers need for ANF to occur in greater numbers.

---

[51]Lynda McDonnell, "The Work-Family Equation," *St. Paul Pioneer Press*, Nov. 26, 1990.

[52]R.A. Zaldivar, "Businesses adjusting to dad's needs: parental leave policies permit time with kids," *St. Paul Pioneer Press*, June 15, 1991, p. 10A.

When meeting some of the family needs of workers are understood to be in the best interests of employers too through increased profits, then employers will provide them. Being realistic about the profit incentive and appealing to the self-interests of employers may be the best strategy for increasing paternity leave in the future. If that strategy works and the employer finds that it is true, then fathers may have the freedom they need to develop a bond with the newborn or to care for a sick child.

DOES THE ENTRY OF WOMEN INTO THE LABOR FORCE PROMOTE ANF?

Statistical evidence has indicated that fathers spent more time in family work and that there was greater equity between parents if the mother was employed than if she was not employed. The implication of this evidence was that policies which facilitate women's entry into the labor force would also promote ANF. Upon closer examination, it appears that while the entry of women into the labor force leads to more than incremental increases in fathering activity, this entry alone does not result in ANF. To provide more effective support of ANF, substantial improvements in the employment status of women are required, not merely measures to facilitate women's entry into the labor force.

In the FIS study cited earlier, the most significant correlation between a father's amount of family work and any other factor was the link with the employment or non-employment of his wife.[53] When the wife was employed, the husband did more family work than fathers in families where the wife was not employed. Family chores and child rearing

---

[53]Bohen and Viveros-Long, p. 134.

were shared more equally in two-earner families (generally 60:40 versus 75:25 in families with non-employed wives).[54]

These findings and their role in clarifying the implications of the study were summarized in theoretical terms:

> In ecological terms, it is when an individual (a wife) from a family system (the microsystem) establishes a functional link with the work system (the mesosystem) that the division of labor in the family changes. The policy of the work system examined in our study (flexitime) did not significantly influence the shift in the division of family work. In this kind of structural analysis, however, the work policies and practices leading to the greater employment of women (along with other factors) appear to be the major forces leading to changes in the sharing of family work.[55]

> In family systems theory, the domestic work roles within the family seem to shift as a result of changes in the behavior of one member of the system: that is, when the wife is employed, the husband does more family work than he does in families where the wife is not employed.[56]

> (In terms of the study design) the dependent variable (schedule) is a much less powerful influence on the dependent variable (increasing equity in family work) than a control variable, namely, spouse employment status.[57]

---

[54]Bohen and Viveros-Long, p. 137.

[55]Bohen and Viveros-Long, p. 138.

[56]Bohen and Viveros-Long, p. 138.

[57]Bohen and Viveros-Long, p. 135.

Joseph Pleck observed that working men with employed wives did 1.8 hours per week more in housework than employed husbands with non-employed wives. This was the "first finding of non-trivial increments in husbands' family work associated with wives' employment in a study assessing family work absolutely in terms of a large representative sample.[58]

David Maklan compared men who worked four ten-hour days instead of five eight-hour days. Those who worked this schedule gave four hours a week more to child care.[59] John Robinson concluded in his sample that husbands of women who were employed full time are more involved in child care than husbands of women who are not employed or who work only part time.[60]

Graeme Russell found that when both parents are employed, fathers doubled their contribution to child care, but mothers still carried most of the burden of routine caretaking.[61] Russell also studied fifty families in which the parents shared more equally (mothers doing 55 percent and fathers 45 percent of the child care). This was in contrast to traditional fathers who did 12 percent. In these role-sharing

---

[58]Joseph Pleck, "Men's Family Work: Three Perspectives and Some New Data," *The Family Coordinator*, Vol 28, October 1979, p. 487.

[59]David Maklan, "The Four Day Workweek: Blue Collar Adjustment to a Nonconventional Arrangement of Work and Leisure Time," (Ph.D. Dissertation, U. of Michigan, 1976).

[60]John Robinson, *How Americans Use Time* (New York: Praeger, 1977).

[61]Graeme Russell, "Fathers as Caregivers: Possible Antecedents and Consequences" (paper presented to a study group on the "Role of the Father in Child Development, Social Policy, and the Law," University of Haifa, Israel, July 15-17, 1980).

families, fathers did as much feeding, bathing and diapering as mothers.[62]

In a study of a large sample, working women averaged three hours a day on housework while men averaged 17 minutes. Women spent 50 minutes a day with their children while men spent only 12 minutes.[63] Arlie Hochschild concluded from this and other studies that women worked fifteen hours longer each week than men. Over a year, they worked an extra month of twenty-four-hour days. Most women work one shift at the office or factory and a "second shift" at home.[64]

Hochschild explored the nature of the "stalled revolution" with longterm detailed interviews and analysis of the interpersonal ways that equality was sidestepped. Women are changing faster toward employment than men are changing toward sharing of the "second shift." Consequently, there is friction on the homefront between "faster changing women and slower changing men." The "supermom" strategy for getting the work done is taking a great toll of stress on mothers and consequently on fathers and the children as well.[65]

In 1990, there were 24 million working fathers with children under 18 years of age, half of them with children under 6. Thirty-six percent of the male labor force is comprised of working fathers with kids under 18.[66]

---

[62]Graeme Russell, "Fathers as Caregivers."

[63]Alexander Szalai, ed. *The Use of Time* (The Hague: Mouton, 1972).

[64]Arlie Hochschild with Anne Machung, pp. 3-4.

[65]Arlie Hochschild with Anne Machung, p. 13.

[66]R.A. Zaldivar, p. 9A.

Two-job families now make up 58% of all married couples with children.[67] Such working couples have been studied to ascertain what strains have developed in work and family life and how spouses seek to cope with these strains.[68] This research is relevant to the question of whether women's working has a significant impact upon fathers' level of involvement in parenting. These studies have documented the inequality in levels of child care done by mothers and the less involved fathers.

It has been shown that fathering activity in two-earner families has not automatically increased to a level equal to mothering activity. Part of the reason for this fact seems to be connected to the continuing inequality between spouses within dual-career families.

Lynda Lytle Holmstrom's study of two-career families revealed a common pattern in these families: "Even though both (the husband's and wife's) careers were important, typically the man's career was still more important...."[69] Child care tasks were organized in such a way as to maximize the father's opportunities for career success while limiting the mother's opportunities. The fathers perceived that such organization was required because their own jobs were more demanding and inflexible.

In a study of married women who were attorneys, physicians, or college teachers, a great discrepancy was found between their egalitarian ideals and the practices of the family

---

[67] U.S. Department of Labor Statistics, *Employment and Earnings, Characteristics of Families: First Quarter* (Washington, D.C.: U.S. Department of Labor, 1988).

[68] See the bibliography listing multiple works by Rhona and Robert Rapoport.

[69] Lynda Lytle Holmstrom, *The Two-Career Family* (Cambridge: Schenkman, 1972), p. 155.

in coping with strains between work and child care. Fathers seldom requested that work demands be adjusted so that they could meet family needs.[70] Mothers, on the other hand, "generally expect(ed) little and ask(ed) nothing of the family to enable her to adjust better to family and career demands."[71]

In a survey of 200 psychologist couples, the husband appeared to be "the primary beneficiary of the alliance."[72] While sex discrimination in the field was a significant factor, the most influential reasons for lower measures of reward and satisfaction among the women were related more to patterns of parenting and marriage. Respondents reported problems which seemed to arise consistently from the fact that the woman had come to place her career in an order of priority secondary to the needs of the family and the needs of her husband's career. For the husband, his career took priority over family demands and his wife's career needs.[73]

In a study of 86 sociologist couples, similar conclusions were drawn. Women in these couples experienced higher rates of career success than women not married to sociologists. Their careers seemed to be facilitated by the spouse's career in

---

[70]T. Neal Garland, "The Better Half? The Male in the Dual Profession Family," in Safilios-Rothschild, ed, *Toward a Sociology of Women*, pp. 199-215.

[71]Margaret Poloma, "Role Conflict and the Married Professional Woman," in Safilios-Rothschild, ed. *Toward a Sociology of Women*, p. 196.

[72]R. Bryson, J, Bryson, M. Licht, and B. Licht, "The Professional Pair: Husband and Wife Psychologists," *American Psychologist*, Vol. 31, January 1976, p. 10.

[73]N. Heckman, R. Bryson, and J. Bryson, "Problems of Professional Couples: A Content Analysis," *Journal of Marriage and the Family*, May 1977, p. 323.

sociology. However, the career status of sociologist wives in these couples was much lower than the measured success of their husbands in sociology. The husbands had a significantly higher number of doctorates (14% more) and a much higher number of positions of full professorial rank (26% more).[74]

Studying lawyer couples in professional partnership, Cynthia Fuchs Epstein was among the first to document this pattern of women's lower employment status within dual-profession couples in the same field.[75] She pointed out how rules against nepotism and other institutional policies have restricted couples from working together, and/or on an equal basis. Contrary to previous presumptions that lawyer couples in partnership worked on an equal level, Epstein concluded:

> These partnerships are not free from the restraints imposed by the culture, and in many ways reflect the prestige system and division of labor found in the larger society, with the result that they are not usually truly equal partnerships, but they do open options for both husbands and wives to work and engage in family life harmoniously.[76]

Sociologists have proposed a resource theory of family power which links income, education and occupational status

---

[74]T. Martin, K. Berry, and R. B. Jacobsen, "The Impact of Dual-Career Marriages on Female Professional Careers: An Empirical Test of a Parsonian Hypothesis," *Journal of Marriage and the Family,* November 1975, p. 741.

[75]Cynthia Fuchs Epstein, "Law Partners and Marital Partners: Strains and Solutions in the Dual Career Family Enterprise," *Human Relations*, Vol. 24, No. 6 (1971), p. 562.

[76]Epstein, "Law Partners and Marital Partners," p. 562.

(among other items) with power in the marital relationship.[77] One's degree of involvement in the economic-opportunity system (employment) has been associated with one's power to negotiate with the spouse over matters such as who cares for the children and when.[78] While negotiation over parenting is heavily influenced by attitudes on sex-roles, relative power between spouses is quite significant as a factor in most negotiations between spouses on this matter. Generally, there is a more egalitarian balance of power when the mother is employed at a level close to or equal with the status of the employment of the father.

While the balance may shift toward equality, the relative weight of child care responsibilities still rests upon mothers because of the imbalance of employment status between most men and most women. The mother's employment at a lower income and status may only lead to the father "helping" with what both of them consider to be "her" responsibility in child rearing. He may still remain at the periphery and not become equally involved in nurturing. This shift is only minimal when viewed in light of the more extensive goal of ANF.[79]

If the mother's work is secondary to the father's in status, income, and time commitments, she is likely to remain the

---

[77]Letha Scanzoni and John Scanzoni, *Men, Women and Change: A Sociology of Marriage and Family* (New York: McGraw-Hill Books, 1976), pp. 310-322.

[78]Margaret Polatnick, "Why Men Don't Rear Children: A Power Analysis," in John Petras, ed., *Sex:Male/Gender:Masculine* (Port Washington, NY: Alfred, 1975), p. 214.

[79]Martha Blaxall and Barbara Reagan, *Women and the Workplace: The Implications of Occupational Segregation* (Chicago: University of Chicago Press, 1976), p. 299.

primary parent.[80] Her employment is frequently subordinated to her husband's by the working of some or all of the following dynamics:

(1) Being segregated into lower paying, lower status occupations.

(2) Being discriminated against on the job and/or in hiring practices.

(3) Receiving less pay than men for similar work.

(4) Being laid off or fired before male workers.

(5) Being unemployed or underemployed more than male workers.

(6) Being protected out of a particular job or advancement opportunity.

(7) Receiving inadequate and unequal fringe benefits.

(8) Supporting her husband's higher career aspirations while limiting her own.

(9) Moving domicile to accommodate his advancement without reciprocation from him.

(10) Stopping work to raise children beyond a brief maternity leave.

(11) Financially supporting his higher educational attainment without reciprocation from him.[81]

Through a vicious cycle of dynamics, the mother continues to have less power, as a "junior partner" to her husband, in the economics of the family. Having less power of this sort, she is

---

[80] John Scanzoni, "Strategies for Changing Family Roles: Research and Practice Implications," *The Family Coordinator*, Vol. 28 (1979), p. 440.

[81] Epstein, *Woman's Place*, p. 196; Holmstrom, p. 121; Polatnick, pp. 199-235; Safilios-Rothschild, *Toward a Sociology of Women*, p. 68.

not well situated to negotiate for the increased involvement of the child's father in parenting.[82]

John Scanzoni has argued for improvements in the employment status of women as an integral part of strategy to promote ANF. He also has made the related point that changing males' family roles in the direction of ANF leads to greater equality between men and women in paid employment and social power. This is not circular reasoning but simply a reflection of the realities of interdependence between work and family activity.

Scanzoni's study of employed women as co-providers identified spouses who had relatively equal responsibility for work. They were similarly committed to achieve vocationally ("dual achievers"); equally prepared to provide for the family ("co-providers"); and similarly employed in terms of time, status and income ("equal partners"). Because they were role-interchangeable as providers, it was more likely that they would negotiate for equal responsibilities in parenting.[83] In a subsequent article, Scanzoni concluded that "unless a man is prepared to share his provider duties with his wife--unless spouses are genuinely interchangeable on this status---the man is unlikely to be interchangeable with the woman in household duties and child care.[84]

While measures to improve the employment status of women help to promote ANF, they do not remove some major barriers. Neither the institution of relevant work reforms nor the balancing of power between parents leads to ANF if, because of socialization, parents are not personally inclined to

---

[82]John Scanzoni, *Sexual Bargaining: Power Politics in the American Marriage*, p. 130.

[83]John Scanzoni, *Sex Roles, Women's Work and Marital Conflict: A Study of Family Change* (Lexington, MA: Heath/Lexington, 1978), p. 110.

[84]Scanzoni, "Strategies," p. 440.

share parenting. If all of the work innovations discussed in this chapter were available to families, there still is the problem of how to motivate them to utilize these opportunities for activity in ANF rather than in longer work hours, second jobs or recreation. Furthermore, there is the task of motivating fathers themselves to press for change toward ANF in their families, workplaces and in society at large. The strategies of this book are all needed in cooperation and not in isolation from each other.

CHAPTER SEVEN

BRINGING BACK THE BANISHED FATHER

Divorce can be the most devastating divider of fathers and their children. The barriers to ANF which face fathers in marriage become even more pronounced in divorce when they are magnified by the predominant practice of sole custody by mothers. In order to provide opportunities for both fathers and mothers to continue active parenting and for children to continue to receive the benefits of a nurturing relationship with both parents, fathers must utilize and create more opportunities for joint custody.

At least 33 states now make joint custody a preference or allow it as an option.[1] That does not mean that fathers are taking that option. Sole custody by mothers has long been the

---

[1]Judith S. Wallerstein and Sandra Blakeslee. *Second Chances: Men, Women and Children a Decade After Divorce* (New York: Ticknor and Fields, 1989), p. 256.

more common practice with as high as ninety percent of custody arrangements with sole custody mothers.[2]

In discussing how sole custody is more often detrimental than joint custody and why joint custody can be a more loving alternative, I will discuss some personal costs to each member of the family, place custody arrangements within an historical perspective, critique the legal practice of sole custody as a presumption and develop the ethical argument for fathers to continue being actively involved (on an equal basis with mothers) in caregiving with their children after divorce.

DIVORCED AND BANISHED FATHERS

The visitation father is a father who has been separated from his children by the courts through custody decisions, by his ex-wife who refuses for various reasons to let him take care of the children, and/or by himself; because he does not feel the obligation, capability, or he cannot bear to face the pain that he feels when he is alone with his children. His contact with the children is infrequent and he often feels alienated and out of touch with them even when he does visit with them. He feels more like an occasional playmate than a parent. "One moment fathers are supposed to 'share the child' and the next they're being told, 'I'll raise my son alone. Just make sure the support checks are on time.'"[3]

Most divorced fathers try to make the best of a bad situation, but the odds against satisfactory relationships between the weekend father and his children are very high.

---

[2]Mel Roman and William Haddad, *The Disposable Parent: The Case for Joint Custody* (New York: Rinehart and Winston, 1978), p. 23.

[3]Erma Bombeck, "What's dear old dad to do?" *St. Paul Pioneer Press,* June 18, 1987.

The children no longer share a 'home' with him. They may not even be visiting the place where he lives. His short time with them hardly allows for the development of the relationship, and most visitation fathers find themselves entertaining the children but not really relating to them on deeper emotional levels.

Perhaps the most difficult feelings to deal with for the weekend father and his children are the father's guilt that he has abandoned the children or been forced to and the children's fear that somehow they are responsible for his having left. While none of these feelings may accurately represent the situation, the custody arrangements of the sole custody mother and visitation father tend to reinforce and intensify these inaccurate and untested feelings.

The feelings of loss that a father experiences when his children are no longer free to live with him, even for short, frequent periods, is often enduring. In one study, banished fathers reported enormous difficulties overcoming this loss. One father commented:

> They are not near me, so I long to see them. I am forgetting about them, but wonder about their well-being. I know I love them and miss them.[4]

One young father with limited rights to care for his eight-year-old son after divorce expressed his feelings in a letter published in the *Village Voice*. Writing to his son:

> I can't control the history you will live in, and live through, and be part of. Sometimes I have to stay up all night to raise the child support money which is my

---

[4]Irving Stuart and Laurence Abt, eds., *Children of Separation and Divorce* (New York: Grossman, 1972), p. 26.

entry ticket to your life....(After having to leave the child once when the young boy begged his father not to, he wrote further) Jason, forgive me for letting go of your hand that night. There's a whole structure of society and law and government that says that we have to play it this way, for now, but things will get better. And believe me, I will never really let you go either. Never.[5]

When fathers are not able to care for their children on a dependable and frequent schedule, they are less likely to continue being involved with them to any significant extent. Sporadic and short encounters between the father and child have been so painful for most men that they feel like seeing the child less and less.[6] This pattern is common to those situations where the mother has sole custody and the father visits on some weekends. These fathers are also inclined to avoid seeing the child because it brings up the pain of the divorce, it increases interaction with the ex-wife, and it reminds the father that he is becoming more distant from his children. Sole custody accentuates this distance by limiting the father's access to the child's life, thereby increasing the sources of dissatisfaction and in turn driving the father further away.

For mothers who receive sole custody, the court's decisions or the father's relinquishing of the children to her full-time care (without court contesting of custody) is experienced as a relief that she did not lose the children. But, in the process, she also becomes the victim as well as the

[5]Don Miller, "Letters to Jason," *Village Voice*, November 10, 1975, pp. 24-25.

[6]Sally Abrahms, "The Joint-Custody Controversy," *New York*, June 18, 1979, p. 61.

victor. She becomes the burdened mother, whose primary hope is to survive the inequities and nearly insurmountable tasks that sole custody places upon her.

Studies of the effects of divorce on children have concluded that the negative consequences for children are greater when the children lose contact with one parent than when they are able to maintain reliable, frequent contact with both parents.[7]

Of 131 children in a study of sole custody mothers, every child "intensely longed for their father's return," especially during the first year of the divorce.[8] This longing included feelings of loss, rejection, loneliness and disorientation. While every child of divorced parents, or even of parents living together, may have a lot to cope with, the child with a sole custody parent and a visitation parent is being put through stress which could be minimized by more quality and quantity time with the other parent.

CHILD CUSTODY IN HISTORICAL PERSPECTIVE

An interpretative history of child custody, such as that presented by Mel Roman and William Haddad, suggests that women's subordinate position in society explains both the long supremacy of the father in patriarchal family structures and the more recent mystique of motherhood which supports the granting of sole custody to mothers:

Whether the woman is denigrated as less than human or exalted to the very suburbs of heaven, exempted from custody or virtually guaranteed it, her relation to

[7]Roman and Haddad, pp. 48-83; Wallerstein and Blakeslee, p. 257.
[8]Roman and Haddad, p. 67.

her children reflects man's dominant position in society and the forms that have been devised to protect that dominance.[9]

Prior to about 1860, American fathers had exclusive right to custody of their children, because children were regarded as their personal property. In 1860, however, an amendment to the Married Woman's Property Act of New York State named wives and husbands as joint guardians of children.[10] But by the early 1900's, the mother came to be regarded by the courts as the "natural" custodial parent.

The present bias in favor of mothers having sole custody stems most directly from the economic conditions created during the onset of industrialization. The wage labor of men was divided from the private labor of women. The exaltation of motherhood and the creation of the concept of "maternal instinct" made a virtue out of the economic subordination of women in the home while men worked and ruled outside the home. In addition to keeping women home to care for the children so men could work, this mystique prevented women from attaining economic parity.

In an 1872 Supreme Court ruling, Divine sanction was cited to ground the mother's right/obligation to sole custody:

The constitution of the family organization, which is founded in the divine ordinance, as well as the nature of things, indicates the domestic sphere as that which properly belongs to the domain of womanhood.... The paramount destiny and mission of women are to fulfill

---

[9]Roman and Haddad, p. 24.

[10]Daniel Molinoff, "Life with Father: How Men Are winning Custody of Their Kids," *New York Times Magazine*, May 22, 1977, p. 13.

the noble and benign offices of wife and mother. This is the law of the Creator.[11]

In more recent years, the law of the Creator has not been invoked, but a similar argument has been based upon the testimony of social scientists. The presumption, known as the "tender years doctrine," upon which many judges make decisions about custody has traditionally run as follows:

> Between mother and child there exists a natural and vital nurturing relationship that fathers can never, psychologically or physically, hope to duplicate. The child will suffer irreparable harm...if separated from the mother during the "tender years."[12]

The changing economic conditions (more women working but in a discriminatory work world) are still only beginning to touch the periphery of the economic dominance of men and the practice of awarding sole custody to mothers. But at the periphery, the contradiction between the mystique of motherhood and the daily life of two divorcing, active parents, who are both successful in careers, becomes painfully apparent. The courts are still engaged in the practice of protecting the economic dominance of men by a practice which seems geared toward keeping men free from the obligation and disadvantages of caring actively for children. The presumption that *sole custody* is in the best interests of the children must be replaced with the presumption that joint

---

[11]*Bradwell vs. Illinois*, 83 *U.S.* 130, 141 (1872), cited in Lila Tritico, "Child Custody: Preference to the Mother," *Louisiana Law Review*, Vol. 34, Summer 1974, p. 883.

[12]Daniel Molinoff, p. 14.

custody should be granted unless there are sufficient reasons to grant custody to one parent or the other.

BEYOND *BEYOND*

In 1973, *Beyond the Best Interests of the Child* was purported to lay the groundwork for an escape from the dilemma of Solomon: to whom should this child be presented for care and keeping? The guidelines that were presented for deciding child custody cases in divorce proceedings did not go far enough in analyzing the issues of justice at stake or the interests of the child. In fact, these guidelines provide an ideology which help the courts to cover up prejudices in favor of sole custody for mothers. While the book was written almost twenty years ago now, it still reflects the thinking of a generation of parents, lawyers and judges who have the greatest impact upon what is happening in child care after divorce.

The dominant principle in *Beyond* was that a biological parent becomes a "psychological parent" only from "day-to-day interaction, companionship and shared experiences."[13] Developing a child-placement statute from this and related concepts, they recommended that the children be placed in *one home* where they would receive continuity from the person who is, or will become, the psychological parent. On the surface, there is no preference for mothers or fathers as psychological parent, but given the court's previous preference and the different roles fulfilled by mothers and fathers in the traditional family, mothers are "the person" who has the most day-to-day interaction, companionship and shared experiences

---

[13]Joseph Goldstein, Anna Freud and Albert Solnit, *Beyond the Best Interests of the Child* (New York: Free Press, 1973), p. 19.

with the children, not fathers. This definition helps to separate most fathers (merely biological parents) from most mothers (real or psychological parents).

Their guidelines strongly recommended that the child have only *one* custodial parent and that the custodial parent have complete and exclusive control over all aspects of custody:

> Once it is determined who will be the custodial parent, it is that parent, not the court, who must decide under what conditions he or she wishes to raise the child. Thus, the noncustodial parent should have no legally enforceable right to visit the child, and the custodial parent should have the right to decide whether it is desirable for the child to have such visits.[14]

They also emphasized the distance between the noncustodial parent and the children, which coincides with the reports of many weekend fathers about their feelings of loss. A 'visiting' or 'visited' parent has little chance to serve as a true object of love, trust and identification, since this role is based on his being available on a more consistent day-to-day basis.

In the case that both parents appear to the court to be acceptable as "psychological parents," *Beyond* recommended a "judicially supervised drawing of lots...(as the) most rational and least offensive process for resolving the hard choice."[15] Perhaps they regarded this as blind justice because they viewed sole custody as just in itself. Whether sole custody is a just disposition for the parties concerned was not questioned by *Beyond*, but it should have been. In the dilemma of

---

[14]Goldstein, Freud and Solnit, p. 38.

[15]Goldstein, Freud and Solnit, p. 153.

Solomon (which seems to be their model), one of the parents was not really the parent. The custody issue that role-sharing parents face is entirely different, however, because in this case both parents are active nurturant parents and they each have something important to offer to the child. *Beyond* might be appropriately applied only to those cases where only one parent is capable of being *the real parent.*

Beyond argued that sole custody is the only right relationship for the psychological health of the child:

> Unlike adults, who are generally capable of maintaining positive emotional ties with a number of different individuals, unrelated or even hostile to each other, children lack the capacity to do so. They will freely love more than one adult only if the individuals in question feel positively to one another. Failing this, children become prey to severe and crippling loyalty conflicts.[16]

This statement discloses their assumption that divorced parents cannot cooperate with one another, but contradicts the evidence of studies on joint custody parents who are able to separate their marital conflict from their parental responsibilities and behavior.[17] Parents *can* reduce their conflict and cooperate in parenting even after divorce.

The priority in their guidelines was to ensure stability for the child, which they assumed to be possible only through sole

---

[16]Goldstein, Freud and Solnit, p. 12.

[17]Miriam Galper, *Co-Parenting: Sharing Your Child Equally* (Philadelphia: Running Press, 1978); Kristine Rosenthal and Harry Keshet, *Fathers Without Partners: A Study of Fathers and the Family After Separation* (New York: Rowman and Littlefield, 1981); Alice Ruth Abarbanel, "Joint Custody Families: A Case Study Approach," Dissertation, California School of Professional Psychology, 1977.

custody. But what about the stability of the child in the relationship with the other parent? The rights of one parent would be protected by law, while the opportunity of the other parent to continue a close relationship with the child and the freedom of the child to continue a close relationship with the noncustodial parent would be a personal matter resolved privately between the parents.

The language in many divorce decrees guarantees the noncustodial parent "reasonable" visitation privileges. But that is entirely inadequate, because it leaves too much up to the custodial parent who has more power in this situation after divorce. *Beyond* and current custody discussions are all too often based on the assumption that divorcing couples cannot set aside the issues that divided them in order to care for the children cooperatively after dissolving the marital bonds. It is based on the assumption that one home is always better than two for the well-being of the child. However, I will argue that to support ANF and the well-being of children joint custody ought to be the presumed best option unless it can be demonstrated that this option is destructive, unworkable or impossible in a given case.

THE CASE FOR JOINT CUSTODY

While joint custody living arrangements presently in practice are diverse, they are all characterized basically within the legal definition suggested by Roman and Haddad:

> Joint custody is that postdivorce custodial arrangement in which parents agree to share equally the authority for making all decisions that significantly affect the lives of their children. It is also that postdivorce arrangement in which child care is split equally or, at

the most discrepancy, child care resolves into a two-to-one split.[18]

Before presuming that joint custody is too complicated, or that the children suffer, and that the parents are incapable of cooperation because they have decided to divorce, courts, psychologists and parents should hear the evidence that joint custody is working to the satisfaction of many, that it is preferred by many, and that it serves the best interests of many children and parents.

At a meeting of the National Institute of Mental Health, participants agreed "that continuous meaningful contact with the non-custodial parent was a critical factor in the child's post-divorce adjustment."[19] Joint custody provides greater opportunities for continuous, meaningful contact than sole custody, and therefore, it could be added that joint custody best fosters positive post-divorce adjustment for children.

If the parents can cooperate and the father is willing and committed to caregiving, joint custody can provide more opportunity for provision of a vital emotional nutrient prescribed by Wallerstein and Blakeslee: a nurturing relationship with both parents.[20] Nurturing fathers with joint custody can soften some of the losses of the divorce. For example, adolescents are particularly vulnerable when deprived of a relationship with the father. Fathers can provide more quantity and quality of time with joint custody than with sole custody if they are prepared and willing. Good father-child relationships were found by this study to be critically important to the psychological well-being and self-

---

[18]Roman and Haddad, p. 173.

[19]National Institute of Mental Health, *Research Conference on the Consequences of Divorce on Children* (Bethesda, MD, February 1978).

[20]Wallerstein and Blakeslee, p. 257.

esteem of the child. Fathers in joint custody arrangements were "more committed to their children." While 7% of noncustodial fathers stopped spending time with their children, none of the joint custody fathers in this study stopped their involvement with their children.[21]

It should be noted that joint custody as an arrangement provides some stressful features as well as positive ones. Because young children fear abandonment in the early stages after the divorce, moving back and forth from one house to the other can stir up this fear more frequently. It may be especially confusing for pre-school children who may not understand what it is all about. School age children adapt better. They often feel a sense of accomplishment about mastering the schedule. They tend to find the variety in their living places to be pleasantly stimulating. They may feel more wanted as they experience the desire of each parent to be with them and the eager anticipation of seeing the parent they will be with next. They can benefit by the fact that each parent has an opportunity to be refreshed during the absence and tends to pick up the child to begin their turn with enthusiasm that many full-time parents do not have because of the monotony of the daily routine.[22]

Joint custody, unlike the sole-custody household, fosters the child's awareness that he/she has not been abandoned by either parent, is not responsible for the separation, and will not be abandoned for misbehavior (three major concerns of children after divorce). Sole custody, on the other hand, tends to reinforce these worst fears of the child by separating him/her from one parent.

Because the child of joint custody maintains meaningful contact with both parents, not just "visitation," there are

---

[21]Wallerstein and Blakeslee, p. 271.

[22]Wallerstein and Blakeslee, p. 267.

generally more opportunities to work through the fears and anger engendered by the divorce. Both parents can be seen in light of their continued parenting behavior, not just the imagined virtues and vices---the idealization and scapegoating---of a child who knows very little about the life of the noncustodial parent after divorce.

An argument presented against joint custody has been that parents who could not reconcile their conflicts while living together could not possibly work out ways of communicating and cooperating after separation. To the contrary, in personal accounts contained in five joint custody studies, the parents offer their assessment that they have satisfactorily isolated their marital conflicts from their parental responsibilities.[23] While the parents may be angry and still somewhat hostile about the marriage and separation, they have worked to isolate these feelings from the role and their behavior as parents. They have even resolved and gotten beyond the sources of the marital conflict when possible and necessary to continue providing quality care of the children. Not living together has reduced the pressure engendered by the differences that separated them, as well as reduced the need they felt to change the other person. Now they can be friends in order to provide quality care for the children. Conflict seems to be reduced for them by virtue of the agreement to end the marriage while continuing to share in the care of the children.

Both parents have expressed satisfaction with their freedom to have time off *and* involvement in child care. They have come to see the ex-spouse as one who is doing something positive to enhance their opportunities to balance their working and parenting activity as well as their social life with other adults.

---

23 Abarbanel; Galper; Roman and Haddad; Rosenthal and Keshet; and Wallerstein and Blakeslee.

While weekend fathers tend to perceive time spent with the child as a "service to the ex-spouse," joint-custody fathers generally feel that time spent with the child is focused on the father-child relationship itself.[24]

Most joint custody fathers experienced somewhat friendly communication with their ex-wife, talked with her on a frequent basis about the child's well-being, and never had any social contact with her. They gave the most positive evaluation of her as a parent and the most positive description of her, in general, compared to the descriptions by full-time fathers and quarter-timers. Joint custody fathers were also the least likely to share their personal problems with the ex-wife.[25] This contributed to the well being of the child because these fathers were also able to provide the child with a positive image of the other parent. That image was vital for the well being of the child: reducing internal emotional tensions and helping the child to get along well with both parents.

This data suggests that joint custody fathers were best able to separate the parental relationship from the marital relationship because communication between the father and the ex-wife was more open and clear as well as more rational and less conflict-ridden. These fathers felt better about themselves as parents and seemed most likely to remain involved in ANF.

Unlike weekend fathers who nearly always came to the ex-wife's home to pick up and return the child, joint custody fathers nearly always made the transfer through the school or day care center. By picking up the child at a neutral site rather than the other parent's home, the father and mother could feel more directly involved with the child, less controlled by the ex-spouse; and their relationship with the child was less

---

[24]Rosenthal and Keshet, p. 89.

[25]Rosenthal and Keshet, p. 165.

mediated by the other parent. Thereby, the sources of conflict between them were also reduced.

Agreements about schedules for being with the child were more consistent and dependable between joint custody parents than between quarter timers and full timers. Both parents and children knew when they could count on being together. This stability helped the parents to feel that they had a more secure place in the child's life. Joint custody parents felt that they could trust each other more than other parents since they did not have to bargain constantly for opportunities to see the child or for the other parent to care for the child.[26]

Divorced people expressed more respect for each other as parents when child rearing responsibilities were shared more equally. They also gave each other support as parents more often when time with the child was shared more or less equally.[27] Such support and mutual respect helped fathers to remain involved. Without such support, fathers would be more likely to avoid ANF after divorce.

In a study by Judith Greif, it was established that joint-custody fathers were the most satisfied:

> Those fathers who had more contact with, and joint custody of, their children were significantly more satisfied than fathers with less contact and no custodial rights of their children.[28]

Rosenthal and Keshet also found that joint custody was an arrangement preferred over full custody and no custody:

---

[26]Rosenthal and Keshet, p. 105.

[27]Rosenthal and Keshet, p. 104.

[28]Judith Brown Greif, "Child Absence: Father's Perceptions of Their Relationship to Their Children Subsequent to Divorce," Dissertation, Adelphi University, 1977, p. 85.

Unlike the weekend father, his hours with the children are not sharply curtailed or ritualized. Unlike the full-time father, his parental duties are not so demanding that his social life suffers. Of all divorced fathers, the half-timer (joint-custody father) has the lowest level of conflict with his former mate as well as the most positive attitude about becoming a father again.[29]

For the most part, the case which has been presented is a moral case justifying joint custody by the consequential benefits for mothers, fathers and children. It has been shown that joint custody produces more good than bad consequences and more good consequences than any other custody options and less bad than other options.

The moral desirability of joint custody is also grounded in the argument for the moral obligation to ANF. Joint custody enables fathers to be active nurturers and thereby to promote opportunities for both fathers and mothers to find greater satisfaction in parenting, work and life overall. The moral obligation of mothers and fathers to deal justly with each other requires that the most loving, mutually supportive, and fair alternative---joint custody---be adopted when the circumstances would also provide for the well-being of the child.

In Wallerstein's and Kelly's monumental longitudinal study of parents' and children's ways of coping with divorce, "the findings point to the desirability of the child's continuing relationship with *both parents* during the postdivorce years in an arrangement which enables each parent to be responsible for and genuinely concerned with the well-being of the

---

[29]Georgia Dullea, "Divorced Fathers: Who Are the Happiest?" *New York Times*, October 1, 1977.

children."[30] In order to promote joint custody, they suggest that laws be developed to influence parents toward joint psychological and financial responsibility for the children in the event of divorce. Basically, this means passing laws which support and promote legal joint custody.

Without joint custody, the father (or the noncustodial parent) is much less likely to remain involved in child care responsibilities. It was observed in this study that "lacking legal rights to share in decisions about major aspects of their children's lives, many noncustodial parents withdrew from their children in grief and frustration. Their withdrawal was experienced by the children as a rejection and was detrimental in its impact."[31]

As Roman and Haddad have suggested, in order for the courts to support the equality of men and women before the law, "joint custody should be made the presumptive choice in our courts."[32] This would not entirely rule out the possibility of sole custody as an option, but it would make joint custody the preferred choice, unless compelling reasons could be given for the unfairness, incapacity or disinterest of one of the parents in taking that responsibility.

No less than 33 states have laws authorizing joint custody.[33] More frequently, joint custody has been granted when the divorcing parents agreed to this without going to court. They simply presented their agreements as part of the divorce papers and the presiding judge signed them into the

---

[30]Judith Wallerstein and Joan Kelly, *Surviving the Breakup: How Children Actually Cope With Divorce* (New York: Basic Books, 1980), p. 310.

[31]Wallerstein and Kelly, p. 310.

[32]Roman and Haddad, p. 174.

[33]Wallerstein and Blakeslee, p. 256.

official divorce records upon granting the decree of divorce and custody settlement.

What are we to say, in terms of this moral approach, about the situations in which the parents divorced because one of them physically abused the child? Or what must be done when openly expressed hostility between the parents is a severe detriment to the well-being of the child? For every moral obligation there are exceptions. In general, there are some moral priorities which are higher than others. Joint custody is meant to serve the priorities of fairness between the parents, the reciprocity of equal opportunities for fulfillment by both of them, and ultimately (i.e., the top priority) the protection of the best interests of the child who is the least powerful party in the matter. Being unable to protect his/her own interests, the pre-adolescent child must have others to look out for those interests in the divorce proceedings. With this order of priorities, joint custody may not always be the best option but it has been shown to fulfill these priorities more often than not.

In cases where joint custody would subject the child to greater conflict or abuse, joint custody would not be the most loving option and some other alternative would have to be found to assure the well-being of the child. This other option might involve custody by the father *or* the mother; whichever is most fit. The courts should require some proof that one parent is unfit, but should accept only extreme evidence. One of the most destructive patterns of recent years has been the legal strategy of seeking to impugn the character of the opponent to get custody. In most of these cases, there are two capable and fit parents fighting for sole custody. This hostility could be avoided entirely if they shared custody. There would also be less conflict and bitterness later to get in the way of caring for the child if they refrained from attacking each other in court through this legal strategy.

The mother should not be *presumed* to be the best option because "a child needs its mother more" nor should the father be presumed to be the best option even if the man earns more and appears able to provide a higher standard of living (analogous to the patriarchal privilege of ownership not so long ago). If it must come to such proceedings (as indeed the reality of physical and sexual violence in some families requires that it must), then the case should be judged on face value and without presumption for mothers or fathers.

From an historical perspective, it can be seen that joint custody is emerging as the needs of the society change. The overall picture of divorce in America is very different today from thirty years ago. In many cases, divorce has become more mutual and amicable, more often settled out of court, and less hostile; while many postdivorce arrangements for child custody are becoming more cooperative. At the same time, because men and women have been participating more equally in the financial support of the family, property settlements have become more and more complicated and more bitter. Children can sometimes be used as the pawns on the chess board of divorce settlements. Joint custody seeks to prevent this from happening.

While divorce was once only taboo and not positive in any way, the stigma is being lifted. Guilt is presently not as prevalent as a burden for divorcing parents. More women are prepared to work and financially support themselves today than thirty years ago. Today, more fathers are prepared to nurture children than were willing and prepared in 1950. If more parents see how others have shared custody and provided for their own satisfaction and the well being of their children, the percentage of amicable arrangements about child custody may continue to increase while the violent scenes that have impaired the children of divorce may become a smaller part of the overall picture of child custody in the United States.

While the presumption of joint custody would be a necessary condition for support of ANF after divorce, it would not in itself be a sufficient condition to make it possible for great numbers of divorcing fathers to adopt ANF. Without removing the psychological and economic barriers to ANF, joint custody alone is inadequate because of the many cases of divorce where fathers were not prepared, unwilling, or unavailable to share the responsibilities of ANF. Only those fathers with adequate motivation to do so, with past socialization toward nurturing, with supportive structures in their families and relative freedom from domination of family life by the workplace would benefit from the opportunity to share custody, be truly open to the court's encouragement for joint custody or be able to fulfill the nurturing goals of ANF. I agree with Susan Whicher, head of the American Bar Association's special committee on joint custody, who predicted that joint custody will soon be the rule rather than the exception.[34] While this may not happen soon due to some "slowing in the revolution," I firmly believe that it ought to happen as soon as possible for the sake of children, fathers and mothers.

---

[34] "One Child, Two Homes, *Time*, January 29, 1979, p. 61.

CONCLUSION

THE RETURN OF THE PRODIGAL FATHER

Like the son in the parable of the Prodigal Son, the absent father of today is away from his family, squandering, channelling and being taken for his creative energies, time and love in such a way that he has nothing left to give to his children. The prodigal father of today is extravagant with his time and directs little of his time and energy toward the care of his children. He is asked by his children to show tender care and concern, but he is unwilling, exhausted and not prepared emotionally or physically to meet their demands. His impatience boils over to anger quickly. He is implored to spend time with the children, but his work spills over into his time at home and he cannot find a relaxed moment to give.

The prodigal father is told of the new, exciting work by his children in school, but his own work has become so routine and boring that he does not have the capacity any longer to feel excitement about creativity through such work. Or he may have so many work demands that he has no time left for sharing the enthusiasm of his children in their work. As his children experience failure, they reach out to him for encouragement; but his own desperate striving to find self-esteem in his work pushes him too hard and he, in turn, pushes them too hard. He demands from them high performance like that demanded of him on the job. He loses sight of their need for unconditional acceptance partly because he is not in touch with his own need for regularly accepting and affirming God's unconditional love for him.

He has played the prescribed role of breadwinner, giving all the energy he *has* to succeeding professionally or economically so that his family can eat, live in a "nice" place and afford "the good life." Or, he may have come to find a great deal of satisfaction in his work and has slowly withdrawn from his family in pursuit of the strokes he gets on the job; stayed away from them out of commitment to altruistic service; or gone off for long periods of time to advance his career dreams. He may also have withdrawn into a regimen of physical recreation that adds to his absence.

His children require the "bread" of a mutually enriching relationship with their father, but all he offers them is the financial "bread" which turns to stone without his love. He may be a good breadwinner, but without his loving presence the money buys little of the love that they really need. He may tell them he loves them as he leaves town for a long period of work, but without his loving presence these words mean nothing to his children left behind.

The prodigal father of today is starving for self-esteem. Because he is starving his family emotionally and in terms of quality and quantity of time, the money he brings to them is of little consolation. He too feels helpless because the way home is blocked by social pressures, systemic realities, economic inequalities and his past conditioning.

One day, if the work world can be transformed so that he will own more of his own labor, he will experience his own value more fully through that work without excessive absence from his family. He will be more free to determine his work hours and amount of work in conjunction with his responsibilities to share equally in the care of his children. His work will provide opportunities to express himself creatively and with a feeling of his own power to contribute value to the lives of others. He will not have to work for a meager share of the profits produced by his work, but will share in the proceeds more justly. He will have more time for ANF and be required to work fewer hours to support the family, in part, because the mother with whom he shares the care of his children and the breadwinning will also earn fair compensation for her work.

The traditional myths that trap mothers and fathers in complementary roles will be transformed by new mythological images that will set them free for mutuality, for sharing child care equally, for empowering each other, for finding fulfillment in well-compensated labor and for loving.

With major transformations such as those suggested here in *Fathers' Liberation Ethics,* the way home will be more clear and open for fathers. Mothers will no longer have to shout,"Wait 'til your father gets home!" The prodigal father will be truly "at home" with his children to care for them and home will be a more loving place for mothers as well. The prodigal father of tomorrow will become more like the Prodigal Father of the biblical parable (Luke 15:11-32), who graciously offered unconditional love to his son. The prodigal father of tomorrow will have learned to be grateful for the unconditional love that he has found and will have learned to share it generously with his children. On that day, there will be great rejoicing, for their father was dead to them and now he is alive again. He was lost and now he is found!

BIBLIOGRAPHY

Abarbanel, Alice Ruth. "Joint Custody Families: A Case Study Approach," Dissertation. California School of Professional Psychology, 1977.

Abarbanel, Alice Ruth. "Redefining Motherhood." In *The Future of the Family*. Ed. Louise Kapp Howe. New York: Simon and Schuster, 1972, pp. 349ff.

Abarbanel, Alice Ruth. "Shared Parenting After Separation and Divorce: A Study of Joint Custody." *American Journal of Orthopsychiatry*. No. 49 (1979), pp. 320-329.

Abbott, Lyman. *The Home Builder*. New York: Houghton Mifflin Co., 1908.

Abelin, Ernest. As quoted by Robert C. Prall in "The Role of the Father in the Preoedipal Years." *Journal of American Psychoanalytic Association*. Vol. 26, 1978, p. 154.

Aberg, Miriam and Patricia Small. "Middle Class Fathers' Occupational Role and Attitude Toward Children."

American Journal of Orthopsychiatry, No. 22 (1952), pp. 366-378.

Abrahms, Sally. "The Joint Custody Controversy." *New York*, June 18, 1979, pp. 56ff.

Ackerman, Gary. "Child Care Leave for Fathers?" *Ms.* September 1973, p. 118.

Ackerman, N.W. "The Principle of Shared Responsibility of Child Rearing." *International Journal of Sociology*, No. 12 (1957), pp. 280-291.

Ahlstrom, Sydney E. *A Religious History of the American People. Vol. 2*, Garden City, N.Y.: Image Books, 1975.

Alduous, Joan and Marie Osmond and Mary Hicks. "Men's Work and Men's Families." In *Contemporary Theories About the Family. Vol. 1*, Ed. Wesley Burr, et. al. New York: Free Press, 1979.

Alduous, Joan. *Family, Careers and Developmental Changes in Families*. New York: John Wiley, 1978.

Allenspach, Heinz. *Flexible Working Hours*. Geneva: International Labor Office, 1975.

Andersen, Christopher. *Father: The Figure and the Force*. New York: Warner Books, 1983.

Appleton, William. *Fathers and Daughters*. Garden City, NY: Doubleday and Co., 1981.

Araji, Sharon. "Husbands' and Wives' Attitude-Behavior Congruence on Family Roles." *Journal of Marriage and the Family*. No. 2 (1977), pp. 309ff.

Aries, Philippe. *Centuries of Childhood*. New York: Vintage Books, 1962.

Arkin, William and Lynne Dobrofsky. "Job Sharing." In *Working Couples*. Ed. Robert and Rhona Rapoport with Janice Bumstead. New York: Harper, 1978. pp. 122-137.

Arnott, Catherine. "Husband's Attitude and Wives' Commitment to Employment." *Journal of Marriage and the Family*, No. 4 (1973), pp. 673-684.

Arnstein, H. "The Crisis of Becoming a Father." *Sexual Behavior*, No. 4 (1972), pp. 42-48.

Astin, Helen, et. al. *Sex Roles: An Annotated Research Bibliography*. Washington, D.C.: U.S. Government Printing Office, 1975.

Atkin, Edith and Estelle Rubin. *Part-Time Father*. New York: Vanguard, 1976.

Bagchi, Pat. "Job Sharing." *Peninsula*, No. 4 (1976), pp. 12-15.

Bailyn, Lotte. "Career and Family Orientations of Husbands and Wives in Relation to Marital Happiness." *Human Relations*, No. 12 (1970), pp. 97-113.

Baker, Russell. "Fathering." *New York Times Magazine*, June 20, 1982, p. 14.

204

Barlow, Janet Scott. "Fad Fatherhood." *Chronicles,* October 1986, pp. 21-23.

Barnett, John. "Growing Job Demands Shatter the Marriages of More Executives." *Wall Street Journal,* May 10, 1967, p. 1.

Bartlett, Laile. *New Work/New Life.* New York: Harper, 1976.

Baum, Charlotte. "The Best of Both Parents." *New York Times Magazine,* October 31, 1976.

Bebbington, A.C. "The Function of Stress in the Establishment of the Dual-Career Family." *Journal of Marriage and the Family,* August 1973, pp. 530-537.

Becker, Lawrence. *On Justifying Moral Judgments.* New York: Humanities Press, 1973.

Becnel, Barbara Cottman. *Co-dependent Parent.* Los Angeles, CA: Lowell House, 1990.

Bedau, H.A. *Justice and Equality.* Englewood Cliffs, NJ: Prentice-Hall, Inc., 1971.

Bednarik, P. *The Male in Crisis.* New York: Alfred A. Knopf, 1970.

Beels, C. Christian. "Whatever Happened to Father?" *New York Times Magazine,* August 25, 1974.

Beer, William. *Househusbands: Men and Housework in American Families.* South Hadley, MA: J.F. Bergin, 1983.

Behles, Jenny and Daniel Behles. "Equal Rights in Divorce and Separation." *New Mexico Law Review*, No. 3 (1973), pp. 118-132.

Bem, Sandra Lipsitz. "The Measurement of Psychological Androgyny." *Journal of Consulting and Clinical Psychology,* No. 2 (1974), pp. 155-162.

Bender, Marilyn. "Executive Couples, Reluctance to Hire Husbands and Wives is Fading." *New York Times*, October 24, 1971.

Benedek, Elissa and Richard Benedek. "Joint Custody: Solution or Illusion? *American Journal of Psychiatry,* December 1979, pp. 1540-1544.

Benson, Leonard. *Fatherhood: A Sociological Perspective.* New York: Random House, 1968.

Benson, Leonard. *The Family Bond: Marriage, Love and Sex in America.* New York: Random House, 1971.

Benston, Margaret. "The Political Economy of Women's Liberation." *Monthly Review*, No. 4 (1969).

Berger, C.G. "Equal Pay, Equal Employment Opportunity and Equal Enforcement of the Law for Women." *Valparaiso Law Review,* Spring 1970, pp. 326-373.

Berk, R. and S. Berk. "A Simultaneous Equation Model for the Division of Household Labor." *Sociological Methods and Research*, No. 6 (1978), pp. 431-468.

206

Bernard, Jessie. *The Future of Marriage*. New York: Bantam, 1972.

Bernard, Jessie. *The Future of Motherhood*. Baltimore: Penguin, 1974.

Bernard, Jessie. *Women, Wives, Mothers: Values and Options*. Chicago: Aldine, 1975.

Best, F., et. al. *The Future of Work*. Englewood Cliffs, NJ: Prentice-Hall, 1973.

Bettelheim, Bruno. *A Good Enough Parent*. New York: Alfred A. Knopf, 1989.

Bettelheim, Bruno. "Fathers Shouldn't Try to be Mothers." *Parents' Magazine*, October 1956, pp. 124-125.

Bigner, J.J. "Fathering: Research and Practical Implications." *The Family Coordinator*, No. 19 (1970), pp. 357-362.

Biller, Henry and D.L. Meredith. *Father Power*. New York: Doubleday, 1975.

Biller, Henry and D.L. Meredith. "The Invisible American Father." *Sexual Behavior*, No. 2 (1972), pp. 16-22.

Biller, Henry. *Father, Child and Sex Role*. Lexington, MA: Heath Lexington Books, 1971.

Biller, Henry. *Paternal Deprivation*. Lexington, MA: D.C. Heath, 1974.

Biller, Henry. "The Father and Personality Development: Paternal Deprivation and Sex-Role Development." In M.E. Lamb, *The Role of the Father in Child Development.* New York: Wiley, 1976.

Billingsley, Andrew. *Black Families and the Struggle for Survival.* New York: Van Nostrand, 1973.

Bird, Caroline. *The Two-Paycheck Marriage.* New York: Rawson, Wade, 1979.

Bittman, Sam and Sue Rosenberg Zalk. *Expectant Fathers.* New York: Ballantine Books, 1978.

Blanchard, Robert and Henry Biller. "Father Availability and Academic Performance Among Third Grade Boys." *Developmental Psychology*, No. 4 (1971), pp. 301-305.

Blankenhorn, David. "Father who stays with family bucks major new trend." *Star Tribune.* November 10, 1990.

Blaxall, Martha and Barbara Reagan. *Women and the Workplace: The Implications of Occupation Segregation.* Chicago: University of Chicago Press, 1976.

Block, J.A., A. Von der Lippe, and J.H. Block. "Sex Role and Socialization Patterns: Some Personality and Environmental Antecedents." *Journal of Consulting and Clinical Psychology,* No. 41 (1973), pp. 321-341.

Blood, Robert and Donald Wolfe. *Husbands and Wives: The Dynamics of Married Living.* New York: Free Press, 1960.

Bloom-Feshbach, Jonathan. *The Beginnings of Fatherhood.* Unpublished Ph.D. Dissertation, Yale University, 1979.

Bly, Robert. "Finding the Father." In Robert Bly, *Selected Poems.* New York: Harper and Row, 1986, p. 132.

Bly, Robert. *Iron John: A Book About Men.* Reading, MA: Addison-Wesley, 1990.

Bohen, Halcyone and Anamaria Viveros-Long. *Balancing Jobs and Family Life: Do Flexible Work Schedules Help?* Philadelphia: Temple University Press, 1981.

Bombeck, Irma. *Family: The Ties That Bind...and Gag!* New York: McGraw-Hill, 1987.

Bombeck, Irma. "What's dear old dad to do?" *St. Paul Pioneer Press,* June 18, 1989.

Boston Women's Health Book Collective. *Ourselves and Our Children: A Book By and For Parents.* New York: Random House, 1978.

Boyce, William and Larry Jensen. *Moral Reasoning.* Lincoln: University of Nebraska Press, 1978.

Boyd, Cynthia. "Dad Care." *St. Paul Pioneer Press,* June 15, 1991.

Bradel, R.A. *Husband-Coached Childbirth.* New York: Harper and Row, 1965.

Bradwell vs. Illinois. 83 U.S. 130, 141 (1872).

Brandt, R.B. *Value and Obligation*. New York: Harcourt Brace Jovanovich, Inc., 1961.

Brazelton, T. Berry. "What Makes a Good Father," *Redbook*, June 1990.

Brenton, Myron. *The American Male*. Greenwich, CT: Fawcett, 1966.

Bronfenbrenner, Urie. "The Changing American Child---A Speculative Analysis." *Merrill-Palmer Quarterly*, April 1961, pp. 73-84.

Brother: The Newsletter of the National Organization for Changing Men, P.O. Box 24159, St. Louis, MO 63130.

Byrne, Robert and Teresa Skelton. *Every Day is Father's Day*. New York: Atheneum, 1989.

Camerin, Ingrid. "The Ideal and the Reality: Women in Sweden." In *Beyond Intellectual Sexism*. Ed. Joan Roberts. New York: David McKay, 1976.

Cammarata, Jerry and Frances Leighton. *The Fun Book of Fatherhood*. New York: Pinnacle, 1979.

Carlsson, Maj-Britt. "Equality Between Men and Women in Sweden." In *Women and Men: Changing Roles, Relationships and Perceptions*. Eds. Libby Cater, Anne Firor Scott with Wendy Martyna. New York: Aspen Institute for Humanistic Studies, 1976, pp. 245-273.

Carroll, Maurice. "U.S. Backs Childcare Leaves for Men in a School Case Here." *New York Times*, January 6, 1973.

Catalyst, "The Report on a National Study of Parental Leaves." New York: Catalyst, 1986, 250 Park Ave. So., New York, NY 10003.

Causey, Mike. "Flexitime Test Sought by Agency." *Washington Post*, February 6, 1974.

Chafe, William H. *Women and Equality: Changing Patterns in American Culture.* New York: Oxford University Press, 1977.

Chafetz, Janet Saltzman. *Masculine/Feminine or Human?* Itasca, Ill: F.E. Peacock, 1974.

Chambers, David. "Rethinking the Substantive Rules for Custody Disputes in Divorce." *Michigan Law Review*, 83 (1984), pp. 477-569.

Changing Men: Issues in Gender, Sex and Politics. 306 N. Brooks St., Madison, WI 55103.

Chesser, Barbara Jo and Ava Gray. *Marriage: Creating a Partnership.* Iowa: Kendall/Hunt, 1975.

Children's Defense Fund---Minnesota Newsletter, 550 Rice St., Suite 104, St. Paul, MN 55103.

Chodorow, Nancy. *The Reproduction of Mothering: Psychoanalysis and the Sociology of Gender.* Berkeley: University of California Press, 1978.

Clary, Mike. *Daddy's Home.* New York: Seaview Books, 1982.

Clayton, Richard. *The Family, Marriage and Social Change.* Lexington, MA: D.C. Heath, 1975.

Clinebell, Charlotte H. *Meet Me in the Middle: How to Become Human Together.* New York: Harper and Row, 1973.

Cohen, Gaynor. "Absentee Husbands in Spiralist Families." *Journal of Marriage and the Family,* No. 3 (1977), pp. 605ff.

Cohen, Monroe, ed. *Growing Free: Ways to Help Children Overcome Sex Role Stereotypes.* Washington, D.C.: Association for Childhood Education International, 1976.

"Company Couples Flourish." *Business Week,* August 2, 1976, pp. 54-55.

Corneau, Guy. *Absent Fathers, Lost Sons.* Boston: Shambhala, 1991.

Cosby, William. *Fatherhood.* Garden City, NY: Doubleday and Co., 1986.

Cowan, Carolyn and Philip A. Cowan. "Men's Involvement in Parenthood: Identifying the Antecedents and Understanding the Barriers." In *Fathers' Transition to Parenthood.* Ed. P. Berman and F.A. Pedersen. Hillsdale, NJ: Erlbaum, 1986.

Cox, H. "Intra-family Comparison of Loving-Rejecting Child-rearing Practices." *Child Development,* 41 (1970), pp. 437-438.

Cox, L. Norma, Ed. *Dear Dad: Famous People's Loving Letters to Their Fathers.* San Francisco, CA: Saybrook, 1987.

D'Andrea, Ann. "Joint Custody as Related to Paternal Involvement and Paternal Self-Esteem." *Conciliation Courts Review,* 21, 2 (1983), pp. 41-87.

Dahlstrom, Edmund. *The Changing Roles of Men and Women.* Boston: Beacon Press, 1971.

Daley, Eliot. *Father Feelings.* New York: Pocket Books, 1979.

Daly, Margaret. "Part-time Jobs Tend to Exploit Women, Say Trade Unionists." *Toronto Star,* April 25, 1972, p. 8.

David, Deborah S. and Robert Brannon, Eds. *The Forty Nine Percent Majority: The Male Sex Role.* Reading, MA: Addison-Wesley, 1976.

Davidson, K., R. Ginsburg, and H. Kay. *Sex-Based Discrimination.* St. Paul, MN: West, 1974.

Day-Lower, Donna. "Clergy Couples: Are They Working?" In *Daughters of Sarah,* March 1977, pp. 2-3.

DeCrow, Karen. *Sexist Justice.* New York: Random House, 1974.

DeGrazia, S. *Of Time, Work and Leisure.* New York: Simon and Schuster, 1962.

DeLone, Richard. *Small Futures: Inequality, Children and the Failure of Liberal Reform.* New York: Harcourt Brace Jovanovich, 1978.

Derdeyn, Andre' and Norman Stevenson. "Child Custody Contests in Historical Perspective." *American Journal of Psychiatry*, December 1976, pp. 1369-1376.

Deutermann, William, Jr. and Scott Brown. "Voluntary Part-Time Workers: A Growing Part of the Labor Force." *Monthly Labor Review*, No. 6 (1978), pp. 1-6.

Deutscher, Irwin. *What We Say, What We Do: Sentiments and Acts.* Glenview, Ill: Foresman, 1973.

Deutscher, Irwin. "Words and Deeds: Social Science and Social Policy." *Social Problems,* Winter 1966, pp. 235-254.

DeWolf, Rose. *How to Raise Your Man: The Problems of a New Style Woman in Love with an Old Style Man.* New York: Franklin Watts, 1983.

Dickie, Jane and S, Carnahan Gerber. "Training in Social Competence: The Effect on Mothers, Fathers and Infants." *Child Development*, 1980, 51, pp. 1248-1251.

Dickson, Paul. *The Future of the Workplace.* New York: Weybright and Talley, 1975.

Dinnerstein, Dorothy. *The Mermaid and the Minotaur: Sexual Arrangements and Human Malaise.* New York: Random, 1976.

Dizard, Jan. *Social Change in the Family.* Chicago: Community and Family Study Center, University of Chicago, 1968.

Dizard, Jan. "The Price of Success." In *The Future of the Family,* Ed. Howe, pp. 87ff.

214

Doely, Sarah Bentley, ed. *Women's Liberation and the Church: The New Demand for Freedom in the Life of the Christian Church.* New York: Association, 1970.

Dowdall, Jean. "Women's Attitudes Toward Employment and Family Roles." *Sociological Analysis.* Vol. 35 (1974), pp. 251-262.

Dreitzel, Hans Peter. *Family, Marriage and the Struggle of the Sexes.* New York: Macmillan, 1972.

Duberman, Lucile, et. al. *Gender and Sex in Society.* New York: Praeger, 1975.

Dullea, Georgia. "Divorced Fathers: Who Are the Happiest?" *New York Times,* October 1, 1977.

Dullea, Georgia. "Is Joint Custody Good for Children?" *New York Times Magazine,* February 3, 1980, pp. 32ff.

Dullea, Georgia. "Joint Custody: Is Sharing the Child a Dangerous Idea?" *New York Times,* May 24, 1976, p. 24.

Duncan, R. Paul and Carolyn C. Perruci. "Dual Occupation Families and Migration." *American Sociological Review,* April 1976, pp. 252-261.

Dwyer, Jim. "Behold the Single Father." *Signature,* September 1974, p. 32.

Earls, F. "The Fathers (Not the Mothers): Their Importance and Influence with Infants and Young Children." *Psychiatry,* Vol. 39 (1976), pp. 209-226.

Eggebroten, Anne. "Each for the Other and Both for the Lord." *Faith/at/Work*, August 1976, p. 12.

Ehrensaft, Diane. *Parenting Together: Men and Women Sharing the Care of Their Children.* New York: Free Press, 1987.

Elbing, Alvar, Herman Gadon and John Gordon. "Flexible Working Hours: It's About Time." *Harvard Business Review*, January-February, 1974.

Engels, F. *The Origins of the Family, Private Property and the State.* Moscow: Foreign Languages Publishing House, 1948.

English, O.S. and C.J. Foster. *Fathers Are Parents Too.* London: Allen and Unwin, 1953.

Epstein, Cynthia F. "Encountering the Male Establishment: Sex-Status Limits in Women's Careers in the Professions." *American Journal of Sociology*, 6 (1970), pp. 965-982.

Epstein, Cynthia F. "Law Partners and Marital Partners: Strains and Solutions in the Dual Career Family Enterprise." *Human Relations*, No. 6 (1971), pp. 549-564.

Epstein, Cynthia F. *Reflections on the Women's Movement: Assessment of Change and Its Limits.* New York: Institute of Life Insurance, 1975.

Epstein, Cynthia F. *Woman's Place: Options and Limits in Professional Careers.* Berkeley: University of California Press, 1970.

"Equal Custodial Time---A Revolutionary Concept." *Family Law Commentator*, July/August 1975, p. 1.

Erickson, Donna. *Prime Time Together with Kids*. Minneapolis, MN: Augsburg, 1989.

Erikson, Erik. *Childhood and Society*. New York: W.W. Norton, 1963.

Evans, A. *Flexibility in Working Life: Opportunities for Individual Choice*. Paris: Organization for Economic Cooperation and Development, 1973.

"Family Life When Success Keeps the Father Traveling." *New York Times*, March 7, 1973.

Farganis, Sondra. "Liberty: Two Perspectives on the Women's Movement." *Ethics*, October 1977, pp. 62ff.

Farians, Elizabeth. "Justice: The Hard Line." *Andover Newton Quarterly*, Vol. XII, March 1972, pp. 191-200.

Farkas, George. "Education, Wage Rates and the Division of Labor Between Husband and Wife." *Journal of Marriage and the Family*, August 1976, pp. 473ff.

Farrell, Warren. *The Liberated Man*. New York: Bantam, 1973.

Fasteau, Marc. "Men as Parents." In *The Forty-Nine Percent Majority*. Ed. Deborah David and Robert Brannon. Reading, MA: Addison-Wesley, 1976, pp. 60ff.

Fasteau, Marc. *The Male Machine*. New York: McGraw-Hill, 1974.

Father's Network. P.O. Box 882, San Anselmo, CA 94960.

Fatherhood USA: The First National Guide to Programs, Services and Resources for and About Fathers. New York: Garland Press, 1987.

Fathering Support Services. P.O. Box 15862, Chicago, Ill 60614.

Fein, Robert. "Men and Young Children." In *Men and Masculinity.* Ed. Joseph Pleck and Jack Sawyer. Englewood Cliffs, NJ: Prentice-Hall, 1974, pp. 54ff.

Fein, Robert. "Men's Entrance to Parenthood." *Family Coordinator*, October 1976, pp. 341ff.

Fein, Robert. "Research on Fathering: Social Policy and an Emergent Perspective." *Journal of Social Issues,* No. 1 (1978), pp. 122-135.

Feldman, Harold. "The First Child." Unpublished paper quoted in "Companionate Marriages and Sexual Inequality." In *Toward a Sociology of Women.* Ed. Safilios-Rothschild. Lexington, MA: Xerox, 1972, p. 67.

Feldman, S.C., S.C. Nash, and B.G. Aschenbrenner. "Antecedents of Fathering." *Child Development,* 54 (1983), pp. 1628-1636.

Field, T. "Interaction Behaviors of Primary Versus Secondary Caretaker Fathers." *Developmental Psychology,* 1978, 14, pp. 183-185.

Fields, Suzanne. *Like Father, Like Daughter: How Father Shapes the Woman His Daughter Becomes.* Boston: Little, Brown and Company, 1983.

Filene, Peter. *Him/Her Self: Sex Roles in Modern America.* New York: New American Library, 1974.

Fishel, Elizabeth. *The Men in Our Lives.* New York: William Morrow, 1985.

Flaste, Richard. "Fathers and Infants: Getting Close." *New York Times,* December 5, 1975.

"Flexible Work Hours: A Magnet to Attract Talented Women." *Affirmative Action in Progress,* April 1976.

Flexner, Eleanor. *Century of Struggle.* New York: Atheneum, 1974.

Fogarty, Michael, Rhona Rapoport and Robert Rapoport. *Sex, Career and Family.* London: Allen and Unwin, 1972.

Fogarty, Michael. *Women and Top Jobs: The Next Move.* London: Allen and Unwin, 1972.

Forbes, R. "A New Role for Expectant Fathers." *Midwife and Health Visitor,* 8 (1972), pp. 166-168.

Foster, Henry, Jr., Doris Freed and Judith Greif. "Joint Custody." *Trial,* May 15, 1979, pp. 26-33.

Foster, Henry. Jr. and Doris Freed. *Law and the Family---New York.* Rochester, N.Y.: Lawyers Co-Operative Publishing Co., 1972. Vol. 2, p. 512.

Foster, J.E. "Comparison of an Ideal Father Image with Selected Television Father Images." *Journal of Marriage and the Family*, August 1964, pp. 353-355.

Frankena, William. *Ethics*. Englewood Cliffs, NJ: Prentice-Hall, 1973.

Frankena, William. "Love and Principle in Christian Ethics." In *Perspectives on Morality: Essays by William Frankena*. Ed. K.E. Goodpaster. Notre Dame: University of Notre Dame Press, 1976, pp. 79ff.

Fraser, Dorothy Bass. "The Feminine Mystique: 1890-1910." *Union Seminary Quarterly Review*, Summer 1972, pp. 225-239.

Freeman, Jo. *The Politics of Women's Liberation*. New York: David McKay Co., 1975.

Freeman, Jo. *Women: A Feminist Perspective*. Palo Alto, CA: Mayfield, 1975.

Friedan, Betty. *The Feminine Mystique*. New York: Dell, 1963.

Friedman, Leon. " 'Fathers Don't Make Good Mothers,' Said the Judge." *New York Times*, January 28, 1973, IV, p. 12.

Fuchs, Lawrence. "A Family's Need: Fatherhood." *Boston Evening Globe,* January 30, 1973.

Fulman, Ricki. "On Their Own: Single Fathers Meet to Talk About Their Troubles." *New York Daily News*, April 20, 1979, p. 41.

Furstenberg, Frank, F.S. Phillip Morgan, and Paul D. Allison. "Paternal Participation and Children's Well-Being After Marital Dissolution." *American Sociological Review*, 52 (1987), pp. 695-701.

Galinsky, Ellen and William Hooks. *The New Extended Family: Day Care That Works*. Boston: Houghton Mifflin, 1977.

Gallese, Liz Roman. "Two for the Price of One: Colleges Say They Get More for Their Money By Hiring a Couple to Share One Faculty Job." *Wall Street Journal*, April 19, 1974.

Galper, Miriam. *Co-Parenting: A Source Book for the Separated or Divorced Family*. Philadelphia: Running Press, 1978.

Gardner, E. Clinton. "Justice and Love." In *Social Ethics*. Ed. Gibson Winter. New York: Harper and Row, 1968, pp. 69ff.

Garfinkel, Perry. *In a Man's World: Father, Son, Brother, Friend and other Roles Men Play*. New York: New American, 1985.

Garland, T. Neal. "The Better Half? The Male in the Dual Profession Family." In *Toward a Sociology of Women*. Ed. Safilios-Rothschild, pp. 199ff.

Gath, Stanley, Alan Gurwitt and John Munder Ross. *Father and Child*. Boston: Little, Brown and Company, 1982.

Gavron, Hannah. *The Captive Wife*. London: Routledge and Kegan, 1966.

Gecas, Viktor. "The Socialization and Child Care Roles." In *Role Structure and Analysis of the Family.* Ed. F. Ivan Nye. Beverly Hills, CA: Sage, 1976.

Gelder, Van Lindsy and Carrie Carmichael. "But What About Our Sons?" *Ms.*, October 1975, p. 52.

Gersick, K.E. "Fathers BY Choice: Divorced Men Who Receive Custody of Their Children." In G. Levinger and O.C. Moles, eds. *Divorce and Separation.* New York: Basic Books, 1979, p. 320.

Gilbert, L.A. *Men in Dual Career Families.* Hillsdale, NJ: Erlbaum, 1985.

Gilbert, Sara. *What's A Father For?* New York: Warner, 1975.

Gilman, Charlotte Perkins. *The Home: Its Work and Influence.* New York: Charlton, 1903.

Gilman, Charlotte Perkins. *Women and Economics.* Boston: Small and Maynard, 1898.

Ginott, Haim. *Between Parent and Child.* New York: Macmillan, 1975.

Ginzberg, Eli and Alice Yohalem, *Corporate Lib: Women's Challenge to Management.* Baltimore: Johns Hopkins Press, 1973.

Giveans, ed. *Nurturing News,* 187 Caselli Ave. San Francisco, CA 94114.

Gladieux, J.D. "Pregnancy---The Transition to Parenthood: Satisfaction with the Pregnancy Experience as a Function of Sex-Role Conceptions, Marital Relationship and Social Network." In *The First Child and Family Formation.* Eds. W.B. Miller and L.F. Newman. Chapel Hill, N.C.: Carolina Population Center, 1978.

Glickman, Albert and Zenia Brown. *Changing Schedules of Work: Patterns and Implications.* Springfield, VA: National Technical Information Service, 1973.

Goff, Harold. "Father's Day Began in Fairmont." *West Virginia,* 1987, p. 11.

Gold, M. and C. Slater. "Office, Factory, Store---and Family: A Study of Integration Setting." *American Sociological Review,* Vol. 23 (1958), pp. 64-74.

Goldsmith, Mark. "A Radical Work Plan to Free Both Husband and Wife." *San Francisco Chronicle*, February 6, 1976.

Goldsmith, Mark. "Part-Time Jobs Liberate Both Parents." *Christian Science Monitor*, October 9, 1974.

Goldstein, Joseph, Anna Freud and Albert Solnit. *Beyond the Bests Interests of the Child.* New York: Free Press, 1973.

Golembiewski, Robert, Rick Hilles and Munro Kagno. "Longitudinal Study of Flexi-time Effects: Some Consequences of an OD Structural Intervention." *Journal of Applied Behavioral Science,* 10 (1974), pp. 503-532.

Goodman, Ellen. "Dads should forget gifts of perfume and build bridges to span worry-gap." *St. Paul Pioneer Press,* June 12, 1990.

Goodman, Ellen. "Whatever happened to those share-the-housework lists?" *St. Paul Pioneer Press,* August 1, 1989, p. 11a.

Gornick, Vivian and Barbara Moran, eds. *Woman in Sexist Society: Studies in Power and Powerlessness.* New York: Basic Books, 1971.

Gottlieb, Annie. "The Secret Strength of Happy Marriages." *McCall's,* 1990.

Gover, David. "Socio-economic Differentials in the Relationship Between Marital Adjustment and Wife's Employment Status." *Journal of Marriage and the Family,* November 1963, pp. 452-458.

Grady. K., R. Brannon and J. Pleck. *The Male Sex Role: An Annotated Research Bibliography.* Washington, D.C.: U.S. Government Printing Office, 1979.

Grams, Jean D. and Walter Waetjen. *Sex: Does It Make a Difference?* Belmont, CA: Wadsworth Publishing, 1975.

Green, Maureen. *Fathering.* New York: McGraw-Hill, 1976.

Greenberg, Dan. *Dan Greenberg's Confessions of a Pregnant Father.* New York: Macmillan, 1986.

Greenberg, Martin. *Birth of a Father.* New York: Continuum, 1985.

Greenberg, Martin. "The Male Early Childhood Teacher: An Appraisal." *Young Children,* 32 (1977), pp. 34-37.

Greene, Bob. *Good Morning, Merry Sunshine: A Fathers Journal of His Child's First Year.* New York: Penguin, 1985.

Greenwald, Carol and J. Lisa. "Part-Time Workers Can Bring Higher Productivity." *Harvard Business Review,* September 1973, pp. 20ff.

Greenwald, Carol. "Part-Time Work: When Less is More." *Ms.* May 1976, pp. 41-42.

Greenwald, Carol. "Working Mothers: The Need for More Part-Time Jobs." *New England Economic Review,* September/October 1972, p. 21.

Greif, Geoffrey. *Single Fathers.* Lexington, MA: Lexington Books, 1985.

Greif, Judith Brown. "Child Absence: Fathers' Perceptions of Their Relationship to Their Children Subsequent to Divorce." Dissertation. Adelphi University, 1977.

Gronseth, Erik. "The Breadwinner Trap." In *The Future of the Family.* Ed. Howe, pp. 175-191.

Gronseth, Erik. "Work Sharing: A Norwegian Example." In *Working Couples.* Eds. Robert Rapoport, Rhona Rapoport with Janice Bumstead. New York: Harper Colophon Books, 1978, pp. 108-121.

Gronseth, Erik. "Work-Sharing Families: Husband and Wife in Part-Time Employment." *Acta Sociologica*, October 1975.

Grossman, Allyson Sherman. *Employment in Perspective: Working Women.* Report #565. Bureau of Labor Statistics. Washington, D.C.: U.S. Department of Labor, 1979.

Grossman, F.K., et. al. *Pregnancy, Birth and Parenthood.* San Francisco, CA: Jossey Bass, 1980.

Grote, Douglas and Jeff Weinstein. "Joint Custody: A Viable and Ideal Alternative." *Journal of Divorce*, Fall 1977, pp. 43-53.

Gump, J.P. "Sex Role Attitudes and Psychological Well-Being." *Journal of Social Issues*, No. 2 (1972), pp. 79-91.

Gutman, Herbert. *The Black Family in Slavery and Freedom, 1750-1925.* New York: Pantheon, 1976.

Guttenberg, M and H. Bray. "Teachers as Mediators of Sex-Role Standards." In *Beyond Sex Roles.* Ed. Alice Sargent. St. Paul, MN: West, 1977, pp. 395-411.

Guttenberg, Marcia and Susan Salasin. "Women, Men and Mental Health." In *Women and Men: Changing Roles, Relationships and Perceptions.* Ed. Libby Cater, et. al. New York: Aspen Institute for Humanistic Studies, 1976, pp. 153-180.

Haavio-Mannila, Elina. "Satisfaction with Family, Work, Leisure and Life Among Men and Women." *Human Relations*, No. 6 (1971), pp. 585-601.

226

Haberstein, Robert and Charles Mindell. *Ethnic Families in America: Patterns and Variations.* New York: Elsevier, 1976.

Hacker, Helen Mayer. "Class and Race Differences in Gender Roles." In *Gender and Sex in Society.* Ed. Duberman. New York: Praeger, 1975, pp. 134-184.

Hal, Nathan. *The Birth of a Family: The New Role of the Father in Childbirth.* New York: Anchor Press, 1979.

Hallaire, Jean. *Part-Time Employment: Its Extent and Problems.* Paris: Organization for Economic Cooperation and Development, 1968.

Hallowell, Christopher. *Father to the Man: A Journal.* New York: William Morrow, 1987.

Hamilton, M.L. *Father's Influence on Children.* Chicago: Nelson-Hall, 1977.

Hamilton, Mildred. "A Couple Pioneers in Job Sharing." *San Francisco Examiner and Chronicle,* April 25, 1976.

Hareven, Tamara. "The Family and Gender Roles in Historical Perspective." In *Women and Men: Changing Roles, Relationships and Perceptions.* Ed. Libby Cater, et. al. New York: Aspen Institute for Humanistic Studies, 1976, pp. 93-118.

Hargleroad, Bobbi Wells, ed. *Women's Work Is...Resources on Working Women.* Chicago: Institute on the Church in Urban Industrial Society, 1978.

Harrison, Fraser. *A Father's Diary.* New York: Pantheon, 1985.

Harrison, James. "A Critical Evaluation on 'Masculinity/Femininity' and a Proposal for an Alternative Paradigm for Research on Psychological Differences and Similarities Between the Sexes." Dissertation. New York University, 1974.

Harrison, James. "Warning: The Male Sex Role May be Dangerous to Your Health." *Journal of Social Issues,* No. 1 (1978), pp. 65-86.

Hayden, Dolores. *Redesigning the American Dream.* New York: W.W. Norton, 1984.

Hayes, Cheryl and Sheila Kamerman, eds. *Children of Working Parents: Experiences and Outcomes.* Washington, D.C.: National Academy Press, 1983.

Hayghe, H. "Marital and Family Characteristics of the Labor Force." *Monthly Labor Review,* No. 2 (1978), pp. 51-54.

Hayghe. H. "Families and the Rise of Working Wives---An Overview." *Monthly Labor Review,* May 1976, pp. 12-19.

Heckman, Norma A., Rebecca Bryson and Jeff Bryson. "Problems of Professional Couples: A Content Analysis." *Journal of Marriage and the Family,* No. 2 (1977), pp. 323ff.

Hedges, Janice Neipert and Stephen J. Gallogly. "Full and Part-time: A Review of Definitions." *Monthly Labor Review,* March 1977, pp. 21-28.

Hedges, Janice Neipert. "Flexible Schedules: Problems and Issues." *Monthly Labor Review,* No. 2 (1977), pp. 62-65.

Heer, David. "The Measurement and Bases of Family Power: An Overview." *Journal of Marriage and the Family,* 25 (1963), pp. 133-139.

Heiskanen, V.S. and Elina Haavio-Mannila. "The Position of Women in Society: Formal Ideology and Everyday Ethic." *Social Service Information,* December 1967.

Heiss, Jerold, ed. *Family Roles and Interaction: An Anthology.* Chicago: Rand McNally, 1968.

Henle, Peter and Paul Rycavage. "The Distribution of Earnings Among Men and Women, 1958-1977." *Monthly Labor Review,* No. 4 (1980).

Hennig, Margaret and Anne Jardin. *Women and Management.* New York: Doubleday, 1977.

Herman, S.R. "Sex Roles and Sexual Attitudes in Sweden: The New Phase." *The Massachusetts Review,* 13 (1972), pp. 45-64.

Herron, Bud. "Report Says 'Sexism' Hurts Clergy Couples." *Bread,* 1975.

HEW, Report of a Special Task Force. *Work in America.* Cambridge: MIT press, 1973.

Heyward, Carter. *Touching Our Strength.* San Francisco: Harper and Row, 1989.

Hochschild, A.R. "A Review of Sex Role Research." *American Journal of Sociology,* February 1978, pp. 1011-1029.

Hochschild, Arlie with Anne Machung. *The Second Shift.* New York: Avon Books, 1989.

Hoffman, L.W. and I. Nye, eds. *Working Mothers: An Evaluative Review of the Consequences for Wife, Husband and Child.* San Francisco: Jossey-Bass, 1974.

Hoffman, L.W. "Early Childhood Experiences and Women's Achievement Motives." *Journal of Social Issues,* 28 1972), pp. 129-155.

Hoffman, L.W. "Effects of Maternal Employment on the Child--- A Review of Research." *Developmental Psychology,* 10 (1974), pp. 204-228.

Hoffman, L.W. "Effects of the Employment of Mothers on Parental Power Relations and the Division of Household Tasks." *Marriage and Family Living,* 22 (1960), pp. 33ff.

Hoffman, Leonore and Gloria DeSole. *Careers and Couples: An Academic Question.* Edited for the MLA Commission on the Status of Women, first edition, 1974.

Holly, Marcia. "Joint Custody: The New Haven Plan." *Ms.* September 1976, p. 71.

Holmstrom, Lynda Lytle. *The Two-Career Family.* Cambridge: Schenkman, 1972.

230

Holter, Harriet. "Sex Roles and Social Change." In *Toward a Sociology of Women*, Ed. Safilios-Rothschild. Lexington, MA: Xerox, 1972, pp. 331-343.

Holter, Harriet. *Sex Roles and Social Structure*. Oslo: Oslo University Press, 1970.

Hood, Jane and Susan Godden. "Beating Time/Making Time: The Impact of Work Scheduling on Men's Family Roles." *The Family Coordinator*, October 1979, pp. 575-582.

Hood, Janet. *Becoming a Two-Job Family*. New York: Praeger, 1983.

Howard, John R. *The Cutting Edge: Social Movements and Social Change in America*.. Philadelphia: Lippincott, 1974.

Howe, Louise Kapp, ed. *The Future of the Family*. New York: Simon and Schuster, 1972.

Howell, M.C. "Can Fathers be Parents?" *Justice*, 1 (1974).

Howell, M.C. "Employed Mothers and Their Families." *Pediatrics*, No. 2 (1973), p. 7.

Howells, J. "Fathering." In *Modern Perspectives in International Child Psychiatry: Vol. 3*. Ed. J. Howells. Edinburgh: Oliver and Boyd, 1969.

Howells, J.G. "Fallacies in Child Care---That Fathering Is Unimportant." *Acta Paedopsychiatrica*, No. 2-3 (1970), pp. 46-55.

Huber, Joan and Glenda Spitze. *Sex Stratification: Children, Housework and Jobs.* New York: Academic Press, 1983.

Humez, A. and K. Stavely. *Family Men: What Men Feel About Their Wives, Their Children, Their Parents and Themselves.* Chicago: Contemporary Books, 1978.

"International Survey of Part-Time Employment." *International Labour Review,* Nos. 4/5 (1963).

Interactive Journal for Caregiver Fathers. P.O. Box 120773, St. Paul, MN 55112.

Jackson, J.C. "Permanent Part-Time." *Physics Today,* June 1972, p. 15.

Jacob, Bonnie. "Single fathers are demanding respect." *USA Today,* Sept. 1, 1987.

Jacobson, Edith. "Development of the Wish for a Child in Boys." *Psychoanalytic Study of the Child,* 5 (1950), pp. 139-152.

Jameson, Dee Dee and Armin Grams. "Changing Roles for Men and Women." *Childhood Education,* No. 4 (1973), pp. 184-190.

Janeway, Elizabeth. *Between Myth and Morning: Women Awakening.* New York: William Morrow, 1975.

Janeway, Elizabeth. *Man's World, Woman's Place.* New York: Delta, 1971.

"Job Sharing." *Business Week,* October 25, 1976, p. 112.

232

Joffe, Carole. "Sex Role Socialization and the Nursery School: As the Twig Is Bent." In *Sex:Male/Gender:Masculine*. Ed. John Petras. Port Washington, N.Y.: Alfred Publishing Co., 1975, pp. 104-119.

Johnson, Laurie Olsen, ed. *Nonsexist Curriculum Materials for Elementary Schools*. Old Westbury, N.Y.: Clearing House on Women's Studies, Feminist Press, 1974.

Johnson, Spencer. *The One-Minute Father*. New York: Delta, 1979.

Josselyn, Irene. "Cultural Forces, Motherliness and Fatherliness." *American Journal of Orthopsychiatry*, April 1956, pp. 270ff.

Julty, Sam. *Men's Bodies/Men's Selves*. New York: Delta, 1979.

Kahan, Stuart. *For Divorced Fathers Only*. New York: Monarch, 1978.

Kaley, Maureen. "Attitudes Toward Dual Roles of the Married Professional Woman." *American Psychologist*, No. 3 (1971), pp. 301-306.

Kamerman, Sheila and Alfred Kahn. *Family Policy: Government and Families in Fourteen Countries*. New York: Columbia University Press, 1978.

Kamerman, Sheila. *Child Care, Family Benefits and Working Parents*. New York: Columbia University Press, 1980.

Kamerman, Sheila. *Parenting in an Unresponsive Society: Managing Work and Family Life.* New York: Free Press, 1980.

Kanter, Rosabeth Moss. *Men and Women of the Corporation.* New York: Basic Books, 1977.

Kanter, Rosabeth Moss. *Work and Family in the United States: A Critical Review and Agenda for Research and Policy.* New York: Russell Sage Foundation, 1977.

Kaufman, Walter. *Without Guilt and Justice.* New York: Peter H. Wyden, 1973.

Keniston, Kenneth and the Carnegie Council on Children. *All Our Children: The American Family Under Pressure.* New York: Harcourt Brace Jovanovich, 1977.

Keniston, Kenneth. *The Uncommitted: Alienated Youth in American Society.* New York: Dell, 1965.

Kennedy, Shawn. "Paternity Leave for Teaching Fathers: An Idea That Has Not Caught Fire." *New York Times,* July 9, 1975., p. 43.

Keshet, Harry Finkelstein and Kristine Rosenthal. "Father as Caretaker After Marital Separation." *Social Work,* No. 1 (1978).

Keshet, Harry. "Part-Time Fathers: A Study of Separated and Divorced Men." Dissertation. University of Michigan, 1977.

Kilgore, James. *The Intimate Man.* Nashville: Abingdon, 1984.

234

Kimball, Gayle. *50-50 Marriage*. Boston: Beacon Press, 1983.

Kinney, William. "Paternal Attachment." *New England Journal of Medicine,* Vol. 18 (1972), pp. 939ff.

Kleiman, Carol. "Daddies may also need fast track to parenting." *St. Paul Pioneer Press*, July 16, 1989.

Klein, Ted. *The Father's Book*. New York: William Morrow and Co., 1968.

Koch, Stephen. "The Guilty Sex: How American Men Became Irrelevant." *Esquire,* July 1975, pp. 53-54.

Kohn, H. and A.J. Wiener. *The Year 2000: A Framework for Speculation in the Next 33 Years*. New York: Macmillan and Co., 1967.

Komarovsky, Mirra. *Blue-Collar Marriage*. New York: Random House, 1964.

Komarovsky, Mirra. *Dilemmas of Masculinity*. New York: Norton, 1977.

Kort, Carol and Ronnie Friedland, eds. *The Father's Book: Shared Experiences*. Boston: G.K. Hal and Co., 1986.

Kraditor, Aileen, ed. *Up From the Pedestal*. Chicago: Quadrangle, 1968.

Kraditor, Aileen. *The Ideas of the Woman Suffrage Movement, 1890-1920*. New York: Random House, 1965.

Kreps, Juanita. *Sex in the Marketplace: American Women at Work.* Baltimore: Johns Hopkins University Press, 1971.

Krucoff, Carol. "Families: Fathers and the Big Business of Raising Children." *Washington Post,* May 18, 1979.

Kuhne, Robert and Courtney O. Blair. "Flexitime." *Business Horizons,* 21, pp. 29-44.

Lacey, Carol. "More dads today facing 'Mommy Track' detours." *St. Paul Pioneer Press,* October 28, 1990.

Lacey, Carol. "Spend more on kids---more time, that is." *St. Paul Pioneer Press,* December 29, 1990.

Lamb, Michael and Jamie Lamb. "The Nature and Importance of the Father-Infant Relationship." *The Family Coordinator,* October 1975, pp. 71-73.

Lamb, Michael E., ed. *Nontraditional Families: Parenting and Child Development.* Hillsdale, NJ: Erlbaum, 1982.

Lamb, Michael E., ed. "Qualitative Aspects of Mother-ands-Father-Infant Attachments." *Infant Behavior and Development,* 1 (1978), pp. 265-275.

Lamb, Michael E., ed. "The Development of a Parent-Infant Attachment in the First Two Years of Life." In *The Father-Infant Relationship.* Ed. Frank Pedersen. New York: Praeger, 1980.

Lamb, Michael E., ed. *The Father's Role: Applied Perspectives.* New York: Wiley-Interscience, 1986.

Lamb, Michael E., ed. *The Role of the Father in Child Development*. New York: John Wiley and Sons, 1976.

Lamb, Michael E., ed. "Why Swedish Fathers Aren't Liberated." *Psychology Today,* October 1982, pp. 74-77.

Lamb, Michael. "A Defense of the Concept of Attachment." *Human Development*, No. 17 (1974), pp. 245-266.

Lamb, Michael. "Fathers: Forgotten Contributors to Child Development." *Human Development*, No. 18 (1975), pp. 245-266.

Land, H. "The Myth of the Male Breadwinner." *New Society,* October 1975, pp. 71-73.

Lasch, Christopher. *The Culture of Narcissism: American Life In An Age of Diminishing Expectations*. New York: W.W. Norton, 1979.

Lazar, Ellen. *Constructing an Employee Benefit Package for Part-Time Workers; A Rationale for Arriving at an Equitable Benefit Package at No Extra Cost to the Employer*. New York: Catalyst, 1975.

Lazarre, Jane. *The Mother Knot*. New York: McGraw-Hill, 1976.

Lazer, Ellen. "Job Sharing As a Pattern for Permanent Part-time Work." *The Conference Record,* October 1975, p. 57.

Lee, P.C. and A.L. Wolinsky. "Male Teachers of Young Children: A Preliminary Study." *Young Children*, Vol 28 (1973), pp. 342-352.

Lee, P.C. and N. Gropper. "Sex-Role Culture and Educational Review." *Harvard Educational Review*, Vol. 44 (1974), pp. 369-410.

Legge, K. "Flexible Working Hours: Panacea or Placebo?" *Management Decision*, 12 (5), pp. 264-279.

Lein, L. "Male Participation in Home Life: Impact of Social Supports and Breadwinner Responsibility on the Allocation of Tasks." *Family Coordinator,* 28 (1979), pp. 489-495.

Lein, Laura. "Male Participation in Home Life: Impact of Social Supports and Breadwinner Responsibility on the Allocation of Tasks." *The Family Coordinator*, October 1979, pp. 489-495.

Levant, Ronald and John Kelly. *Between Father and Child: How to Become the Kind of Father You Want to Be.* New York: Viking, 1989.

Levine, James. "Parents' Passages." *Psychology Today,* November 1980, p. 112.

Levine, James. "Redefining the Child Care 'Problem'---Men as Child Nurturers." *Childhood Education.* November/December 1977, pp. 55-61.

Levine, James. *Who Will Raise the Children?: New Options for Fathers (And Mothers).* New York: Lippincott, 1976.

Levine, Jo Ann. "Parents Agree to Joint Custody." *Christian Science Monitor,* May 5, 1975, p. 18.

Levy, B. "The School's Role in the Sex-Role Stereotyping of Girls: A Feminist Review of the Literature." *Feminist Studies*, Vol. 1 (1972), pp. 5-23.

Lewis, Robert. ed. *Men in Difficult Times.* Englewood Cliffs, NJ: Prentice-Hall, 1981.

Liebenberg, B. "Expectant Fathers." *American Journal of Orthopsychiatry*, Vol. 37 (1967), pp. 359-369.

Liljestrom, R. "The Parent's Role in Production and Reproduction." *Sweden Now*, 11 (1977), pp. 359-369.

Lipman-Blumen, J. and A.R. Tickmayer. "Sex Roles in Transition: A Ten-Year Perspective." *Annual Review of Sociology*, 1 (1976).

Lloyd, Cynthia, ed. *Sex, Discrimination and the Division of Labor.* New York: Columbia University Press, 1975.

Logan Nancy, et. al. "Job Satisfaction Among Part-Time and Full-Time Employees." *Journal of Vocational Behavior*, January 1973.

Lopata, Helena Znaniecki. *Occupation: Housewife.* New York: Oxford University Press, 1971.

Lott, Bernice E. "Who Wants the Children?" *American Psychologist*, July 1973, pp. 573-582.

Louisell, D.W. and C. Carroll. "The Father as Non-Parent." *The Catholic World.* 210 (1969), pp. 108-110.

Luce, Robert. "From Hero to Robot: Masculinity in America---Stereotype and Reality." *Psychoanalytic Review*, No. 4 (1967), pp. 53-74.

Lynn, David. *The Father: His Role in Child Development.* Belmont, CA: Wadsworth, 1974.

Lynn, David. "The Husband-Father Role in the Family." *Marriage and Family Living*, August 1961, pp. 295-296.

M/R: A Magazine About Men. 2600 Dwight Way, Berkeley, CA 94704.

Maccoby, Eleanor and Carol Nagy Jacklin. *The Psychology of Sex Differences.* Stanford: Stanford University Press, 1974.

Maccoby, Eleanor, ed. *The Development of Sex Differences.* Stanford: Stanford University Press, 1972.

MacDonald, Gordon. *The Effective Father.* Wheaton, Ill: Tyndale House, 1977.

Mack, Delores. "The Power Relationship in Black and White Families." *Journal of Personality and Social Psychology*, No. 3 (1974), pp. 409-413.

Madden, Janice Fanning. "Discrimination---A Manifestation of Male Market Power?" In *Sex, Discrimination and Division of Labor.* Ed. Cynthia Lloyd. New York: Columbia University Press, 1975, pp. 146-174.

Maklan, David. "The Four Day Workweek: Blue Collar Adjustment to a Nonconventional Arrangement of Work and Leisure Time." Ph.D. Dissertation, University of Michigan, 1976.

Manion, J. "A Study of Fathers and Infant Caretaking." *Birth and the Family Journal*, No. 4 (1977), pp. 174-179.

Markus, M. "Women and Work: Emancipation at an Impasse." *Impact of Science on Society*, January-March, 1970, pp. 61-72.

Martin, Stanley. *New Patterns of Work.* Scarsdale, NY: Work in America Institute, 1979.

Martin, Thomas, Kenneth Berry and R. Brooke Jacobsen. "The Impact of Dual-Career Marriages on Female Professional Careers: An Empirical Test of a Parsonian Hypothesis." *Journal of Marriage and the Family*, No. 4 (1975), pp. 734ff.

Martin, Virginia and Jo Hartley, eds. *Hours of Work When Workers Can Choose: The Experience of 59 Organizations with Employee-Chosen Staggered Hours and Flexitime.* Washington, D.C.: Business and Professional Women's Foundation, 1972.

Martin, Virginia. "Recruiting Woman Managers Through Flexible Hours." *Advanced Management Journal*, July 1974.

Matthews, Shailer. *The Social Teaching of Jesus.* New York: Macmillan, 1909.

Maxwell, Joseph. "The Keeping Fathers of America." *The Family Coordinator*, October 1976, pp. 387-392.

McCain, Nina. "Paternity Leave---Its Time Has Come." *Boston Globe,* October 15, 1972.

McDonnell, Lynda. "The Work-Family Equation." *St. Paul Pioneer Press*, Nov, 26, 1990.

McFadden, Michael. *Bachelor Fatherhood.* New York: Ace, 1974.

McGrath, Lee Pair and Joan Scobey. *What Is a Father? Children's Responses.* New York: Simon and Schuster, 1973.

McGuigan, Dorothy. *New Research on Women and Sex Roles.* Ann Arbor: University of Michigan Press, 1976.

McKee, L. and M. O'Brien, eds. *The Father Figure.* London: Tavistock Publications, 1982.

McMillan, Marvin. "Attitudes of College Men Toward Career Involvement of Married Women." *Vocational Guidance Quarterly*, September 1972, p. 8.

Mead, Margaret. *Male and Female.* New York: Dell, 1949.

Mead, Margaret. *Sex and Temperament in Three Primitive Societies.* New York: Dell, 1935.

Meier, Gretl. Barbara Marmen, Barney Olmstead and Linda Schuck. *Job Sharing in the Schools: A Study of Nine Bay Area Districts,* Palo Alto, CA: New Ways to Work, 1976.

Meier, Gretl. *Job Sharing.* Kalamazoo, MI: W.E. Upjohn Institute for Employment Research, 1978.

Meislin, Richard. "Poll Finds More Liberal Beliefs in Marriage and Sex Roles, Especially Among Young." *New York Times*, November 27, 1977.

Meissner, M., E. Humphreys, C. Meis and J. Scheu. "No Exit for Wives: Sexual Division of Household Demands." *Canadian Review of Sociology and Anthropology*, 12 (1975), pp. 424-439.

Meissner, Martin. "The Long Arm of the Job: A Study of Work and Leisure." *Industrial Relations*, 10 (1971), pp. 239-260.

Meister, Robert. *Fathers: Daughters, Sons, Fathers Reveal Their Deepest Feelings.* New York: Ballantine, 1981.

Men's Studies Newsletter. Men's Studies task force of the National Organization for Changing Men, P.O. Box 32, Harriman, TN 37748.

Miles, Herbert and Fern Harrington Miles. *Husband-Wife Equality.* Old Tappan, N.J.: Green, 1978.

Mill, John Stuart. "Prestige for the Other Sex." In *The Feminist Papers.* Ed. Alice Rossi. New York: Bantam Press, 1973, pp. 235-236.

Mill, John Stuart. "The Subjection of Women." In *Essays on Equality.* Ed. Alice Rossi. Chicago: University of Chicago Press, 1970, pp. 125-242.

Miller, Don. "Letters to Jason." *Village Voice.* November 10, 1975, pp. 24-25.

Miller, J. "Fathers in the Delivery Room." *Child and Family*, 3 (1964).

Miller, J. "Return the Joy of Home Delivery with Fathers in the Delivery Room." *Hospital Topics,* 1966.

Mitchell, G, W.K. Redican and J. Gomber. "Males Can Raise Babies." *Psychology Today,* 7 (1974), pp. 63-68.

Mitchell, G.D. "Paternalistic Behavior in Primates." *Psychological Bulletin,* 71 (1969), pp. 399-417.

Mitchell, Juliet. *Woman's Estate.* New York: Pantheon Books, 1971.

Mitscherlich, Alexander. *Society Without the Father.* New York: Harcourt Brace Jovanovich, 1973.

Molinoff, Daniel. "After Divorce, Give Them a Father Too." *Newsday,* October 5, 1975.

Molinoff, Daniel. "Life With Father: How Men Are Winning Custody of Their Kids." *New York Times Magazine,* May 22, 1977, pp. 131ff.

Money, J. and A.A. Erhardt. *Man and Woman, Boy and Girl.* Baltimore: Johns Hopkins University Press, 1972.

Money, John. *Sexual Signatures: On Being a Man or a Woman.* Boston: Little and Brown, 1975.

Montagu, Ashley. *The Natural Superiority of Women.* New York: Collier Books, 1952, 1974.

244

Morgenthau, Eric. "Sweden Offers Fathers Paid Paternity Leaves: About Ten Percent Take Them." *Wall Street Journal,* January 30, 1979.

Morse, Nancy and R.S. Weiss. "The Function and Meaning of Work and the Job." *American Sociological Review*, April 1955, pp. 191-198.

Murray, Pauli. "Economic and Educational Inequality Based on Sex: An Overview." *Valparaiso University Law Review*, 5 (1971).

Myrdal, A. and Viola Klein. *Women's Two Roles.* London: Routledge and Kegan Paul Ltd., 1968.

Naifeh, Steven and Gregory Smith White. *Why Can't Men Open Up? Overcoming Men's Fear of Intimacy.* New York: Potter, 1984.

Nandy, L. and D. Nandy. "Education for Equal Parenthood." *Family Planning.* October 1975.

Nash, John. "The Father in Contemporary Culture and Current Psychological Literature." *Child Development,* Vol. 36 (1965), pp. 262-266.

National Congress for Men. Washington, D.C. 202-FATHERS.

National Institute of Mental Health. *Research Conference on the Consequences of Divorce on Children.* Bethesda, MD: NIMH, 1978.

Nemerowicz, Gloria Morris. *Children's Perceptions of Gender and Work Roles.* New York: Praeger, 1979.

New Ways to Work. *A Booklet of General Information About Job Sharing.* Palo Alto, CA: New Ways to Work, 1977.

New Ways to Work. *Job Sharing in the School: A Study of Nine Bay Area Districts.* Palo Alto, CA: New Ways to Work, 1976.

Nichols, Jack. *Men's Liberation: A New Definition of Masculinity.* Baltimore: Penguin, 1975.

Nollen, Stanley and Virginia Martin. *Alternative Work Schedules, Pt. 1: Flexitime.* New York: AMCOM, a Division of American Managements Association, 1978.

Nollen, Stanley. *New Patterns of Work.* Scarsdale, N.Y.: Work in America Institute, 1979.

Novitski, A. and M. Babkina. "Part-Time Work and Employment." *Problems of Economics,* January 1974.

Nurturing News: Quarterly for Nurturing Men. 187 Caselli Ave., San Francisco, CA 94114.

Oakley, Ann. *Woman's Work: The Housewife, Past and Present.* New York: Vintage Books, 1974.

Oakley, Ann. "The Myth of Motherhood." *New Society,* February 26, 1970.

Oakley, Ann. *The Sociology of Housework.* New York: Random House, 1974.

246

Oakley, Ann. *Woman Confined: Towards a Sociology of Childbirth*. New York: Schocken Books, 1980.

Oaxaca, Ronald. "Male-Female Wage Differentials in Urban Labor Markets." *International Economic Review,* October 1973, pp. 693-709.

Odhnoff, Camilla. "Equality is For Children Too." *Current Sweden,* March 1976, p. 3.

"One Child, Two Homes." *Time,* January 29, 1979, p. 61.

Orden, S.T. and N.M. Bradburn. "Dimensions of Marriage Happiness." *American Journal of Sociology,* 73, pp. 715-731.

Orthner, Dennis and Ken Lewis. "Evidence of Single-Father Competence in Childrearing." *Family Law Quarterly,* Spring 1979.

Osherson, Samuel. *Finding Our Fathers: How a Man's Life Is Shaped by His Relationship with His Father*. New York: Fawcett Columbine, 1986.

Ostwald, Martin, trans. *Nicomachean Ethics*. By Aristotle. New York: Bobbs-Merrill, 1962.

Outka, Gene. *Agape: An Ethical Analysis*. New Haven: Yale University Press, 1972.

Outka, Gene. "Character, Conduct and the Love Commandment." In *Norm and Context in Christian Ethics*. Ed. Gene Outka and Paul Ramsey. New York: Charles Scribner's Sons, 1968, pp. 37-66.

Owen, John. "Why Part-Time Workers Tend to Be in Low Wage Jobs." *Monthly Labor Review*, No. 6 (1978).

Palme, Olaf. "Lesson from Sweden: The Emancipation of Man." In *The Future of the Family*. Ed. Louise Kapp Howe. New York: Simon and Schuster, 1972, pp. 247ff.

Parelius, Ross D. "Emerging Sex-Role Attitudes, Expectations and Strains Among College Women." *Journal of Marriage and the Family*, No. 1 (1975), p. 146.

Parents Without Partners. International Headquarters, 8807 Colesville Rd., Silver Spring, MD 20910.

Parke, Ross and Sandra O'Leary. "Father-Mother Infant Interaction in the Newborn Period: Some Findings, Observations and Some Unresolved Issues." In *The Developing Individual in a Changing World. Vol. II.* Eds. K. Riegel and K. Meachem. Hague: International, 1975.

Parke, Ross D. and Douglas B. Sawin. "Fathering: It's A Major Role." *Psychology Today*, November 1977, pp. 109ff.

Parke, Ross, "Infant Characteristics and Behavior as Elicitors of Maternal and Paternal Responsibility in the Newborn Period." Paper presented at the Annual Convention of the American Psychological Association, Chicago, September, 1975.

Parke, Ross, S.E. O'Leary and S. West. "Mother-Father-Infant Interaction: Effects of Maternal Medication, Labor and Sex of Infant." *Proceedings of the American Psychological Association,* 1972, pp. 85-86.

Parke, Ross. *Fathers*. Cambridge, MA: Harvard University Press, 1981.

Parke, Ross. "Perspectives in Father Infant Interaction," In *The Handbook of Infant Development*. Ed. J.D. Osofsky. New York: Wiley, 1979.

Parke, Ross. "The Father's Role in Infancy: A Re-Evaluation." *The Family Coordinator*, October 1976, p. 365.

Parson, Talcott and R.F. Bales. *Family, Socialization and Interaction Process*. New York: Free Press, 1955.

Parson, Talcott. "The Father Symbol: An Appraisal in Light of Psychoanalytic and Sociological Theory." In *Social Structure and Personality*. Ed. Parsons. Glencoe, N.Y.: Free Press, 1964.

Parsons, Talcott. "The Social Structure of the Family." In *The Family: Its Function and Destiny,* Ed. R.N. Anshen, New York: Harper and Row, 1949.

"Part-Timers and Affirmative Action Goals." *Fair Employment Practices*, April 15, 1976, p. 4.

Peck, Ellen. *The Baby Trap*. New York: Bernard Geis Associates, 1971.

Pedersen, Frank and Phyllis Berman, eds. *Men's Transitions to Parenthood: Longitudinal Studies of Early Family Experience*. New York: Erlbaum, 1988.

Pedersen, Frank, B.J. Anderson and R.L. Cain. "An Approach to Understanding Linkages between Parent-Infant and Spouse Relationships." Paper presented at the Society for Research in Child Development, New Orleans, March 1977.

Pedersen, Frank, ed. "Infant Development in Father-Absent Families." *Journal of Genetic Psychology,* 135 (1979), pp. 51-61.

Pedersen, Frank, ed. *The Father-Infant Relationship.* New York: Praeger, 1980.

Pedersen, Frank, M.T. Zaslow, R.L. Cain, and B.J. Anderson. "Caesarean Birth: The Importance of a Family Perspective." Paper presented at the International Conference on Infant Studies, New Haven, CT, April 1980.

Pedersen. F.A. and K.S. Robson. "Father Participation in Infancy." *American Journal of Orthopsychiatry,* April 1969, pp. 466-472.

Petras, John, ed. *Sex:Male/Gender:Masculine.* Port Washington, N.Y.: Alfred Publishing Co., 1975.

Phillips, C.R. and J.T. Anzalone. *Fathering: Participation in Labor and Birth.* St. Louis: Mosby, 1978.

Pinegar, Ed. *Fatherhood.* Salt Lake City: Deseret, 1976.

Pleck, Joseph and Jack Sawyer, eds. *Men and Masculinity.* Englewood Cliffs, N.J.: Prentice-Hall, 1974.

Pleck, Joseph. Masculinity-Femininity: Current and Alternative Paradigms." *Sex Roles,* No. 1 (1975), pp. 161-178.

Pleck, Joseph. "Men's Family Work: Three Perspectives and Some New Data." *The Family Coordinator*, No. 4 (1979), pp. 481-488.

Pleck, Joseph. *Men's New Roles in the Family: Housework and Childcare*. Ann Arbor: Institute for Social Research, University of Michigan, 1976.

Pleck, Joseph. "Psychological Frontiers for Men." *Rough Times*, June-July 1973, pp. 14-15.

Pleck, Joseph. *The Myth of Masculinity*. Cambridge, MA: MIT Press, 1982.

Pleck, Joseph. "The Psychology of Sex Roles: Traditional and New Views." In *Women and Men: Changing Roles, Relationships and Perceptions*. Ed. Cater, et. al., pp. 181-199.

Pleck, Joseph. "The Work-Family Role System." *Social Problems*, 24 (1977), pp. 417-427.

Pleck, Joseph. *Working Wives, Working Husbands*. Beverly Hills: Sage Publications, 1985.

Plummer, Ava-dale. "Book documents father's key role in child raising." *St. Paul Pioneer Press*, June 6, 1987.

Polatnick, Margaret. "Why Men Don't Rear Children: A Power Analysis." In *Sex:Male/Gender:Masculine*. Ed. Petras. Port Washington, N.Y.: Alfred Publishing Co., 1975, pp. 199-235.

Polk, Lon. "Involuntary Overtime and the Liberation of Men." Hearings Before Committee on Labor. Michigan State House of Representatives, June 25, 1971.

Poloma, Margaret and Neal T. Garland. "The Married Professional Woman: A Study in the Tolerance of Domestication." *Journal of Marriage and the Family*, Vol. 33 (1971), pp. 531-540.

Poloma, Margaret and Neal T. Garland. "The Myth of the Egalitarian Family: Familial Roles and the Professionally Employed Wife." In *The Professional Woman*. Ed. A. Theodore. Cambridge, MA: Schenkman Publishing, 1971.

Poloma, Margaret. "Role Conflict and the Married Professional Woman." In *Toward a Sociology of Women*. Ed. Safilios-Rothschild, pp. 187-198.

Price-Bonham, Sharon. "Bibliography of Literature Related to Roles of Fathers." *The Family Coordinator*, October 1976, pp. 489-512.

Prichard, H.A. *Moral Obligation*. New York: Oxford University Press, 1950.

Pruett, Kyle. *The Nurturing Father: Journey Toward the Complete Man*. New York: Warner Books, 1987.

Rabinowitz, Nancy and Peter. "Some Thoughts on Job Sharing." In *Careers and Couples: An Academic Question*. Ed. Leonore Hoffman and Gloria DeSolle, pp. 37-41.

Radin, Norma and Graeme Russell. "Increased Father Participation and Child Development Outcomes." In

252

Nontraditional Families: Parenting and Child Development.
Ed. M.E. Lamb. Hillsdale, NJ: Erlbaum, pp. 191-218.

Radin, Norma and R. Goldsmith. "Caregiving Fathers of
Preschoolers: Four Years Later." *Merrill Palmer Quarterly,*
31 (1985), pp. 375-383.

Radin, Norma. "Primary Caregiving and Role Sharing Fathers of
Preschoolers," In *Nontraditional Families: Parenting and
Child Development.* Ed. M.E. Lamb. Hillsdale, NJ: Erlbaum,
1982.

Radl, Shirley. *Mother's Day Is Over.* New York: Charterhouse,
1973.

Rapoport, Rhona and Robert Rapoport and V. Thiessen. "Couple
Symmetry and Enjoyment." *Journal of Marriage and the
Family,* Vol. 36 (1974), pp. 588-591.

Rapoport, Rhona and Robert Rapoport and Ziona Strelitz with
Stephen Kew. *Fathers, Mothers and Society: Towards New
Alliances.* New York: Basic Books, 1977.

Rapoport, Rhona and Robert Rapoport and Ziona Strelitz.
Leisure and the Family Life Cycle. Boston: Routledge and
Kegan Paul, 1975.

Rapoport, Rhona and Robert Rapoport with Janice Bumstead,
eds. *Working Couples.* New York: Harper Colophon Books,
1978.

Rapoport, Rhona and Robert Rapoport. *Dual Career Families Re-
examined: New Integrations of Work and Family.* New
York: Harper and Row, 1976.

Rapoport, Rhona and Robert Rapoport. *Dual Career Families.* Baltimore: Pelican Books, 1971.

Rapoport, Rhona and Robert Rapoport. "Early and Later Experiences as Determinants of Adult Behavior: Women's Family and Career Patterns." *British Journal of Sociology,* March 1971, pp. 16-30.

Rapoport, Rhona and Robert Rapoport. "Family Enabling Processes: The Facilitating Husband in Dual-Career Families." In *Support, Innovation and Autonomy.* Ed. R. Gosling. London: Tavistock Institute, 1973, pp. 245-264.

Rapoport, Rhona and Robert Rapoport. "Men, Women and Equity." *The Family Coordinator,* October 1975, pp. 421-432.

Rapoport, Rhona and Robert Rapoport. "The Dual Career Family." *Human Relations,* No. 1 (1969), pp. 3-30.

Rapoport, Rhona and Robert Rapoport. "Work and Family in Contemporary Society." *American Sociological Review,* Vol. 30 (1965), pp. 381-394.

Rausch, H.L., W.A. Barry, R.K. Hertel and M.A. Swain. *Communication, Conflict and Marriage.* San Francisco: Jossey-Bass, 1974.

Rebelsky, F. and C. Hanks. "Fathers' Verbal Interaction with Infants in the First Three Months of Life." *Child Development,* Vol. 42 (1971), pp. 63-68.

254

Redican, W.K. and G. Mitchell. "The Social Behavior of Adult Male-Infant Pairs of Rhesus Monkeys in a Laboratory Experiment." *American Journal of Physical Anthropology,* Vol. 38 (1973), pp. 523-526.

Rehn, Gosta. "For Greater Flexibility of Working Life." *OECD Observer,* February 1973, pp. 3ff.

Reiber, V.D. "Is the Nurturing Role Natural to Fathers?" *American Journal of Maternal Child Nursing,* No. 1 (1976), pp. 366-371.

Reinhold, Robert. "The Trend Toward Sexual Equality: Depth of Transformation Uncertain." *New York Times,* November 30, 1977.

"Reluctant Fathers." *Wall St. Journal,* December 19, 1988.

Rendina, Irma and Jean D, Dickerscheid. "Father Involvement with First-Born Infants." *The Family Coordinator,* October 1976, pp. 373-378.

Renne, Karen. "Correlates of Dissatisfaction in Marriage." *Journal of Marriage and the Family,* Vol. 32 (1970), p. 1.

Rescher, Nicholas. *Distributive Justice.* Indianapolis: Bobbs-Merrill, 1966.

Reuter, M. and H.B. Biller. "Perceived Paternal Nurturance Availability and Personality Adjustment Among College Males." *Journal of Consultative Psychology,* Vol. 40 (1973), pp. 339-342.

Reynolds, Pamela. "The Daddy Track." *St. Paul Pioneer Press,* March 25, 1989.

Reynolds, William. *The American Father: A New Approach to Understanding Himself, His Woman, His Child.* New York: Paddington Press, Ltd., 1978.

Rhoads, John. "Overwork." *Journal of the American Medical Association,* No. 24 (1977), pp. 2615-2618.

Ricci, Isolina. *Mom's House, Dad's House: Making Shared Custody Work.* New York: Macmillan, 1980.

Rich, Adrienne. *Of Woman Born! Motherhood as Experience and Institution.* New York: W.W. Norton, 1980.

Richard, M.P.M., J.F. Dunn and B. Antonis, "Caretaking in the First Year of Life: The Role of Fathers and Mothers' Social Isolation," In *Child Care, Health and Development,* 1977, 3, pp. 23-26.

Richman, J. et. al. "Fathers in Labour." *New Society,* October 16, 1975, pp. 145ff.

Rickfels, Roger. "Employees, Employers Both Discover the Joys of Part-time Positions." *Wall Street Journal,* March 7, 1973.

Ricks, F. and S. Pyke. "Teacher Perceptions and Attitudes that Foster or Maintain Sex Role Differences." *Interchange,* 4 (1973), pp. 26-33.

Ridley, Carl. "Exploring the Impact of Work Satisfaction and Involvement on Marital Interaction When Both Partners are Employed." *Journal of Marriage and the Family,* Vol. 35 (1973), pp. 2ff.

Robinson, B. "Men Caring for Young Children: An Androgynous Perspective." *The Family Coordinator,* October 1979, pp. 553-556.

Robinson, J. *How Americans Use Time: A Social-Psychological Analysis.* New York: Praeger, 1977.

Robinson, John. *How Americans Use Time,* New York: Praeger, 1977.

Roby, Pamela. ed. *Child Care---Who Cares?* New York: Basic Books, 1973.

Roby, Pamela. "Shared Parenting: Perspectives for other Nations." *School Review,* May 1975, pp. 21-24.

Rollings, Boyd and Harold Feldman. "Marital Separation over the Family Life Cycle." *Journal of Marriage and the Family,* No. 1 (1970), pp. 20-28.

Roman, Mel and William Haddad. "The Case for Joint Custody." *Psychology Today,* September 12, 1978, p. 96.

Roman, Mel and William Haddad. *The Disposable Parent: The Case for Joint Custody.* New York: Holt, Rinehart and Winston, 1978.

Roscow, Jerome. ed. *The Changing World of Work.* Englewood Cliffs, N.J.: Prentice-Hall, 1974.

Rosenthal, Kristine and Harry Keshet. *Fathers Without Partners: A Study of Fathers and the Family After Separation.* New York: Rowman and Littlefield, 1981.

Rossi, Alice. "A Bio-Social Perspective on Parenting." In *The Family.* Ed. Rossi, et. al. New York: W.W. Norton, 1978.

Rossi, Alice. "Equality Between the Sexes: An Immodest Proposal." *Daedalus,* Spring 1964, pp. 638-646.

Rossi, Alice. "Sex Equality: The Beginnings of Ideology." In *Toward a Sociology of Women.* Ed. Safilios-Rothschild, pp. 352-353.

Rossi, Alice. "Transition to Parenthood." In *The Marriage Game.* Ed. C. Greenblatt, et. al. New York: Random House, 1974.

Roszak, Betty and Theodore. *Masculine/Feminine: Readings in Sexual Mythology and the Liberation of Women.* New York: Harper and Row, 1969.

Rowe, M. "That Parents May Work and Love and Children May Thrive." In *Raising Children in Modern America.* Ed. N. Talbot. Boston: Little and Brown, 1976.

Rubin, J. and B. Brown. *The Social Psychology of Bargaining and Negotiation.* New York: Academix, 1975.

Ruether, Rosemary, ed. *Religion and Sexism: Images of Women in the Jewish and Christian Traditions.* New York: Simon and Schuster, 1974.

258

Ruether, Rosemary. "Working Women and the Male Work Day." *Christianity and Crisis,* February 7, 1977.

Russell, Candyce Smith. "Transition to Parenthood: Problems and Gratification." *Journal of Marriage and the Family,* Vol. 36 (1974), pp. 294-301.

Russell, Graeme. "Fathers as Caregivers: Possible Antecedents and Consequences." Paper presented to a study group on The Role of the Father in Child Development, Social Policy and the Law, University of Haifa, Israel, July 15-17, 1980.

Russell, Graeme. "The Father Role and Its Relation to Masculinity, Femininity and Androgyny," *Child Development,* 1978, 49, pp. 1174-1181.

Rutter, Michael. *Maternal Deprivation Reassessed.* Baltimore: Penguin Books, 1972.

Rypma, Craig. "Biological Bases of the Paternal Response." *The Family Coordinator,* October 1976, pp. 335-340.

Saario, Terry, Carol Jacklin and Carol Tittle. "Sex Role Stereotyping in the Public Schools." *Harvard Educational Review,* 43 (1973), pp. 386-416.

Safilios-Rothschild, Constantina and John Georgiopoulos. "A Comparative Study of Parental and Filial Roles." *Journal of Marriage and the Family,* August 1970.

Safilios-Rothschild, Constantina. "Companionate Marriages and Sexual Inequality: Are They Compatible?" In *Toward a Sociology of Women*, Ed. Safilios-Rothschild, pp. 63-70.

Safilios-Rothschild, Constantina. "Dual Linkages Between the Occupational and Family System: A Macrosocial Analysis." *Signs: Journal of Women in Culture and Society.* December 1975.

Safilios-Rothschild, Constantina. "The Influence of the Wife's Degree of Work Commitment Upon Some Aspects of Family Organization and Dynamic." *Journal of Marriage and the Family,* Vol. 32 (1970), pp. 681-691.

Safilios-Rothschild, Constantina. "The Study of Family Power Structure: A Review 1960-1969." *Journal of Marriage and the Family,* Vol. 32 (1970), pp. 539-552.

Safilios-Rothschild, Constantina. *Toward a Sociology of Women.* Lexington, MA: Xerox, 1972.

Safilios-Rothschild, Constantina. *Women and Social Policy.* Englewood Cliffs, NJ: Prentice-Hall, 1974.

Sagi, A. "Antecedents and Consequences of Various Degrees of Paternal Involvement in Child-Rearing: The Israeli Project." In *Nontraditional Families: Parenting and Child Development.* Ed. Lamb. Hillsdale, NJ: Erlbaum, 1982.

Salk, Lee. "Raising Boys, Raising Girls." *McCall's,* December 1990.

Sampson, Roland. *The Psychology of Power.* New York: Pantheon, 1966.

Sandlund, Maj-Britt. "The Status of Women in Sweden: Report to the United Nations." In *The Changing Roles of Men and*

Women. Ed. Edmund Dahlstrom. Boston: Beacon Press, 1971.

Santrock, J.W. and R. Warshak. "Father Custody and Social Development in Boys and Girls." *Journal of Social Issues*, 1979, 35, p. 113.

Sargent, Alice. ed. *Beyond Sex Roles*. St. Paul, MN: West Publishing, 1977.

Sawhill, Isabel. "The Economics of Discrimination Against Women: Some New Findings." *Journal of Human Resources*, Summer 1973, pp. 383-395.

Sawin, Douglas and Ross Parke. "Fathers' Affectionate Stimulation and Caregiving Behaviors with Newborn Infants." *The Family Coordinator*, October 1979, pp. 509-513.

Scanzoni, John. *Opportunity and the Family*. New York: Free Press, 1970.

Scanzoni, John. "Sex Roles, Economic Factors and Marital Solidarity in Black and White Marriages." *Journal of Marriage and the Family*, February 1975, pp. 130ff.

Scanzoni, John. *Sex Roles, Life Styles and Childbearing*. New York: Free Press, 1975.

Scanzoni, John. *Sex Roles, Women's Work and Marital Conflict: A Study of Family Change*. Lexington, MA: Heath/Lexington, 1978.

Scanzoni, John. *Sexual Bargaining: Power Politics in American Marriage.* Englewood Cliffs, NJ: Prentice-Hall, 1972.

Scanzoni, John. "Strategies for Changing Male Family Roles: Research and Practice Implications." *The Family Coordinator,* October 1970, pp. 435-442.

Scanzoni, Letha and John Scanzoni. *Men, Women and Change: A Sociology of Marriage and the Family.* New York: McGraw-Hill, 1976.

Scanzoni, Letha and Nancy Hardesty. *All We're Meant to Be.* Waco, Texas: Word Books, 1974.

Schaefer, George. *The Expectant Father.* New York: Barnes and Noble Books, 1972.

Schonberger, Richard. "Private Lives Versus Job Demands." *Human Resource Management,* Summer 1975, pp. 27-32.

Schroeder, Pat. "A Promise of parental leave is pro-family." *St. Paul Pioneer Press,* April 6, 1990.

Schultz, David and Stanley Rogers. *Marriage, Family and Personal Fulfillment.* Englewood Cliffs, NJ: Prentice-Hall, 1975.

Schultz, David. *The Changing Family: Its Function and Future.* Englewood Cliffs, NJ: Prentice-Hall, 1972.

Schultz, Theodore. ed. *Economics of the Family: Marriage, Children and Human Capital.* Chicago: University of Chicago Press, 1975.

Schwartz, Felice, Margaret Schifter and Susan Gilloti. *How to Go to Work When Your Husband is Against It, Your Children Aren't Old Enough and There's Nothing You Can Do Anyhow.* New York: Simon and Schuster, 1972.

Scott, Hilda. *Does Socialism Liberate Women?* Boston: Beacon Press, 1974.

Schwartz, Eleanor Brantley. *The Sex Barrier in Business.* Atlanta: Georgia State University, 1971.

Sebald, Hans. *Momism: The Silent Disease of America.* Chicago: Nelson Hall, 1976.

Seidenberg, Robert. *Corporate Wives: Corporate Casualties.* Garden City, NY: Anchor Press, 1975.

Seidenberg, Robert. *Marriage Between Equals.* New York: Anchor Books, 1973.

Sennett, Richard and Jonathan Cobb. *The Hidden Injuries of Class.* New York: Vintage Books, 1972.

Seward, G.H. and R.C. Williamson. *Sex Roles in Changing Society.* New York: Random House, 1970.

Shapiro, Stephen. *Manhood: A New Definition.* New York: Putnam, 1985.

Shavin, Susan. "Joint Parenting After Divorce: An Alternative to Traditional Child Custody." Master's Thesis. The California School of Professional Psychology, 1976.

Shedd, Charlie. *Smart Dads I Know*. New York: Sheed and Ward, 1975.

Shedd, Charlie. *The Best Dad Is a Good Lover*. Mission, Kansas: Universal Press Syndicate, 1977.

Sheehy, Gail. *Passages*. New York: Bantam Books, 1977.

Sheridan, G. "Flexing Time." *New Society*, No. 256, November 2, 1972.

Shostak, Arthur and William Gomberg, eds. *Blue-Collar World: Studies of the American Worker*. Englewood Cliffs, NJ: Prentice-Hall, 1964.

Sidgwick, Henry. *Methods of Ethics*. Chicago: University of Chicago Press, 1907, 1964.

Sidgwick, Henry. *Outlines of the History of Ethics*. New York: St. Martin's Press, 1967.

Silverberg, Marjorie and Lorraine Eyde. "Career Part-time employment: Personnel Implications of the HEW Professional and Executive Corps." *Good Government*, Fall 1971, pp. 11-20.

Singer, Wenda Goodhart, Stephen Schechtman and Mark Singer. *Real Men Enjoy Their Kids!: How to Spend Quality Time With Your Kids*. Nashville, TN: Abingdon, 1983.

Skolnick, Arlene. *The Intimate Environment: Exploring Marriage and Family*. Boston: Little and Brown, 1973.

Skrzycki, Cindy. "More men trying to juggle career, family." *St. Paul Pioneer Press,* December 30, 1990.

Slater, Philip. *Footholds: Understanding the Shifting Sexual and Family Tension in Our Culture.* Boston: Beacon, 1977.

Slater, Philip. *The Pursuit of Loneliness: American Culture at the Breaking Point.* Boston: Beacon Press, 1970.

Slobin, K. "Stress." *New York Times Magazine,* November 20, 1977, pp. 48ff.

Smith, A.D. and W. Reid. *Role Sharing Marriage.* New York: Columbia University Press, 1986.

Smith, C.W. *Will They Love Me When I Leave?: A Weekend Father's Struggle to Stay Close to His Kids.* New York: G.P. Putnam's Sons, 1987.

Spelke, E., P. Zelazo, J. Kagan and M. Kotelchuck. "Father Interaction and Separation Protest." *Developmental Psychology,* 9 (1973), pp. 83-90.

Spiegel, Irving. "Paternity Leaves Offered in New City University Contract." *New York Times,* September 24, 1972.

Spock, Benjamin. *Baby and Child Care.* New York: Pocket Books, 1976.

Spock, Benjamin. *Bringing Up Children in a Difficult Time.* New York: W.W. Norton, 1974.

Spock, Benjamin. "Joint Custody and the Father's Role," *Redbook,* October 1979, p. 77.

Spock, Benjamin. *The Common Sense Book of Baby and Child Care.* New York: Duell, Sloan and Pearce, 1945.

Spock, Benjamin."Women and Children: Male Chauvinist Spock Recants---Almost." In *The Future of the Family.* Ed. Howe, pp. 151ff.

Stacey, J., S. Bereaud, and J. Daniels. *And Jill Came Tumbling After: Sexism in American Education.* New York: Dell, 1974.

Staines, Graham and Robert Quinn." American Workers Evaluate the Quality of Their Jobs." *Monthly Labor Review,* Vol. 102 (1979), pp. 3-12.

Stapleton, Jean and Richard Bright. *Equal Marriage.* Nashville, TN: Abingdon, 1976.

Stein, Barry, Allan Cohen and Herman Gadon. "Flexitime: Work When You Want To." *Psychology Today,* June 10, 1976.

Stein, Edward, ed. *Fathering: Fact or Fiction.* Nashville, TN: Abingdon, 1977.

Steinberg, David. "Redefining Fatherhood: Notes After Six Months." In *The Future of the Family.* Ed. Howe, pp. 368-378.

Steinfels, Margaret O'Brien. *Who's Minding the Children? The History and Politics of Day Care in America.* New York: Simon and Schuster, 1973.

Steinman, Susan, Steven E. Zemmelman, and Thomas M. Knoblauch. "A Study of Parents Who Sought Joint Custody Following Divorce: Who Reaches Agreement and Sustains Joint Custody and Who Returns to Court." *Journal of American Academy of Child Psychiatry* 24 (1985), pp. 545-554.

Steinman, Susan. "The Experience of Children in a Joint Custody Arrangement: A Report of a Study." *American Journal of Orthopsychiatry* 51, No. 3 (1981), pp. 403-414.

Steinmann, Ann and David Fox. *The Male Dilemma*. New York: Jason Aronson, 1973.

Stewart, D.L. *Fathers Are People Too*. Indianapolis: Bobbs-Merrill Co., 1980.

Stoll, C. *Female and Male: Socialization, Social Roles and Social Structure*. New York: Brown, 1974.

Stoller, Robert. *Sex and Gender*. New York: Jason Aronson, 1974.

Strober, Myra. "Women and Men in the World of Work: Present and Future." In *Women and Men: Changing Roles, Relationships and Perceptions*. Ed. Cater, et. al., pp. 119-152.

Stronge, Michael. "Guidelines for Fathers." *Brother*, Summer 1972.

Stuart, Irving and Laurence Abt, eds. *Children of Separation and Divorce*. New York: Grossman, 1972.

Sullivan, S. Adams. *The Father's Almanac.* Garden City, NY: Dolphin, 1980.

Survey Research Center. *Men's Two Roles: Work and Family.* Ann Arbor: University of Michigan, 1977.

Szalai, Alexander. *The Use of Time.* The Hague: Mouton, 1972.

Tavris, C. "Men ands Women Report Their Views on Masculinity." *Psychology Today,* 10 (1977), pp. 34-43.

Terkel, Studs. *Working.* New York: Avon, 1972.

Terrebonne, Nancy and Bob Terrebonne. "On Sharing an Academic Appointment." In *Careers and Couples: An Academic Question.* Ed. L. Hoffman and G. DeSolle, pp. 30-32.

"The First Weeks of Fathering: The Importance of Choices and Supports for New Parents." *Birth and Family Journal,* 3, No. 2, 1976, pp. 53-58.

Thiessen, V., Rhona Rapoport and Robert Rapoport. "Enjoyment, Careers and the Family Life Cycle." In *The Life Cycle in European Societies.* Ed. J. Cuisenier. The Hague: Mouton, 1977.

Thingvall, Joel. "Fatherhood a tough job but immensely gratifying." *St. Paul Pioneer Press,* June 19, 1987.

Thompson, Doug Cooper. *As Boys Become Men: Learning New Male Roles.* New York: Irvington Publishers, 1985.

Tibbets, S. "Sex-Role Stereotyping in the Lower Grades: Part of the Solution." *Journal of Vocational Behavior,* 6, pp. 255-261.

Tillich, Paul. *Love, Power and Justice.* New York: Oxford University Press, 1954.

Tobias, Sheila and Margaret Reembarger. "Full Status Part-Time Faculty." In *Women in Higher Education.* Ed. W. Todd Furniss and Patricia A. Graham. Washington, D.C.: American Council on Education, 1974.

Tognoli, Jerome. "In Flight from Domestic Space: Men's Roles in the Household." *The Family Coordinator,* October 1979, pp. 599-607.

Trethowan, W.H. and M.F. Conolon, "The Couvade Syndrome." *British Journal of Psychiatry,* 1965, 111, pp. 57-66.

Tritico, Lila. "Child Custody: Preference to the Mother." *Louisiana Law Review,* Summer 1974, pp. 883ff.

U.S. Comptroller General. *Benefits from Flexible Work Schedules---Legal Limitations Remain.* Washington, D.C.: General Accounting Office, 1977.

U.S. Congress, House of Representatives. Committee on Post Office and Civil Service. *Part-Time Employment and Flexible Work Hours: Hearings on H.R. 2732, and H.R. 1026.* Serial No. 95-28. Ninety-fifth Congress, First Session, May 24, June 29, July 8, October 4, 1978.

U.S. Congress, Senate. Committee on Governmental Affairs. *Flexitime and Part-Time Legislation: Hearings on S 517, S*

269

518, H.R. 7814, H.R. 1026. Ninety-fifth Congress, Second Session, June 19, 1978.

U.S. Department of Labor Statistics, Employment and Earnings, Characteristics of Families: First Quarter. Washington, D.C.: U.S. Department of Labor, 1988.

U.S. Department of Labor, Employment Standards Administration. *Twenty Facts on Women Workers.* Washington, D.C.: U.S. Government Printing Office, 1973.

U.S. Department of Labor, Women's Bureau. *Fact Sheet on the Earnings Gap.* Washington, D.C.: U.S. Government Printing Office, 1972.

U.S. Department of Labor, Women's Bureau. *Laws on Sex Discrimination in Employment.* Washington, D.C.: U.S. Government Printing Office, 1970.

U.S. Department of Labor. *Manpower Report of the President.* Washington, D.C.: U.S. Government Printing Office, 1975.

Van Beek, Rex, ed. *Clergy Couples: Dynamic Duals in Ministry.* Nashville, TN: Board of Higher Education and Ministry, United Methodist Church (1976-1979.

Vanek, Joann. "Time Spent in Housework." *Scientific American,* November 1974, pp. 116-120.

Victor, Ira and Win Anne Winkler. *Fathers and Custody.* New York: Hawthorn Books, 1977.

Vlastos, Gregory. "Justice and Equality." In *Social Justice.* Ed. Richard Brandt. Englewood Cliffs, NJ: Prentice-Hall, 1962.

Von Lackum, Nancy Jo and John von Lackum, III. *Clergy Couples: A Report on Clergy Couples and the Ecumenical Clergy Couple Consultation.* New York: National Council of Churches, 1979.

Wade, Michael. *Flexible Working Hours in Practice.* Epping, England: Gower Press, 1973.

Waldron, I. "Why Do Women Live Longer Than Men?" *Journal of Human Stress,* No. 2 (1976), pp. 1-13.

Walker, Kathryn and Margaret Woods. *Time Use: A Measure of Household Production of Family Goods and Services.* Washington, D.C.: American Home Economics Association, 1976.

Walker, Kathryn. "Time Spent by Husbands in Household Work." *Family Economics Review,* June 1970, pp. 8-11.

Walker, Kathryn. "Time-Use Patterns for Household Work Related to Homemaker's Employment." Talk presented to 1970 National Agricultural Outlook Conference, Washington, D.C., February 18, 1970.

Wallerstein, Judith and Joan Kelly. *Surviving the Breakup: How Children Actually Cope with Divorce.* New York: Basic Books, 1980.

Wallerstein, Judith and Joan Kelly. "California's Children of Divorce." *Psychology Today,* January 1980, pp. 67-76.

Wallerstein, Judith and Joan Kelly. "The Father Child Relationship: Changes After Divorce." In *Father and Child.* Ed. Stanley Gath.

Wallerstein, Judith and Sandra Blakeslee. *Second Chances: Men, Women and Children a Decade After Divorce.* New York: Ticknor and Fields, 1989.

Walster, E. and G.W. Walster. "Equity and Social Justice." *Journal of Social Issues,* Vol. 31, (1975), pp. 21-44.

Walters, J. and N. Stinnett. "Parent-Child Relationships: A Decade Review of Research." *Journal of Marriage and the Family,* Vol. 33 (1971), pp. 70-111.

Wapner, J. "The Attitudes, Feelings and Behaviors of Expectant Fathers Attending Lamaze Classes." *Birth and Family Journal,* 3 (1976), pp. 5-14.

Ware, Ciji. "Joint Custody: One Way to End the War." *New West,* February 26, 1979, p. 42.

Wells, J. Gipson. *Current Issues in Marriage and the Family.* New York: Macmillan, 1975.

Wente, Arel and Susan Crockenberg. "Transition to Fatherhood: Lamaze Preparation, Adjustment Difficulty and the Husband-Wife Relationship." *The Family Coordinator,* October 1976, pp. 351-358.

Werther, William B. Jr. "Part-Timers: Overlooked and Undervalued." *Business Horizons,* February 1975.

272

Whittaker, William. *Alternative Work Schedules and Part-Time Career Opportunities in the Federal Government: A Legislative Review*. Washington, D.C.: Congressional Research Service, 1978.

Williams, Bruce. "A Symposium: Men in Young Children's Lives." *Childhood Education*, December 1970, pp. 139-143.

Williams, Patricia. *Working Wonders: The Success Story of Wives Engaged in Professional Work Part-Time*. London: Hodder and Stoughton, 1969.

Wilmott, Peter. "Family, Work and Leisure Conflicts Among Male Employees." *Human Relations*, No. 6 (1971), pp. 575-584.

Winter, Gibson. *Elements for a Social Ethics: The Role of Social Science in Public Policy*. New York: Macmillan, 1966.

Winter, Ruth. "Psychologists Sound Off on What Makes a Good Father." *Science Digest*, June 1973, p. 14.

Withers, Merren, et. al. "Sex and Sexism: A Comparison of Male and Female Sex-Role Attitudes." *Journal of Marriage and the Family*, No. 4 (1975), pp. 744ff.

Women Employed. *Women in the Economy: Preferential Mistreatment*. Chicago: Women Employed, 1977.

Woolley, Persia. *The Custody Handbook*. New York: Summit Books, 1979.

"Working Fathers: Views of Ten Fathers." *Ms*. May 1974, pp. 54-55.

Wortis, Rochelle Paul. "The Acceptance of the Concept of Maternal Role by Behavioral Scientists: Its Effect on Women." *American Journal of Orthopsychiatry*, No. 5 (1971) , pp. 738ff.

Wright, James. "Are Working Women Really More Satisfied? Evidence From Recent National Surveys." *Journal of Marriage and the Family,* 40 (1978), pp. 301-314.

Yablonsky, Lewis. *Fathers and Sons.* New York: Simon and Schuster, 1982.

Yorburg, B. *Sexual Identity: Sex Roles and Social Change.* New York: Wiley, 1973.

Young, Michael and Peter Wilmott. *The Symmetrical Family.* New York: Penguin Books, 1973.

Zaldivar, R.A. "Businesses adjusting to dad's needs: parental leave policies permit time with kids." *St. Paul Pioneer Press,* June 15, 1991, p. 9A.

Zaretsky, Eli. *Capitalism, The Family and Personal Life.* New York: Harper and Row, 1976.

Zelazo, Philip, M. Kotelchuck, L. Barber and J. David. "Fathers and Sons: An Experimental Facilitation of Attachment Behaviors." Unpublished paper cited in Ross Parke, *Fathers.*

Zellner, H. "Discrimination Against Women, Occupational Segregation and the Relative Wage." *American Economic Review*, Vol. 62 (1972), pp. 157-160.

INDEX